ONE-MINUTE COIN EXPERT

ONE-MINUTE
COIN EXPERT

SCOTT A. TRAVERS

FIFTH EDITION

House of Collectibles
Random House Reference
New York

House of Collectibles and colophon are registered trademarks of Random House, Inc.

RANDOM HOUSE is a registered trademark of Random House, Inc.

This book is available for special discounts for bulk purchases for sales promotions or premiums. Special editions, including personalized covers, excerpts of existing books, and corporate imprints, can be created in large quantities for special needs. For more information, write to Special Markets/Premium Sales, 1745 Broadway, MD 6-2, New York, NY, 10019 or e-mail specialmarkets@randomhouse.com.

Please address inquiries about electronic licensing of reference products for use on a network, in software or on CD-ROM to the Subsidiary Rights Department, Random House Reference, fax 212-572-6003.

Visit the Random House Web site: www.randomhouse.com

Manufactured in the United States of America

Fifth Edition: November 2004

0 9 8 7 6 5 4 3 2

Library of Congress Cataloging-in-Publication data is available.

ISBN: 0-375-72039-1

ON THE COVER: 1955 Doubled Die Lincoln cent PCGS MS65RD (photo courtesy Heritage Galleries); 1913 Liberty head nickel found at the bottom of a closet by the Walton family (photo courtesy and copyright American Numismatic Association); and 1932-D Washington quarter PCGS MS66 (photo courtesy Heritage Galleries)

To my parents

CONTENTS

ACKNOWLEDGMENTS

I especially appreciate the knowledge and advice given to me by so many persons during the preparation of this book. Given the uncertain nature of some of the issues addressed, this book is really a consensus of opinion of many of the contributors consulted. Those contributors are:

John Albanese; David T. Alexander; Michael Alster; Richard A. Bagg; Dennis Baker; Q. David Bowers; Ruthann Brettell; H. Robert Campbell; Jeanne Cavelos; Christopher Cipoletti; William L. Corsa, Sr.; John W. Dannreuther; Beth Deisher; Thomas K. DeLorey; John P. Dessauer; Silvano DiGenova; Shane Downing; Al Doyle; William Fivaz; Harry Forman; Leo Frese; Michael Fuljenz; David L. Ganz; Klaus W. Geipel; Salvatore Germano; Marcy Gibbel; William T. Gibbs; Lindsey Glass; Ira Goldberg; David Hall; James L. Halperin; David C. Harper; Dorothy Harris; Michael R. Haynes; Leon Hendrickson; Brian Hendelson; Robert L. Hughes; Jay W. Johnson; Steve Ivy; R. W. Julian; Christine Karstedt; Melissa Karstedt; Charles H. Knull; Timothy J. Kochuba; Chester L. Krause; Randy Ladenheim-Gil; David W. Lange; Julian Leidman; Robert J. Leuver; Kevin J. Lipton; Steve Markoff; Steve Mayer; Raymond N. Merena; Bob Merrill; Lee S. Minshull; Richard Nachbar; Laura Paczosa; John Pasciuti, Sr.; Martin Paul; Donn Pearlman; Ed Reiter; Robert S. Riemer; Maurice H. Rosen; Deborah G. Rosenthal; Michael Keith Ruben; Howard Ruff; John Sack; Stephen H. Spahn; Mark Salzberg; Hugh Sconyers; Michael W. Sherman; Jeff Shoop; John Slack; Harvey Stack; Michael J. Standish; Kari Stone; David Sundman; Rick Sundman; Marilyn Van Allen; Armen Vartian; Fred Weinberg; Leigh H. Weiss; Bob Wilhite; Mark Yaffe; Marc D. Zand, and Keith M. Zaner.

Maurice H. Rosen was of supreme importance in his assistance in understanding market psychology and issues relating to the performance of gold. John Dessauer's help was invaluable for his expression of ideas regarding coins and precious metals. Marilyn Van Allen and Keith Zaner compiled many of the photographs and coin prices. Ed Reiter served as my numismatic editor and carefully reviewed and assisted in revising the finished manuscript. And John Albanese helped to make chapter 14 a viable working reality by reviewing the manuscript and sharing his vast knowledge of treasure buried at sea.

Information and coins for chapter 3 was graciously provided by Fred Weinberg & Co., 16311 Ventura Blvd., Suite #1298, Encino, CA 91436, tel. 818-986-3733.

Scott A. Travers
travers@pocketchangelottery.com
New York
November 2004

ONE-MINUTE COIN EXPERT

INTRODUCTION

Small change can be worth big money.

In the late 1980s, rare coins became the hottest new game in the world of high finance. Promoters pointed to studies showing that coins had outperformed all other major forms of investment, and this attracted thousands of new buyers to the coin market. The hype faded thereafter, and many rare coins fell in price. But that actually makes them better values today. And these very good values are within the reach of almost everyone.

At times, the only reach needed is into your pocket or purse. Coins worth hundreds—even thousands—of dollars can be found in otherwise ordinary pocket change. True, it doesn't happen every day. But bettors don't hit the lottery very often either, and that doesn't stop them from playing their numbers religiously week after week. You're much more likely to find a valuable coin in pocket change than you are to win a bundle in the lottery. And the cost—just the face value (or spending value) of the coin—is cheaper by a long shot than what people spend on lottery games.

One-Minute Coin Expert will tell you how to maximize your chances to reap big profits from *your own* small change. It also will provide you with all the tools you need to buy and sell coins effectively, shrewdly—and profitably—in the bustling coin marketplace, an international network of dealers, collectors, and investors where rare cents are no penny-ante proposition and scarce nickels and dimes are much more than merely a five-and-ten-cent business. By following a series of quick, easy steps, you'll soon be able to transform your coin col-

1913 Liberty head nickel worth $2.5-million dollars that was found at the bottom of a closet in the summer of 2003. (Photo courtesy Donn Pearlman)

1804 silver dollar that sold for $4,140,000 in 1999. (Photo courtesy Auctions by Bowers and Merena, Inc.)

lection into a healthy bankroll of that other highly popular form of money—the kind you spend!

While certainly important, profit is just one reason why millions of people all around the world collect coins. The hobby is richly rewarding in other ways, as well.

Pick up an old coin and you're literally holding history in your hand. Coins are mirrors of the civilizations that issued them, and they frequently furnish fascinating insights into the life and times of those who made them.

They're more than just mirrors, of course: They're tangible mementos of the cultures in which they were produced; in fact, they're among our most important links with some of mankind's greatest, most glorious eras. The temples of ancient Athens have vanished or lie in ruins, but many lovely coins endure as tangible reminders of the grandeur that was Greece.

Coins are also tiny works of art. Although they may be only millimeters wide, many are exquisitely beautiful and their owners take great pride in possessing and displaying them.

Collectors enjoy assembling sets of coins. Finding a coin you need—whether in pocket change, a piggy bank, or even a dealer's display case—is a source of satisfaction and even exhilaration. It's just like digging up buried treasure.

Coin collecting didn't come into its own as a pastime for the masses until relatively recently. At one time, it was known as "The Hobby of Kings" because only noblemen had the time and money to indulge in it. During the last few decades, interest and involvement in this stimulating pastime have multiplied geometrically, and "The Hobby of Kings" has now become "The King of Hobbies" instead.

The coin market, too, has undergone major changes in recent years. A generation ago, it was populated almost exclusively by mom-and-pop dealers and small collectors. But now, well-heeled investors have joined the hunt, altering the ground rules fundamentally and raising the stakes—and many of the prices—enormously.

Coin collecting still holds great appeal for small collectors; it's avidly pursued by multitudes of people—including several million Americans—in virtually every age group and income bracket. This widespread demand provides a solid base for the coin market, serving as an important underpinning for the price structure. Today, however, rare coins are no longer mere collectibles. In a word, they have become an *investment*—an investment whose returns can be spectacular.

Investors' interest in coins peaked in the late 1980s, when several Wall Street firms became active, aggressive participants in the coin market. Unfortunately, that involvement proved to be premature. Coin prices soared initially amid the euphoria generated by these new "players," but after the frenzy subsided, price levels also fell back. Far from being a source of concern, this represented a wonderful opportunity: The lower prices made the market even more attractive for potential investors.

The coin market has grown not only in size but also in sophistication. For example, a 70-point grading system is now used to denote coins' "condition," or state of preservation. The number 70 refers to a coin which is perfect— which has no nicks or scratches and never has been passed from hand to hand. As a coin goes from hand to hand, the metal wears down and that coin loses detail which can never be recovered. Coins that have lost this detail are said to be "circulated."

The market's greater complexity is evident, as well, from the way coins are now bought and sold. Dealers conduct transactions on computerized trading networks; and neighborhood coin shops, while far from extinct, are dwarfed today by large, high-profile dealerships with international clienteles and multimillion-dollar inventories and sales. In other ways, however, buying and selling coins is really simpler—for those who know what they're doing and where they're going.

Some people have trouble telling the difference between coins which have no scratches, and have not been spent, and other coins which have passed through many hands and been worn down. "Certification" services give people an impartial opinion as to how worn—or how new—a coin is. These organizations seal each coin in a special plastic holder designed so the coin cannot be easily removed. A paper insert stating the service's grading is sealed inside this holder with the coin. Any attempt to remove the coin or insert, or to change the grading on the insert, can be easily detected.

Independent grading services have removed much of the guesswork—and much of the risk—from buying and selling coins. A number of certified coins are so widely accepted, in fact, that many dealers feel comfortable making offers for them on a sight-unseen basis. Although most buyers now prefer to look at coins first, and purchase them on a sight-seen basis, the sight-unseen concept has made it possible for even neophytes to participate successfully in the coin market.

The ability to grade coins accurately is partly a science, partly an art. *You* don't need to be an expert grader; the grading services' expertise provides you with a fine security blanket. Still, you should equip yourself with a fundamental knowledge of what's involved—and once understood, the elements are simple.

One-Minute Coin Expert makes them even simpler by showing you an easy, enjoyable way to determine the grade of a coin by reviewing its key components.

Like any investment field, the rare coin market goes up and down. And how you "play the game" goes a long way toward determining how much money you make. *One-Minute Coin Expert* gives you a big head start and an inside track. Knowledge is the key. Many current players lack the knowledge they need to be successful—but after reading this book, you'll be ready to compete like a seasoned veteran.

One-Minute Coin Expert will tell you what to look for. Whether you're simply a casual accumulator—someone who pulls odd-looking coins out of pocket change and sticks them away in a drawer—or a high-powered investor who buys expensive coins for thousands of dollars apiece, this book will give you all the information you need to maximize your return on the time and money you spend.

I'll tell you how to cash in your profits when the coin market is strong. And I'll also explain how to ride out the storm comfortably when hard times hit.

One-Minute Coin Expert provides you with a maximum of information in a minimum of time. I'll give you a simple, straightforward blueprint of how the market works and how it can be made to work for you, enabling you to turn your small change into big money.

I'll start by explaining why people save coins, and examine the four different categories into which most of these people fall. Then I'll tell you more about coins in general, including how to spot the mint marks on U.S. coins—small symbols that can add enormous value.

In Chapter Two, I'll give you a checklist of valuable coins that can and do appear in ordinary pocket change. Then, in Chapters Three and Four, I'll tell you about still other worthwhile coins that won't be in your pocket change but may very well turn up around your home—perhaps in a cigar box or dresser drawer.

Once you know which dates and mint marks to look for, I'll take you on a guided tour of the coin market, showing you what makes it tick and how you can get the edge on everyone else when buying or selling coins. I'll make you an instant expert not only on grading coins but also on trading them. And I'll tell you how to spot the coins with the greatest potential—the ones that are likely to go up in value faster and farther than all the rest. I'll even give you a secret list of my personal Top Twelve recommendations.

Coins and precious metals are closely interrelated. I'll show you just how they work together, and how this can provide you with golden opportunities to pocket sizable profits.

Before we're through, I'll also take you behind the scenes in a captivating real-life drama featuring drug dealers, coin dealers, and the U.S. government. And I will take you on a journey of discovery of golden treasures buried at sea and rescued from their watery graves.

As this book is written, the coin market is enjoying a renaissance, thanks in large measure to the new quarter dollars honoring the fifty states of the Union. Still, many prices are well below the levels they enjoyed at the market's last big peak in mid-1989. Many analysts see this as a great opportunity. In traditional investment areas such as stocks, long bear markets frequently are followed by especially dramatic bull-market upturns. Although there is no guarantee that the coin market will come back to the price levels of the past, you're sure to be a winner if you follow the recommendations in this book. You may not always reap huge profits from the coins you find and buy, but you'll have a lifelong sense of appreciation for the beauty, romance, and history they possess.

One-Minute Coin Expert is meant to do just what the title suggests: make you an expert.

You'll learn how to spot bargains . . . how to pick coins that will rise in value quickly . . . how to grade coins . . . how to buy and sell . . . how to understand market psychology . . . how to protect your investments from the tax man. In short, you'll learn how to play this intriguing, potentially lucrative money game—and how to win!

CHAPTER 1

YOU CAN BE AN EXPERT

This is a book on how to become an expert on coins.

Expertise on coins can take many forms. It can mean becoming adroit at checking pocket change for coins that will bring you a financial windfall. It also can mean becoming astute at spending money on coins, whether you're reaching into your pocket for one hundred dollars to buy a rare coin, or even reaching deep into your bank account for many thousands of dollars to spend on extremely rare coins in hopes of achieving a profit.

Whatever your degree of involvement, this book will make you an expert. And if you become an expert, you can profit from rare coins at every level of involvement, regardless of whether current market conditions are good or bad.

At one time or another, possibly without even realizing it, just about everyone thinks about coins as an investment. It happens, for example, when a really old coin turns up in your change or in your travels, or when you get a coin that just doesn't look right—one, for example, on which the date and some of the words are misprinted.

Many of us have had this experience. And when it happens, we invariably want to know two things: What's it worth, and will I make more money if I sell it now or later?

You don't have to wait for scarce and valuable coins to come along; you can go looking for them. And you can make money by buying and selling scarce coins. Many such coins today are authenticated and graded by independent experts and then encased in special plastic holders. This process assures the buyer that the grade, or level of preservation, is being properly stated by the seller. "Certified" coins change hands readily on nationwide trading networks and greatly enhance the appeal of rare coins to traditional investors.

I've come up with simple, easy-to-follow guidelines that will take you step by step through the process of identifying good values at all levels of the coin-buying spectrum. Follow these steps and you'll not only know what to look for, but also what to do with the coins once you have them.

Coins go up and down in value frequently; the coin market has peaks and valleys. But I'll show you how to make money in all kinds of markets—when coins are red-hot and also when prices are in a tailspin. That, after all, is the sign of a real expert: knowing how to thrive whether the coin market is rallying or is in one of its characteristic cyclical downturns.

WHY PEOPLE ACQUIRE COINS

People save coins for a number of different reasons. Some find them appealing as miniature works of art. Others are intrigued by the rich historical significance they possess. Many simply enjoy the challenge of pursuing something rare, elusive, and valuable. And, not least of all, many are attracted by the marvelous track record rare coins have achieved as good investments. Obviously, a great many people collect rare coins for *all* these different reasons, to a greater or lesser degree.

Finding something valuable is understandably thrilling, and many scarce coins do turn up in ordinary pocket change. I'll furnish a list of such coins in Chapter Two. Realistically, though, many rare coins have to be purchased.

Billions of dollars are spent on rare coins every year, and U.S. coins are by far the biggest segment of that market. In large part, that's because Americans account for the single biggest group of collectors in the world, as well as being among the most affluent. But other factors also have a bearing. For one thing, U.S. coins require less in-depth knowledge than ancient coins or international coins from the modern era. For another thing, the U.S. coin market is an easy-entry, easy-exit field with no regulation by the government—and many entrepreneurs find this appealing.

THE COIN BUYER SPECTRUM

The rare coin market is really a spectrum of different kinds of buyers. While one group of buyers may have different motivations from other groups, all are integral parts of the overall market—and all, in a real sense, are interdependent.

We can better understand who buys and saves coins, and why, by looking at the following graphic:

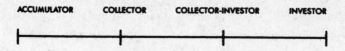

Accumulators   Accumulators are people who save coins haphazardly, without a particular pattern or plan of action. Many are undoubtedly attracted by the same positive qualities that motivate collectors and investors: the physical appeal of the coins and the notion of selling them for a profit, for example. But these objectives are only vaguely defined.

An accumulator may have sugar bowls or jars filled with coins, but they're probably not arranged in any special order and he probably doesn't have a very good idea what they're worth—even though some of them may be worth a great deal.

Collectors   In theory, a collector is someone who purchases coins with no regard at all for their profit potential—someone who is motivated strictly by such factors as aesthetics and historical significance. If a collector purchased a coin for $100 and its value went up to $1,000, he wouldn't even consider selling that coin, since he wouldn't have any interest in the coin's financial aspects. Theoretically, a collector also wouldn't concern himself with how much he had to pay to obtain a coin.

Collectors enjoy assembling coins in sets, and they strive for completeness in those sets. Lincoln cents with wheat stalks on the reverse were issued, for example, from 1909 to 1958. A collector would be interested in putting together representative Lincoln cents from each of those years so that she would have a complete set. Some collectors also like to assemble "type" collections, consisting of one coin from each of a number of different series. A twentieth-century type set of U.S. coins, for instance, would include one example of every different U.S. coin issued since 1901. A "type" coin is a representative example of a major coin variety but not a rare date of that variety.

Investors   On the other end of the spectrum, at the right-hand side of our graphic, is the investor. Unlike the collector, the investor pays close attention to inflation, interest rates, the size of the money supply—and, in short, the economic justification for purchasing rare coins. The quintessential investor, in fact, would be concerned *only* with profit, and not at all with coins' aesthetics and history.

Collector/Investors   In practical terms, no one is ever a totally solid collector or solid investor. Even the most dedicated collectors can't be completely oblivious to the cost and the value of their coins. And even the most profit-oriented investor can't completely ignore the intangible allure of beautiful coins.

The collector/investor combines the best of both worlds. This is a person who buys coins not only for their cultural, historical, and artistic appeal, but also to make a profit. The collector/investor represents a new breed of coin buyer, and a very healthy one.

OLD-TIME COLLECTING

Years ago, many people set aside interesting coins: circulated coins they found in pocket change, rolls of brand new coins they obtained at face value from the bank, or possibly government proof sets they purchased for modest premiums from the Mint. These coins may not have been particularly valuable at the time, but over the years coin collecting has evolved from a small hobby into a big business. And today, these tiny treasures may very well command enormous premiums.

As with anything else, it's a matter of supply and demand. Many of these coins, rolls, and proof sets have been in small supply since the day they were made. But years ago, the number of collectors was also relatively small, so demand for these coins remained at moderate levels. That served to hold down their prices.

Coin collecting became much more popular in the early 1960s. Thousands and thousands of newcomers started looking for low-mintage coins in their pocket change; many would go to the bank and get rolls of coins every week, then take them home and pick out the scarcer pieces. During that period, many people also began to purchase proof sets from the government every year. The expansion continued and accelerated during the 1970s and into the 1980s.

THE COMING OF THE INVESTOR

Investors began to enter the coin market in large numbers in the mid to late 1970s. The timing was no accident: Coins, like precious metals, have come to be viewed as hedges against economic calamities, and the late 1970s were years of unusual turbulence economically. Inflation was on the rise and many people were skeptical of the government's ability to control it. They also were wary of conventional investments such as stocks.

Driven by these fears, many turned to tangible assets and diverted large sums of money into gold, silver, and other such investments—including coins. Some combined their interest in coins and precious metals by buying *bullion coins*. These are coins whose value goes up or down in accordance with the value of the metal they contain—usually gold or silver. We'll discuss these in greater detail in a later chapter.

During the period ending in early 1980, the coin market experienced the most tremendous boom it has ever enjoyed.

THE GROWTH OF COLLECTING/INVESTING

As the number of collectors and investors expanded, so did the demand for better-date coins. The results were entirely predictable: As market demand increased for a fixed (and small) supply, prices began to escalate dramatically. At the same time, more and more people began to approach rare coins as both a collecting outlet and an investment.

Many collector/investors are baby boomers grown up: people who possibly started collecting coins when they were twelve or thirteen years old and built a solid foundation, then took a hiatus to pursue other interests such as college, courtship, and careers. Many of these collector/investors returned to the field in the mid to late 1980s and returned with a vengeance, bringing with them not only their strong foundation in coins but also finely honed minds and high incomes—testaments to their high degree of success at institutions of higher learning and in their careers.

These people are buying coins like there's no tomorrow. They have substantial sums of money at their disposal and they're savoring the chance to spend it on desirable coins. They appreciate every aspect of coins, including the one which can benefit *your* pocketbook: the financial aspect.

Collector/investors have added to the market's volatile nature—its susceptibility to going up or down in value very quickly.

Collectors and investors—and collector/investors—come in different degrees. Many, for example, would fall between the *Collector* and *Collector/Investor* locations on our graphic. The coin buyer spectrum is broad, diverse, and continuous, and buyers can be found across that spectrum.

THREE KINDS OF RARE COINS

For the purposes of this book, there are basically three different kinds of valuable coins.

One group consists of coins that are possible to come across in pocket change. These coins are described in Chapter Two.

Another group consists of coins you'd have to purchase. These tend to be coins with very low mintages and in very high grades or levels of preservation. They're the kind of coins investors favor. We'll look at these in greater detail in later chapters.

The third group of coins consists of what might be called "cigar-box rarities." They're coins that you might find in a cigar box up in the attic, or stashed away in a shoe box on a shelf at the back of a closet.

"Cigar-box rarities" probably wouldn't be found in pocket change. Many are coins that aren't being minted anymore. But most people have such coins sitting around the house, or know of a friend or relative who does. Often, they've been handed down by relatives who found them—or maybe even purchased them—years ago. If so, they may be quite valuable. Many coins that were looked upon as common fifty years ago, or even twenty-five years ago, are worth large sums of money in the current marketplace.

The cigar-box rarities which are most valuable—and which you might have a chance of finding—are listed in Chapter Three, along with their fair market value.

There's an excellent chance that some of these scarce coins—coins that have become quite valuable over the years—may be sitting in *your* attic, or perhaps in a jewelry case in the back of a dresser drawer. Perhaps your father put them there many years ago, when they were still regarded as not of great consequence, then forgot them. Or maybe they've been handed down through generations that go back even farther.

PROOF SETS AND MINT SETS

A proof set is a group of specimen-quality coins, usually bearing a uniform date and housed in protective packaging. Proof coins are made by taking special, highly polished coin blanks and striking them several times with highly polished dies. These are considered the highest-quality coins available. The United States Mint offers proof sets for sale to the public every year.

A mint set, by contrast, consists of business-strike coins: the kind that are produced for circulation. A mint set contains one example of each different coin struck for circulation in any given year by each of the different mints. The coins in such a set may have been chosen carefully, but they're business strikes just the same.

Normally, a proof set costs more than a mint set when purchased from the government and also has higher value in the resale market. However, on occasion a mint set may be more valuable in the resale market than the corresponding proof set for that year. This may happen, for example, if the mint set contains a coin that wasn't actually made for general use. Since the mint set then contains the only circulation-quality example, that coin and that set will command an added premium.

MINT MARKS AND HOW TO LOCATE THEM

Many coins' values are enhanced by the presence of *mint marks*. These are little letters denoting the mint facility where the coins were manufactured.

During its earliest years, the United States Mint had only one production plant—in Philadelphia—and so there was no need to identify the source of any coins. As the nation grew and coinage requirements rose, branch mints were established in cities around the country. Each of these branches placed a mint mark on its coins to distinguish them readily from those being made at other mints.

Following are the letters used on U.S. coins to denote branch mints:

C—Charlotte, North Carolina (1838–1861, gold coins only)
CC—Carson City, Nevada (1870–1893)
D—Dahlonega, Georgia (1838–1861, gold coins only)
D—Denver (1906 to date)
O—New Orleans (1838–1909)
S—San Francisco (1854 to date)
W—West Point, New York (1984 to date)

Throughout most of U.S. history, coins produced at the main mint in Philadelphia carried no mint mark. Their origin was denoted by the *absence* of any such mark. In recent years, however, a small P has been placed on most coins produced in Philadelphia. This practice began in 1979, when the P mint mark was used on the Susan B. Anthony dollar. The following year, it was added to all other coins with one exception: No P has been used on Lincoln cents.

A Philadelphia mint mark was used one other time. During World War II, nickel was urgently needed for war-related purposes, so from 1942 through

1945 the Mint used a substitute alloy without any nickel in making five-cent pieces. The emergency alloy's components were copper, silver, and manganese. To denote this change in composition, the Mint placed large mint marks above Monticello's dome on the coins' reverse—including a large, slender P on non-nickel "nickels" produced during those years in Philadelphia. (The reverse of a coin is what is commonly known as the "tails" side and carries the monetary value of the coin. The obverse or "heads" side commonly carries a portrait and the year of the coin's issue.)

On nineteenth-century coins, the mint mark was usually placed at the base of the reverse, below the wreath or eagle depicted on that side. Mint marks' locations have varied a great deal more on twentieth-century coins, and some coins have carried them in several different places at different times.

Here's a checklist of where to look for mint marks on some of the coins you're most likely to encounter in current pocket change or older hoards:

- Lincoln cent (1909 to date)—below the date.

- Indian Head cent (1859–1909)—below the wreath (mint marks appear only on coins dated 1908 and 1909).

- Jefferson nickel (1938 to date)—on the reverse, to the right of Monticello, on most dates from 1938 to 1964; above Monticello on war nickels from 1942 to 1945; below the date from 1968 to the present.

- Buffalo nickel (1913–1938)—on the reverse, below the words *FIVE CENTS*.

- Liberty Head nickel (1883–1912)—on the reverse, to the left of the word *CENTS* (mint marks appear only on coins dated 1912).

- Roosevelt dime (1946 to date)—on the reverse, to the left of the torch's base, from 1946 to 1964; above the date from 1968 to the present.

- "Mercury" dime (1916–1945)—on the reverse, to the left of the fasces (the symbolic bundle of rods).

- Barber dime (1892–1916)—below the wreath.

- Washington quarter (1932 to date)—below the wreath from 1932 to 1964; to the right of George Washington's pigtail from 1968 to the present.

- Standing Liberty quarter (1916–1930)—to the left of the date. (*NOTE:* The M to the right of the date is not a mint mark; it stands for Hermon MacNeil, the coin's designer.)

- Barber quarter (1892–1916)—below the eagle.

- Kennedy half dollar (1964 to date)—to the left of the eagle's tail feathers in 1964; below John F. Kennedy's neck from 1968 to the present.

- Walking Liberty half dollar (1916–1947)—on the front, below *IN GOD WE TRUST*, in 1916 and 1917; on the reverse, above and to the left of *HALF DOLLAR*, from 1917 to 1947 (1917 examples come in both varieties).

- Barber half dollar (1892–1915)—below the eagle.

- Anthony dollar (1979–1981)—above Susan B. Anthony's right shoulder.

- Eisenhower dollar (1971–1978)—below Dwight D. Eisenhower's neck.

- Peace silver dollar (1921–1935)—on the reverse, below the word *ONE*.

- Morgan silver dollar (1878–1921)—below the wreath.

- Saint-Gaudens $20 gold piece (1907–1933)—above the date.

- Liberty Head $20 gold piece (1850–1907)—below the eagle.

Now that you have some idea of where you fall on the collector/investor spectrum and the different types of coins that are available to you, it's time to take a closer look at the coins you already have—in your pocket change.

CHAPTER 2

A FORTUNE IN POCKET CHANGE

A penny saved isn't always a penny earned. It can be *thousands* or *millions* of pennies earned if the penny in question is rare.

A client of mine discovered this recently when he looked through a box of old coins in the attic of his grandmother's home. Included in that hoard were several Lincoln cents dated 1909. They turned out to be extremely scarce coins worth hundreds of dollars apiece—yet they had been pulled out of pocket change many years before. Thus, the initial "investment" had been just a penny apiece.

That wasn't *all* my client found. Altogether, that box of coins probably contained only a few hundred dollars in face value—but because some of the coins were rare and especially well preserved, the tiny keepsakes were worth more than *a quarter of a million dollars* as collector's items. And they hadn't cost a penny more than "face" when the grandmother and other family members set them aside.

This experience is hardly an isolated case. Over the years, untold thousands of people have come across valuable coins in their pockets or purses, or set aside coins for sentimental reasons and learned later to their amazement that those coins had soared in value as collectibles.

MISSTRIKES AND MINT MARKS

Sometimes the value of such coins stems from the fact that they are "misstrikes": coins with obvious errors that somehow eluded detection at the mint where they were made. Other times, they're valuable because they display an important identifying mark, such as a mint mark. As I explained in Chapter One, coins produced at certain mints are stamped with little letters denoting the place of manufacture. Coins made at the Denver Mint have a small letter D, while those produced at the San Francisco Mint have an S.

Worth $200. *1970 Roosevelt dime struck off-center and too many times at the Denver Mint. (Photo courtesy* Coin World)

The presence—or absence—of a mint mark can sometimes make a difference of hundreds or thousands of dollars in the value of certain coins. Those 1909 Lincoln cents found by my client, for instance, had a small letter S under the date. That means they were made at the San Francisco Mint. They also had the letters V.D.B. at the base of the reverse, or "tails" side. These are the initials of Victor D. Brenner, the artist who designed the Lincoln cent. Without the S mint mark and the initials of the designer, those pennies would be worth just two or three dollars apiece. Those letters were missing on most of the Lincoln cents produced in 1909. Only a few displayed them—and with coins as with anything else, value is determined by supply and demand. The supply of these coins is small, the demand is great, and therefore the value is high.

Worth $600. *1909-S V.D.B. Lincoln cent received in change at a supermarket. (Photo courtesy* Coin World)

Most of these 1909-S V.D.B. cents were put away years ago by collectors. But some turn up in ordinary pocket change even now. A few years ago, a hospital employee in Los Angeles got an unusual cent in change at a local supermarket. She showed it to a friend at the hospital, seventy-nine-year-old Sid Lindenbaum, who worked there as a volunteer. Lindenbaum, a longtime coin collector, looked at the strange cent under a magnifying glass—and sure enough, it had both the S and the V.D.B.

"Miracles can still happen!" Lindenbaum exclaimed in an interview with a newspaper reporter. "I've been collecting coins for over sixty years and this is a first."

The coin had some wear, but wasn't in bad condition considering its age— two years older than Lindenbaum himself. Buying one would have cost the veteran hobbyist a couple of hundred dollars. Doing the right thing, he compensated his friend and both shared the joy of the occasion.

"I paid her more than she ever dreamt a Lincoln penny could possibly be worth, and she was as deliriously happy as I was," Lindenbaum told the reporter.

Some coins are valuable because they *lack* a mint mark. A case in point occurred in 1982, when the Philadelphia Mint made a small number of dimes without the mint mark P which normally appears just above the date on coins from that mint. Because of that omission and the scarcity of these dimes, collectors soon began to bid up the price. If one of these coins shows up in your change next time you go to the store, put it in a safe place: It's worth at least $50—and possibly several times more, depending on what condition it's in.

PROFITABLE MISTAKES

"Mint errors"—oddball coins—make great conversation pieces, and finding one can sometimes be the next best thing to digging up buried treasure.

Consider these examples:

- In 1955, odd-looking cents began appearing in upstate New York and New England. The date and lettering on the "heads" side of these coins (the side called the "obverse" by collectors) had a double image—a sort of shadow effect. Thousands of these pennies popped up in people's change.

At that time, cigarettes cost eighteen cents a pack and people who bought them in vending machines would insert twenty cents and get their two cents change tucked inside the cellophane in the pack. On occasion, both these coins would be double-

Worth $600. *1955 doubled-die Lincoln cent, a mint error. This example is circulated or worn. (Photo courtesy* Coin World)

image cents. Lots of people saved them as curiosities—and today they're glad they did: These 1955 "doubled-die" cents, as collectors call them, are now worth almost $400 even in used condition. Brand new, they're worth well over $1,000 apiece.

• In 1972, similar double-image cents began turning up in the East, especially in and around Philadelphia. These weren't quite as obvious as the ones from 1955, and they seemed to be somewhat more numerous. Nonetheless, they were soon bringing premiums of well over $100 apiece. Some show up in pocket change even now—and when they do, they're readily salable to dealers and collectors for $50 to $200, depending on how well preserved they are.

Worth $250. *1972 doubled-die Lincoln cent, a mint error. This example is new and has not been spent. Notice the prominent doubling of the letters, as the close-up indicates. (Photo courtesy* Coin World)

Worth $120. *1995 doubled-die Lincoln cent, a mint error. Doubling is most visible on LIBERTY, and IN GOD WE TRUST, shown here blown up. (Photo courtesy Heritage)*

- In 1995, thousands of Lincoln cents minted in Philadelphia (without a mint mark) turned up with doubling on the obverse. The error is most obvious in the word *LIBERTY*. These coins were being sold for $40 or so by the end of the year. Values are highest in top mint condition. The gem pictured sold for auction for $120.

- In 1937, an especially fascinating error was discovered on certain Buffalo nickels. For those of you too young to remember them, let me explain that these well-loved coins had the portrait of an Indian on the "heads" side and a realistic likeness of a bison on the reverse.

On a small number of 1937 nickels made at the Denver Mint, the bison's right front leg appeared to be missing. These "three-legged" nickels became extremely popular with collectors, and remain in great demand to this day. You won't find Buffalo nickels in pocket change today, but chances are good that you—or a member of your family—may have a few stuck away in a dresser or desk. If so, check the dates and if you find any dated 1937, count the legs on the bison. A three-legged nickel can be worth many hundreds of dollars in top condition.

Worth $450. *1937 Buffalo nickel struck by the Denver Mint. The weakness of the right leg (left to you) has led to collectors calling this the "three-legged Buffalo." (Photo courtesy* Coin World)

LOW-MINTAGE COINS

In 1950, the government made only about two million Jefferson nickels at the branch mint in Denver. That's far below normal production levels. Each of these Denver nickels carried a small letter D just to the right of the building on the back of the coin (Monticello, the home of Thomas Jefferson). Collectors got wind that the nickels were scarce and rushed to their banks. They saved so many that hardly any entered circulation. Within a few years, these nickels were selling for $30 apiece. Some can still be found in circulation, and even in worn condition they're worth about $5 each.

Sometimes people put away coins from special years—years that have personal meaning to them, or years when new coins first appear. Many people saved Kennedy half dollars when those were first produced in 1964.

I know of one woman born in 1921 whose parents assembled a set of all the U.S. coins bearing that date. They did this soon after their child's birth, putting together the set from coins they obtained at their local bank—coins that had never been spent and were still mint fresh. Twenty-one years later, on their daughter's wedding day, they gave her the coins. As luck would have it, the mintage levels of most U.S. coins were unusually low during 1921. As a result, the coins in this set are extremely desirable to dealers and collectors. In fact, this meticulously preserved set—formed by noncollectors for a total of just a few dollars—is now worth more than $50,000. This felicitous set of coins, a birth memento that later became a wedding gift, is now a valued nest egg, helping to secure the woman's golden years.

PROOF SETS

Birth-year tributes are much more common now than they were back in 1921. But rather than obtaining ordinary coins from a bank, parents today frequently purchase current-year "proof sets" from the government or a coin shop.

The U.S. Mint makes two or three million proof sets every year. Each set contains special, high-quality examples of all the current coins—one example each of the cent, nickel, dime, quarter, and half dollar. These coins are produced by a painstaking process which gives them shimmering mirror-like surfaces and a frosty appearance on the high points. Each set is housed in a plastic presentation case suitable for display. Up to and including 1998, the cost of these sets was $12.50 apiece. In 1999, the Mint struck the first five statehood Washington quarters and included all five in the regular proof set, raising the issue price to $19.95. It also offered a five-coin proof set with only the quarters for $13.95.

Proof sets, too, contain mint errors now and then. And, when they do, the coins in question can be worth a lot of money.

As in the case of regular coins, the error often takes the form of a missing mint mark. That happened, for instance, in 1970, when someone forgot to stamp the letter S above the date on a small number of dimes produced for that year's proof sets. All the proof coins were made at the branch mint in San Francisco and should have carried the mint mark—but an estimated 2,200 dimes did not. Today, those dimes are worth $700 apiece.

A similar error occurred with nickels in 1971. In an estimated 1,655 proof sets that year, the Jefferson nickel was missing the S mint mark. Today, each one is worth close to $1,000.

Worth $1,500. *1971 no-S proof Jefferson nickel. All of the proof coins were struck in San Francisco and were supposed to have carried the S mint mark. (Photo courtesy* Coin World*)*

History has a way of repeating itself at Uncle Sam's mints. In 1983, the S turned up missing again on the dimes in a small number of proof sets. These mint errors are now bringing $200 to $300 apiece. And in 1990, the S was missing on Lincoln cents in 3,555 proof sets. One collector in Washington State bought four 1990 proof sets from the Mint and all four contained no-S cents. He sold the sets to a dealer for $1,400 apiece, or a total of $5,600—a very tidy return on his $44 investment. The near-perfect example shown here sold at auction in 2004 for $15,000, although most examples are worth a bit more than a third of that.

Worth $6,000. *1990 no-S proof Lincoln cent. Again, someone at the mint left off the S. It should have appeared just under the date. (Photo courtesy Heritage)*

One of the most desirable of these mint-error proof coins is the no-S proof dime of 1968. It's thought that fewer than five hundred examples of this coin were produced, and each has a market value of $6,000 to $7,000 at this writing.

Obviously, your chances of finding a $6,000 coin in pocket change, or in a low-cost proof set, are remote. But they're no more remote than your chances of scoring a $6,000 win in a lottery. And I'd be willing to bet you'll spend a lot less money—and have a lot more fun—seeking your fortune in pennies, nickels, and dimes than in random numbers.

A 1989 RARITY

Finding a rare coin in a proof set isn't quite the same as finding one in pocket change. You do have to spend a modest premium above the face value to get the proof set. But the thrill of discovery, the sense of satisfaction, and the joy of ownership are really no different at all. And the profits are equally real and equally high.

Proof sets aren't the only special coins sold to the public by the government. In recent years, the U.S. Mint has also made a number of "commemorative" coins—coins produced in honor of noteworthy people or events. In 1986, for example, the

Mint made three coins for the one hundredth anniversary of the Statue of Liberty. And in 1987, it produced two special coins as a two hundredth-birthday tribute to the nation's Constitution.

In 1989, the Mint produced three special coins to honor the U.S. Congress on its two hundredth anniversary. One of these, a silver dollar, was sold to collectors and other interested purchasers for $23 each. A few of the Congress silver dollars were found to have a seldom-seen error—and, as this is written, coins with this error are being bought and sold for prices in excess of $300 apiece.

The error involves a feature known as the "rotation" of the coin. On most U.S. coins, the "heads" and "tails" designs are engraved in diametrically opposite positions; when the obverse design is right side up, the reverse design is upside down. To see what I mean, take a quarter out of your pocket and hold it in your hand. Position it so that George Washington's portrait is right side up, with the date at the bottom. Flip the coin over, from north to south, and the eagle should be standing straight up. (If it isn't, you've got an error coin that may be worth a premium to collectors.)

On a small number of 1989 Congress silver dollars, the reverse is rotated 180 degrees from this normal position. If you flip one of *these* coins in the manner I just described, from north to south, it will look upside down.

This may not seem like much of an error to you, but many collectors view it as a great rarity and they're willing to pay a correspondingly great premium.

A VALUABLE 1997 NICKEL

Jefferson nickels are minted each year by the hundreds of millions. In 1997, however, the U.S. Mint made one kind of Jefferson nickel that was so scarce—and so highly desired by collectors—that within a matter of weeks it was being sold for several hundred dollars.

The Mint produced the unusual nickels as part of a special collector set honoring the U.S. Botanic Garden in Washington, D.C. The centerpiece of the set—ostensibly, at least—was a silver dollar bearing a design emblematic of the famous national garden. But the set—the Botanic Garden Coinage and Currency Set—also contained a crisp new $1 bill and a 1997 Jefferson nickel because the two presidents depicted on these pieces of money, George Washington and Thomas Jefferson, both were identified closely with horticulture. And while the silver dollar and the $1 bill could be obtained elsewhere as well, the nickel was a type available only as part of this special set.

The nickel was distinctive because of the way it was made: Unlike regular Jefferson nickels, which have a shiny appearance when they are new, this one exhibited a dull "matte" finish because the dies used to produce it were subjected to chemical treatment. Mint technicians applied a combination of aluminum oxide and silver dioxide to the dies, spraying them with this mixture under high pressure. The nickels made from these dies are readily identifiable—and since the Mint limited production to 25,000 Botanic Garden Coinage and Currency Sets, and the nickels could be obtained nowhere else, the 1997 "matte-finish" coin was viewed at once by collectors as an instant rarity—the lowest-mintage issue in the whole Jefferson series.

Worth $175. *1997 matte-finish Jefferson nickel from U.S. Botanic Garden Coinage and Currency Set. (Photo courtesy Heritage)*

As you might expect, the Botanic Garden set was also an instant sellout. All 25,000 sets were sold almost immediately, even though the Mint cut multiple orders to a maximum of five sets per customer. The lucky buyers got their sets for $36 apiece from Uncle Sam, and could have sold them for ten times that amount within days. As of June 2000, the matte-finish nickel was trading in the resale market for $175 or more, making it one of 1997's very best investments. Indeed, for those who bought it from the Mint, this curious five-cent piece was an even better buy than most stocks—and, at a time when bulls were running rampant on Wall Street, that was quite an accomplishment! The virtually flawless example pictured sold at auction in 2004 for $630.

A SCARCE 1998 HALF DOLLAR

In 1998 the U.S. Mint produced another "matte"-finish coin—this time a Kennedy half dollar. And like its Jefferson nickel counterpart from the previous year, it proved to be a winner for those who bought it.

The matte half dollar was offered to Mint customers as part of a two-coin "Kennedy Collectors Set," also including an uncirculated example of the 1998 Robert F. Kennedy silver dollar. The dollar was a one-year commemorative coin marking the 30th anniversary of Robert Kennedy's death. The Mint did not limit the number of sets it would produce, as it had done with the 1997 Botanic Garden set. However, it did establish a time limit, accepting only orders submitted by that date.

Orders were higher this time than they had been for the set containing the 1997 matte nickel—but not by very much. When the Mint announced that the all-but-final figure was approximately 62,000, the price of the set rose sharply in the secondary market. Within a short time, it was selling for more than twice its $59.95 issue price, and some were predicting it would go up considerably more. Like the matte nickel, this new half dollar became overnight the lowest-mintage coin in its series. And it has the added advantage of the Kennedy mystique: Admirers of John F. Kennedy, not only in this country but also around the world, have helped make the Kennedy half dollar one of the most popular of all U.S. coins.

THE 1943 'COPPER' CENT

One of the most famous of all U.S. coins is the 1943 bronze Lincoln cent—widely and inaccurately referred to by many laypersons as the 1943 "copper" cent. (The actual coinage metal, bronze, is an alloy of copper, tin, and zinc.) Millions of non-collectors—people who don't know the first thing about coin collecting—have heard about this coin, know it's worth a great deal of money, and have made at least a cursory attempt to locate one in their pocket change.

By 1943, World War II was at a crucial stage and the war effort permeated every aspect of American society. Coinage was no exception. Copper was urgently needed for battlefield uses, and to help conserve the supply of this critical metal the U.S. Mint suspended production of bronze ("copper") cents and made the coins instead from steel with a coating of zinc. These "white" cents proved unsuitable almost at once. For one thing, people confused them with the dime; for another, they rusted rapidly. As a result, they were minted for just that one year.

Official government records make no mention of regular bronze cents dated 1943; as far as the Mint was concerned, it never made any. However, it's well established that a few such coins—probably fewer than twenty—do exist. Apparently, a few bronze coin blanks were still in a hopper at the end of production in 1942 and somehow got stamped along with the new steel cents in 1943.

Worth $87,500. *1943-S bronze Lincoln cent should have been struck in zinc-coated steel. (Photo courtesy Superior Stamp & Coin)*

For many years, a story made the rounds that the Ford Motor Company would give a new car to anyone finding a 1943 "copper" cent. That story was unfounded, but anyone fortunate enough to find such a coin today could certainly parlay it into a new car. It wouldn't be surprising, in fact, to see the former owner of some 1943 bronze cents driving around today in a Jaguar or a Porsche. One of these coins, a 1943-D cent (struck at the Denver Mint) changed hands at a Beverly Hills, Calif., auction in February 2003 for $212,750—the highest price ever paid for any Lincoln cent. That nearly doubled the record set three years earlier, in February 2000, when a 1943-S bronze cent (struck at the San Francisco Mint) sold for $115,000 at a Los Angeles auction. The 1943-D specimen is the only "copper-alloy" 1943 cent known to have been made at the Denver Mint. It was authenticated by the Professional Coin Grading Service (PCGS), which certified it as Mint State-64 Brown—an unusually high level of preservation for a 1943 bronze cent. Most of the examples that have come to light over the years have been in less-than-mint condition, indicating that these coins saw actual use in circulation. Ira Goldberg, a principal of the auction firm that conducted the February 2003 sale, Ira & Larry Goldberg Coins and Collectibles, said the coin originally belonged to the heirs of a Denver Mint employee. The same coin had brought $82,500 in its last previous sale, at an auction in May 1996, so its price level jumped more than two-and-a-half times in less than seven years—dramatic evidence of just how dynamic the market is for these famous mint errors.

As spectacular as those prices seemed at the time, as this book goes to press in October 2004, most of those values are up substantially.

The Philadelphia Mint produced the lion's share of the 1943 bronze cents— or at least those that have surfaced to date. As a result, specimens from that mint

Worth $165,000. *1943-S "copper" cent graded Mint State-61 Brown by NGC. (Photo courtesy Ira and Larry Goldberg Coins & Collectibles, Beverly Hills, California)*

(distinguishable by the absence of any mint mark below the date) bring somewhat lower premiums than their scarcer "D" and "S" counterparts. But they, too, cost about the same as some very snazzy cars. At the same auction in February 2003 where the 1943-D cent broke the record, a 1943 Philadelphia specimen went for an impressive $97,750—to the very same buyer. That coin had been certified as MS-61 by PCGS.

In December 1999, a different 1943 bronze cent from the Philadelphia Mint was sold in a private transaction for $112,500. That piece had been certified as MS-61 Red-Brown by ANACS. Some circulated specimens also came on the market that year—and did well enough to put their former owners in, say, a Lincoln Continental or a Cadillac. A Philadelphia piece graded Extremely Fine-40 changed hands for $32,200, and a 1943-S graded Very Fine-35 brought $51,750 I can vouch for the excitement surrounding the latter coin's sale, since I was in the gallery—bidding on the coin on behalf of a client—and ended up being the underbidder.

The flurry of excitement surrounding these rare wartime cents undoubtedly got a boost in February 1999 when the news media carried a report—which proved to be highly misleading—concerning the disappearance of a purported 1943 "copper penny" owned by an Idaho businessman. The man told The Associated Press that his wife had inadvertently spent the coin, which he said he had kept in plain view, in a dish atop his refrigerator, to avoid calling attention to it. The AP story was filled with inaccuracies, including a claim that the coin could be worth up to $500,000. Nonetheless, its wide dissemination triggered a wave of new public in-

Worth $80,000. *1943-S "copper" cent graded VF-35 by PCGS. I was the underbidder on this coin when it sold at auction in August 1999. (Photo courtesy Auctions by Bowers and Merena, Inc.)*

Worth $65,000. *Another 1943-S bronze Lincoln cent in a slightly lower grade level. (Photo courtesy Heritage Numismatic Auctions, Inc.)*

terest in the '43 bronze cent, helping pave the way for the round of record sales in the year that followed.

A similar media report in January 2004 sparked another burst of excitement among the general public—but again the story had an unhappy ending. The protagonist this time was a Staten Island, New York man who claimed to have found a 1943 "copper" cent in his storage box. A local coin dealer apparently tested the coin with a magnet—and it passed. (Steel cents are attracted to a magnet, but bronze cents are not—and this man's coin was not attracted.) At this point, the man, who is not a collector, contacted both me and, at my recommendation, Asa Aarons, the award-winning consumer reporter for WNBC-TV in New York. I had appeared on television with Asa in a series about the 1943 "copper" cent after my firm brokered one for nearly $100,000. When the Staten Island man told me that his coin had passed the magnet test, I advised him to submit it to a certification service so that its authenticity could be verified. He replied that he wouldn't let the coin out of his sight.

When Asa Aarons learned that I was just leaving to attend the Florida United Numismatists (FUN) coin show in Orlando, Fla., and that the major certification services would also be participating in the show, he agreed to have the man take his coin to Orlando and let the experts examine it on the spot, while television cameras captured the instant drama. The TV people took the unusual step of reimbursing the man for his trip—in return they were able to cover the story, which they did for NBC affiliates from coast to coast.

Sadly, the coin turned out to be an impostor: Someone had taken a 1945 cent (which was made of copper alloy) and altered the "5" in the date to resemble a "3." Expert authenticator Miles Standish and his skilled team at the Professional Coin Grading Service needed only seconds to spot the alteration and pass the news along to the coin's now crestfallen owner. Instead of being rare and worth a small fortune, the coin was just an ordinary cent. But again, as in the Idaho case five years earlier, the story produced enormous publicity for the coin hobby in general and 1943 cents in particular. For days afterward, NBC affiliates continued to carry reports detailing the man's quest and his ultimate disappointment—and each time the story aired, the mystique of the *real* 1943 bronze cent became even more ingrained in the public's subconscious.

HOW TO TELL IF YOU HAVE A REAL BRONZE 1943 CENT

There are many, many fakes of the 1943 bronze cent—some produced initially as novelty items, others made with malice aforethought by con artists in hopes of victimizing the unwary. The most common fakes are copper-plated steel 1943 cents. As noted, these can be detected quite easily with a magnet: Being made of steel, they'll be attracted to the magnet, while genuine bronze cents will not. Simply applying a magnet to a 1943 cent will unmask the typical pretender, even though it may look very realistic to the naked eye.

Altered-date coins can be trickier to identify, as the man in New York discovered. In their effort to fleece unknowledgeable victims, fast-buck artists have tinkered with the dates of many cents that were bronze to begin with. Alterations are seen most frequently on cents made in 1945 and 1948, but also on those originally dated 1933 and 1953. In each of these cases, only one numeral had to be modified to change the date to 1943. Most of these alterations can be detected by examining a coin with a simple 5-power magnifying glass. For one thing, this will often reveal scratches on the surface, where the con artist applied a tool in reworking the metal. For another, the numerals in the date of a genuine 1943 cent are highly distinctive and differ significantly with those in many other dates, including 1945 and 1948. On a real 1943 cent, the "9" and "3" in the date are much longer than the "1" and "4." On both 1945 and 1948 cents, the last digit (either "5" or "8") is the same height as the "4." Similarly, the last "3" on 1933 cents is shaped much differently from the "3" on real 1943 cents, making it almost impossible to duplicate the appearance—even if the first "3" could be molded somehow into a convincing-looking "4." The 1953 cents have a "3" very much like those of 1943. But on all but the most professional alterations, scratches or other signs of finagling should be visible in the area where the "5" was changed to a "4."

Sophisticated fakes do exist. Fakes have been made, for instance, by using steel cents to produce new steel dies, then striking bronze cents with those dies. This technique would be impractical with any other cents, for copper is too soft for use in preparing dies. But, because of its hardness, the steel in the 1943 cent will withstand the pressure required to impart its image to another piece of steel. Counterfeits produced in this manner can be spotted by the softness—or "mushiness"—of elements in the design. The genuine 1943 bronze cents are exceptionally sharp; the Mint had to use extra pressure to bring up the design on the steel cents, so bronze cents struck under similar pressure have greater sharpness than normal bronze cents.

Because of the existence of so many fakes, some of which are good enough to fool even experienced collectors, it is imperative never to buy a 1943 bronze cent unless it has been authenticated and certified by a reputable third-party grading service. And if you should be fortunate enough to find one of these coins—or what *appears* to be one of these coins—you should have it certified immediately.

THE AURA OF THE 1943 CENTS

More than 60 years have passed since the 1943 bronze cents were produced, and since they presumably entered circulation. At this point, they have entered something else—the imagination of the American people—and achieved a status few, if any, other U.S. coins now enjoy: They are the stuff of legends. I have appeared frequently on Asa Aarons' consumer affairs segments on WNBC-TV News programs in New York, and on several occasions Asa and I have discussed the 1943 bronze cents—both genuine and fake. These segments have never failed to generate overwhelming response from the public. After several of these appearances, I created a number of web pages on wnbc.com, knbc.com and msnbc.com, and they all stirred tremendous interest. In fact, NBC's on-line services director told me that the weather was the only other subject that drew as much interest while the 1943 cents were on the Web sites for a period of over a year. My web work for NBC News was later given a "best mass-market web site" award.

1943 "copper" cent sold by the author's firm to a collector for nearly $100,000. This coin and Scott Travers were widely publicized on television for the sale. (Photo courtesy Scott Travers Rare Coin Galleries, LLC)

The odds are long against finding a genuine bronze 1943 cent in your pocket change, or stashed away in a cubbyhole in that old desk in your attic. But it could happen—and the fact is, it *has* happened for other lucky people over the years.

OTHER WARTIME RARITIES

Oddball coins seem to be produced more frequently at times when the nation is at war. There are several reasons for this. The need to conserve strategic metals may lead to experimentation with new compositions—as happened with Lincoln cents in 1943—and this may result in unintended coinage consequences. Wartime economies may cause the Mint to stretch the normal working life of its equipment, including coinage dies, and this may lead to coins with weak strikes and other deficiencies. And skilled Mint technicians may be off fighting the war, leaving their jobs at the Mint in the hands of less experienced personnel, more prone to making mistakes that will turn up in the hands of John Q. and Jane Q. Public.

World War II gave rise to an unusually high number and variety of offbeat U.S. coins. All of the factors just mentioned contributed to this. Beyond these elements, though, the nation's coinage needs were exceptionally high; the war shoved the U.S. economy into high gear, and after more than a decade of unusually low Depression-era mintages, Americans needed new coins in unprecedented numbers. The conditions were ideal for mint-error coins, and the bumper crop that resulted has been a boon for collectors ever since.

The 1943 bronze cents are surely the most famous of the World War II mint errors, but they have some distinguished—and extremely valuable—company. Here are a few others that you should be on the lookout for when checking your pocket change or old accumulations:

• The 1942 "white-metal" Lincoln cent.

   The experiments that resulted in the 1943 steel cents actually began in 1942, and during that year the Mint produced numerous test coins in various compositions—including not only new metals but also glass and Bakelite. Almost all of those die-trial pieces later were destroyed, but at least one is known to have escaped. The piece in question carries the same design as the regular Lincoln cent but is made of white metal.

   In offering this coin for sale at an auction in August 1997, Heritage Numismatic Auctions of Dallas said that it has "almost the appearance of steel, being bright and nearly white . . ." Its actual composition had not yet been

Worth $12,500. *Experimental 1942 white-metal Lincoln cent. (Photo courtesy Heritage Numismatic Auctions, Inc.)*

determined, but there can be no question about its value: The coin—believed to be unique—brought the eye-popping sum of $12,500 at the sale.

• The 1944 steel Lincoln cent.

Widespread public dissatisfaction with the "white"1943 cents prompted the Mint to abandon the experiment after just one year. When cent production resumed in 1944, the zinc-coated steel gave way to brass, an alloy very much like the previous bronze, containing copper and zinc but lacking tin. Just as wartime requirements had dictated the removal of copper a year earlier, war conditions now provided the needed raw material: The Mint obtained the brass from salvaged cartridge shell casings.

While millions of people know about the off-metal bronze cents of 1943, few are aware that similar minting mistakes occurred in 1944, this time in reverse. Small numbers of steel cent blanks remained in the pipeline at the start of 1944, and these were then struck with the new date. A few escaped detection and reached collectors' hands, and these now command substantial premiums.

Worth $12,500. *1944 zinc-coated steel Lincoln cent should have been struck in brass. (Photo courtesy Heritage Numismatic Auctions, Inc.)*

Worth $20,000. *1944-D zinc-coated steel Lincoln cent. (Photo courtesy* Coin World.*)*

The 1944 steel cents have never captured the public's imagination in the same way as the 1943 "coppers," so they've trailed behind in value—but their market level has risen impressively through the years. In 1997, an AU-58 example from the Denver Mint brought $5,000 at a Heritage auction. By February 2003, the market had advanced to the point where two specimens in slightly lower grades both sold for more than six times that amount: A P-mint piece graded AU-55 by PCGS brought $31,050 and a 1944-D graded AU-53 by PCGS went for $35,650. As with the 1943 coppers, certification is a must when buying or selling these appealing mint errors.

- Wartime Jefferson nickels struck on prewar planchets.

The Lincoln cent wasn't the only U.S. coin to undergo a change of composition during World War II. The Jefferson nickel got a make-over, too, and for much the same reason: Combat requirements led to the removal of nickel as a component of U.S. coinage. Up until 1942, the five-cent piece had been 75-percent copper and 25-percent nickel. Midway through production that year, the coin was changed to an alloy of 56-percent copper, 35-percent silver, and 9-percent manganese. This alloy would be retained through the end of 1945—and to underscore the change, the Mint placed a large mint mark above

Worth $5,000. *1944-P Jefferson nickel of standard copper-nickel composition should have been struck in wartime alloy of copper, silver, and manganese. (Photo courtesy Superior Stamp & Coin)*

the portrait of Monticello, Thomas Jefferson's home, on each coin's reverse. A large "P" appeared on wartime Jefferson nickels from the Philadelphia Mint, coins which normally wouldn't have carried any mint mark at all.

Recently, a collector came across a 1944-P nickel made from the prewar alloy of 75-percent copper and 25-percent nickel. The coin had a large "P" above Monticello, suggesting along with its date that it should have been made of the substitute alloy, but tests confirmed that it was of standard composition. This coin, a circulated piece graded Very Fine-30, was offered for sale by Superior Stamp & Coin, but failed to attract the minimum required bid of $5,000. Still, it is clearly a major rarity and worth a pretty penny—in fact, many thousands of pretty pennies.

• The 1942-over-1 Mercury dimes.

The three silver U.S. coins—the half dollar, quarter, and dime—didn't get new alloys during World War II. It seems ironic today, with precious metal gone from our everyday coins, but while copper and nickel needed to be conserved to aid the war effort, silver was relatively plentiful, even being added to the nickel. As noted previously, however, the war affected coinage in other ways, as well, and one of those impacts—the stretching of Mint resources—probably was responsible for a fascinating and valuable error on a wartime U.S. dime.

Worth $22,500. *1942-over-1 Mercury dime, with the "2" engraved over the final "1" of "1941."* *(Photo courtesy Superior Stamp & Coin)*

In 1942, with a budget squeeze being applied, Mint technicians decided not to discard some of the dies used in the production of dimes dated 1941, as they would have done in normal times. Instead, they cut a "2" over the final "1" in the date. Since the dies were not yet worn out, this seemed like a good way to maximize their working life and thus save the government money. But people soon noticed the dimes produced with these dies, for the 1 was clearly visible under the 2. In fact, the date appeared to be 1942/1. The "overdate" dimes were quickly removed from circulation, and it soon became apparent that they were quite scarce. A superb example, graded Mint State-67 by the Professional Coin Grading Service, fetched $15,950 at a 1997 auction held by Superior Stamp & Coin. It would be hard to imagine a better return on any investment costing just ten cents!

1965 SILVER ROOSEVELT DIME

The U.S. Mint officially stopped the manufacture of silver Roosevelt dimes in 1964. So virtually every Roosevelt dime you find dated "1965" will not be silver; it will be composed of copper and nickel "clad." This rare 1965 dime mistake is made of 90% silver and, as such, is 1 of only a few accounted for. You can tell silver from clad by examining the coin's edge: The rare silver coin has a silver edge; *the common clad coin has a strip of brown around the edge.* Experts believe that many hundreds of 1965 silver dimes were manufactured by mistake by the Mint, and are waiting to be discovered hiding in piggy banks and cookie jars. These coins, depending on their condition, can be valued up to $30,000 or more.

Worth up to $30,000. *1965 Silver Roosevelt dime. The U.S. Mint officially stopped manufacturing silver Roosevelt dimes in 1964. The National Star featured this coin and the author in a 2-page spread. (Photo courtesy Scott Travers Rare Coin Galleries, LLC)*

CHECK THAT CHANGE!

Your chances of finding a 1943 copper cent or a 1909-S V.D.B. cent in pocket change are diminished by the fact that in 1959 the Lincoln cent's reverse got a new design. Since that time, the back of the coin has portrayed the Lincoln Memorial. With the passage of time, the earlier Lincoln cents—with two sheaves of wheat displayed on the reverse—have grown steadily harder to find in circulation. As a result, these "wheat-ears" cents are conspicuous when they do appear in change and therefore are quickly set aside. Likewise, a Buffalo nickel (three-legged or otherwise) would stand out from other coins if it showed up in circulation, and that reduces your chances of finding one of these.

There are many scarce and valuable coins waiting for lucky finders in cash drawers, sugar bowls, pockets, and purses today—but, for the most part, these are coins that blend in with the rest of our current coinage. Their basic design is the same, they're made of the same metal, and at first glance they don't look any different.

While they may *look* ordinary, these coins can often be like nuggets of high-grade gold for the prospectors lucky enough to find them.

To give you an idea of the quantity and diversity of these coins, I've compiled a list including some typical illustrations. I've limited this list to coins whose common counterparts are still routinely seen in circulation. It doesn't contain Buffalo nickels or pre-1959 Lincoln cents, for example, since those are seldom encountered anymore and any that did turn up—even common ones—would be set aside almost at once as curiosities. That, of course, would minimize the chances for finding pocket-change rarities of those types.

To readily identify some of the following coins, you may need a magnifying glass. But an inexpensive glass with 5-power magnification will do just fine.

Keep in mind that if you find one of these coins and offer it for sale to a dealer, he's likely to offer substantially less than its current list price. That, after all, is a retail price and dealers must purchase at wholesale in order to turn a profit.

Care to hold a personal treasure hunt? Here's a list of scarce coins—some worth hundreds of dollars—that might turn up in your pocket change today:

• The 1960 small-date Lincoln cents.

  Early in 1960, coin collectors noticed something strange about the new one-cent pieces coming out of the main mint in Philadelphia and the branch

1960-D small- and large-date Lincoln cents. The close-up of the 6 on the left is the large date; the 6 on the right is the small date. The large date has the longer tail on the 6. (Photos courtesy Coin World)

in Denver. The numbers in the date were perceptibly smaller on some of these cents than on others—and the "small-date" coins were significantly scarcer than those with larger numbers.

As word of these "instant rarities" spread around the country, a coast-to-coast scavenger hunt ensued. The small-date cents from the Philadelphia Mint proved to be much more elusive than those from Denver. Before long, the price of these 1960-P cents (which carry no mint mark below the date) jumped to $400 for a roll of fifty coins. That's $8 apiece—a very tidy profit for those who obtained these coins at face value. The Denver small-date cents (with a D below the date) rose as high as $20 a roll, or 40 cents apiece, which is also nothing to sneeze at and also a nice return for those who invested just a penny and a little time.

The premiums on these coins have dropped with the passage of time. Still, both will bring you considerably more than a penny for your thoughts if you're fortunate enough to find them in circulation. The 1960-P small-date cent is now worth between $1 and $2 each, depending on its condition, while the 1960-D is worth between a nickel and a dime.

How can you tell a "small date" from a "large date"? The photos make the distinction clear. Take special note of the 6 on the small-date cent: It looks somewhat squashed and has a shorter upward tail than its large-date counterpart. Also, in the small date, the numbers seem farther apart. And the top of the 1 lines up with the top of the 9.

Cents in 1960 proof sets also came in both varieties, and again the small-date version was quite a bit scarcer. You'd have to pay about $25 today for a 1960 proof set with the small-date cent. That's $10 more than the price of the normal set with the large-date cent.

• The 1960-D cent with a small date punched over a large date.

   The cents of 1960 come in many varieties. This is one case where you'll need magnification. Under a glass, you'll note what appears to be slight double images in the numbers in the date. What you're actually seeing are numbers from both the "small date" and the "large date."

• The 1969-S doubled-die Lincoln cent.

Earlier in this chapter, I wrote in some detail about the double-image cents made by mistake in 1955 and again in 1972 at the Philadelphia Mint. Those are coins you should always be alert for, since both command handsome premiums—and the 1972 cent, in particular, may very well appear in your pocket or purse someday. (The chances of discovering the 1955 cent are more remote since, as I noted earlier, the Lincoln cent's design was modified in 1959 and coins produced before that date are more likely to have been saved.)

While these are the best-known examples of "doubled-die" cents, they're not the only ones. Others exist—and some of these come with similarly fancy price tags.

One was made in 1969 at the San Francisco Mint (denoted by an S below the date). As with the 1955 and 1972 varieties, the features of this coin are doubled on only the obverse (or "heads" side). The date and inscriptions on this side of the coin display distinct doubling. You can see this much more readily under a magnifying glass, and I recommend that you buy one to assist you. It will come in handy not only in identifying doubled-die coins but also in spotting other mint errors and unusual varieties. A 5-power glass is fine for most such purposes, and you can obtain one for only a few dollars. You'll recoup this small investment with a single worthwhile find.

The 1969-S doubled-die cent would be a *very* worthwhile find: Well-known coin dealer Harry J. Forman of Philadelphia is paying between $100 and $200 for typical examples of this coin. And Forman says he would pay $1,000 for a really exceptional example.

• The 1970-S "Atheist" cent.

The motto *IN GOD WE TRUST* has appeared on U.S. coinage since 1864, when religious fervor born of the Civil War gave impetus to this and other expressions of the nation's collective belief in a supreme being. Not all coins carried the inscription right away; it didn't appear on the nickel, for example, until 1938. But it now has been a fixture on every U.S. coin for more than half a century.

The Lincoln cent has borne this familiar motto right from the start—since Abe Lincoln's penny first appeared on the scene in 1909. And the motto has a prominent place along the top of the obverse, right above Lincoln's head.

There are, however, a few Lincoln cents on which the nation's trust in God is compromised. The result is both interesting and potentially profitable for lucky pocket-change treasure hunters.

The compromise occurs because of mint errors which cause part of the motto to be missing. The best-known example of this took place in 1970 at the San Francisco Mint. Part of the metal on one or more of the obverse cent dies—the pieces of metal used to strike the "heads" side of the cent—broke off that year along the upper edge. As a result, that portion of the coin was covered by a "cud," or small lump of metal, instead of getting the imprint of the design. (Since the die metal was missing, the metal in the coin blank simply expanded and filled the empty area.) As luck would have it, the cud completely obliterated the words *WE TRUST* in the motto. Enterprising dealers soon dubbed this the "Atheist cent."

At one time, there was a lively market for Atheist cents and a brand new example would fetch $20 or more. The market isn't as active today—but, even so, a nice Atheist cent will bring about $5. Keep in mind that the error occurred on San Francisco cents, which have an S mint mark below the date.

• The 1970-S small-date Lincoln cent.

Small-date and large-date cents turned up again in 1970—this time on coins from the San Francisco Mint (identified by an S below the date). As in 1960, they appeared on both regular cents and proofs. And, once more, the small-date coins proved to be scarcer and more valuable.

1970-S small- and large-date Lincoln cents. The small date on the right has the top of the 7 and the top of the 0 aligned. (Photos courtesy Krause Publications)

The 1970 small-date cents didn't create as much excitement initially as their predecessors had ten years earlier. But, while the 1960 coins have dipped in value with time, the 1970 versions appear to be getting more popular and desirable. That's because collectors have determined that fewer were made.

To get a 1970-S small-date cent from a coin dealer, you'd have to pay about $17 each for the "business strike"—the regular kind produced for circulation—and

$65 for the proof. However, there's a much cheaper way to pick one up: Check the cents in that jar in your kitchen cupboard! You're not very likely to find one of the proofs; those were sold to collectors in custom-made plastic cases. But the regular kind may very well turn up. And, if it does, you've made yourself close to $20!

As with the 1960 small-date cents, it may take a little time before you can tell the "small" 1970 dates from the "large" ones. But knowing how to spot them is your edge! That's what gives you the inside track over people who don't know the difference. To the untrained eye, these coins—and the scarce 1960 coins, too—blend in with all the other Lincoln cents in a cookie jar or cigar box. The trick is to develop a *trained* eye. And it's really an easy trick.

Take a close look at the photos I've provided. Focus, in particular, on the 7 in each of the dates. In the large date, the tops of the 9 and the 0 are higher than the top of the 7. In the small date, the tops of all four numbers look uniform.

• The 1971-S cent with a doubled-die obverse (or "heads" side).

   This has been far less publicized than the 1972 doubled-die cent described earlier in this chapter, and apparently is far rarer.

• The 1972-D cent without the designer's initials V.D.B.

   Cents without the V.D.B. turned up in significant quantities starting in 1988 (see pages 55–56). The same kind of error has also been discovered on 1972 cents minted in Denver (with a D below the date). These appear to be considerably rarer than those from the late 1980s.

• The 1979-D cent without the designer's initials FG.

   Frank Gasparro had a long and busy career at the U.S. Mint, where he was chief engraver for more than sixteen years. Besides designing the back of the Kennedy half dollar, he also created the Lincoln Memorial design used on the reverse of the current cent. And just as his initials have sometimes been omitted from Kennedy halves, they've also turned up missing on Lincoln cents. The letters "FG" are supposed to appear just to the right of the Lincoln Memorial's base. But in 1979, they were left off a few of the cents from the Denver Mint (identifiable by the D below the date).

• The 1980 D-over-S cent.

   From time to time, more than one mint mark shows up on a coin—not in different places, but with one super-imposed directly above the other. Sometimes this occurs because of misguided economy: In an effort to save a little money, an engraver at one of the mints may take an unused die made for use at the San Francisco Mint (with an S mint mark) and cut a D into the metal right above the S so the die can be used in Denver. Inevitably, an eagle-eyed collector will detect the original letter with a magnifying glass.

"Over-mint-mark" and "overdate" varieties are not routine; this kind of sloppiness is discouraged at the Mint—and when it does take place, the coins that result are eagerly pursued by many collectors. That, in turn, gives them considerable value.

Through the years, several such varieties have been found among Lincoln cents. Under a glass, you'll see that the D mint mark below the date is actually superimposed above an S. This coin is considered very scarce.

• The 1981 D-over-S cent.

The same thing happened again the following year. Only a microscopic trace remains of the original "S" mint mark.

• The 1982 small-date zinc cent.

Most people don't realize that the current one-cent piece is made almost entirely out of zinc. It looks very much like the "copper" cent of yesteryear, but that's because it's plated with pure copper. The core of the coin is 99.2 percent zinc.

The Mint made the change in 1982 because the price of copper had risen to the point where the cent's metal value was approaching its value as money. Zinc is not only cheaper than copper but also lighter-weight, so more coins can be made from the same number of pounds.

The cent had contained zinc for more than a century; from 1864 to 1962, the coin's composition had been bronze (an alloy of copper, tin, and zinc), and since 1962 it had been brass (copper and zinc but no tin). But, in both those alloys, copper accounted for 95 percent of the weight. The present cent, by contrast, is 97.5 percent zinc and just 2.5 percent copper.

During the changeover year of 1982, brass and zinc cents were both produced in very substantial numbers. Both were made at Philadelphia (no mint mark) and also at Denver (a D below the date). And, to make matters even more interesting, the date that year came in both large and small varieties.

In all, there are seven different 1982 cent varieties: large-date brass cents from both Philadelphia and Denver . . . small-date brass cents from Philadelphia . . .

and large- and small-date zinc cents from both mints. For some reason, small-date brass cents weren't made at the Denver Mint—but that was the only missing combination.

None of these varieties turned out to be extremely scarce. But the small-date zinc cent from the Philadelphia Mint is elusive, and coin dealers who specialize in cents are currently paying $25 a roll (or 50 cents per coin) for this variety.

How can you tell the difference? It's relatively easy to distinguish the large date from the small; there's a sharp variation in size. Telling brass from zinc isn't quite so simple, since outwardly the zinc cent looks pretty much like the brass. People who handle coins on a regular basis find the brass cents noticeably heavier, but the difference may not be as apparent to those with less experience.

Until you gain the expertise and confidence to tell the coins apart without external help, I recommend the purchase of a simple scale. For less than a dollar, you can obtain a penny scale marketed by the Whitman Coin Products division of Western Publishing Company (1220 Mound Ave., Racine, WI 53404). With a brass cent, the indicator will dip; with a zinc cent, it will stay up.

• The 1983 doubled-die Lincoln cent.

In 1983, another double-image cent appeared. This time, however, the doubling was on the reverse. Find one of these and you'll be not only seeing double but sitting pretty: Brand new, this coin now retails for about $200—and even in worn condition it's worth between $50 and $100.

Worth $200. *1983 doubled-die Lincoln cent. This blow-up shows the doubled letters on the reverse that make this coin scarce and sought after. (Photo courtesy* Coin World*)*

Worth $100. *1984 doubled-die Lincoln cent. The doubled ear is visible on the blow-up. (Photo courtesy* Coin World)

One expert estimates that no more than 10,000 examples were produced. And most, he says, were released in the vicinity of Lancaster, Pennsylvania. Obviously, you should be especially watchful for this coin if you live within spending distance of that town.

• The 1984 cent without the initials FG.

This coin is similar to the 1979-D cent described a few paragraphs earlier. It's not a great rarity, but it's worth a modest premium to mint-error specialists.

• The 1984 cent with a doubled obverse.

This coin has attracted less publicity than the 1983 cent with the double-image reverse I just described. Nonetheless, it appears to be quite scarce; according to one expert, only about 2,000 have shown up. The doubling is clearest at Lincoln's ear and beard.

• Lincoln cents without the designer's initials V.D.B.

At the start of this chapter, I mentioned that some Lincoln cents derive substantial value from the presence of the letters V.D.B. As I explained, these are the initials of Victor D. Brenner, the artist who designed this durable coin. It now turns out that the *absence* of these initials can also give a coin added value.

Before reviewing the reason, let's go back to 1909, the year the Lincoln cent was introduced. Brenner's initials, along the lower edge on the coin's reverse, caught the eye of many sharp observers—and more than a few objected to the size of this "signature." So many complained, in fact, that the Mint removed the letters within a matter of weeks.

In 1918, the initials were restored—but in much smaller letters and in a location where they wouldn't be nearly as conspicuous: at the base of Abraham

Lincoln's shoulder. They've remained there ever since—or rather, they're *supposed* to be there. In 1988, collectors discovered a number of newly minted cents on which the initials were missing. Apparently, someone at the Mint inadvertently removed them while polishing one of the dies (the pieces of steel that impart the design to a coin, very much like cookie cutters).

The same thing happened again in 1989 and 1990. Pull out your magnifying glass and see if *you* can find some. If you do, there are dealers who will pay you upwards of $5 each. Please note, however, that the premiums will apply only to coins in brand new condition or very nearly so. Once Lincoln cents circulate for a while, the letters V.D.B. tend to wear down and wear off, and those coins naturally don't command a premium based on the absence of the initials.

- The 1939 Jefferson nickel with a doubled reverse.

Despite its age (more than fifty years old), this coin has a good possibility of turning up in pocket change. That's because Jefferson nickels still have the same design and metallic composition today as they did when they first came out in 1938. You'll notice the doubling especially in the words *FIVE CENTS* and *MONTICELLO*. (Don't expect to see a dramatic double image in the building; the doubling isn't that obvious.) This coin is worth $10 or more even in well-worn condition.

- The 1949 D-over-S Jefferson nickel.

You'll certainly need a 5-power glass—and maybe even a 10-power glass—to pick out this rarity; after all, the letters are small and the people who cut the dies were trying to conceal the original mint mark. But, if you're successful in finding one of these coins, the reward can be great.

The 1949 D-over-S nickel was struck at the Denver Mint with a die originally meant for San Francisco. Look very closely and you'll see part of the S directly below the D. You'll also see dollar signs, for this coin can be worth more than $100 in nice condition.

- The 1954 S-over-D Jefferson nickel.

In 1954, the tables were turned: This time, a die made for Denver was recut for use in San Francisco. The S mint mark doesn't completely hide the original D—although, once again, you'll need a decent magnifying glass to detect this. The payoff this time will be a little less, since this coin appears to be more common. Even so, you'll pocket $10 or more—a lot more if the coin is unusually nice.

- The 1955 D-over-S Jefferson nickel.

   In 1955, operations were halted at the San Francisco Mint, not to be resumed for more than a decade. Thus, the temptation was particularly strong to pull an unused San Francisco die off the shelf when the need arose for an extra die in Denver. After all, there wouldn't be any more need for the die in San Francisco.

   Whatever the cause, the result was another crop of D-over-S nickels. These coins are approximately equal in scarcity and value to the S-over-D nickels from one year earlier.

- The 1964-D nickel with E PLURIDUS UNUM.

   E PLURIBUS UNUM ("Out of many, one") is a motto that has graced U.S. coins for nearly two centuries. Once in a while, production problems lead to misspelling of this inscription. That's what happened in 1964 with Jefferson nickels made at the Denver Mint (with a D just to the right of Monticello on the reverse). Heavy polishing of one or more of the dies caused the center of the letter "B" to be obliterated. As a result, the word looks like PLURIDUS instead of PLURIBUS. This isn't an extremely valuable error, but it's certainly an interesting one—and it does command a modest premium.

- The 1983-D nickel with a doubled reverse.

   Again, here's a coin with doubling of some of the features—this time on the reverse. The double image is relatively weak on this 1983 nickel from the Denver Mint (with a D just below and just to the left of the date on the "heads" side). Still, it's worth a premium to dealers and collectors who specialize in this type of error.

- The 1964 dime struck in copper-nickel.

   The rising price of silver forced the U.S. government to discontinue production of silver dimes and quarters starting in 1965. Since then, these coins have been made from an alloy of copper and nickel bonded to a core of pure copper. All dimes and quarters minted during 1964 were made of silver—or rather, they were *supposed* to have been. But experiments with the new "clad" coinage were already under way at that time, and somehow a few dimes dated 1964 were made of copper-nickel, rather than silver. These are extremely rare and quite valuable. Hint: Look for a coppery reddish line around the rim of the coin; if it's there, the chances are good that you've found a "clad" coin, rather than a silver one.

- The 1967 dime with a doubled obverse.

   Again, the Mint produced a coin with a double image, this time on the "heads" side. It's uncertain where this 1967 dime was produced; from 1965 through 1967, the Mint withheld mint marks in order to discourage hoarding of coins by speculators. In any event, the coin is quite scarce. The doubling is most apparent on the mottos and the date.

- The 1970-D dime with a doubled reverse.

   By 1970, mint marks had been restored—and a double-image error was in evidence once again. This 1970 dime from the Denver Mint (with a D just above the date) has doubling on the reverse.

- The 1982 no-P Roosevelt dime.

   Up until recent years, coins that were made at the Philadelphia Mint almost never carried a mint mark. "P-mint" coins were distinguished not by a special letter, but rather by the *absence* of any such letter. But, since 1980, a tiny letter P has been stamped on all Philly coins except the cent.

Worth $150. *1982 no-P Roosevelt dime. (Photo courtesy Heritage)*

   As you might expect, this has given rise to errors now and then when the P has been omitted. One such error occurred in 1982, when collectors began to notice Philadelphia dimes without the mint mark. This error proved embarrassing for the Mint—but make no mistake, it can be a real bonanza for people like you: A typical example will bring you between $25 and $100.

- The 1965 quarter struck in silver.

   This is the flip side of the dime error I listed a few coins back. In that case, a 1964 dime was *supposed* to be silver but was made of copper-nickel instead. In 1965, all dimes and quarters were supposed to be made of copper-nickel—but a very small number of quarters got minted in silver by mistake.

This is a rare and valuable coin. Unlike "clad" coins, it *won't* have a reddish line around the rim.

• The 1970 quarter with a doubled reverse.

Once more, a double-image error appeared in 1970—this time on quarters from the Philadelphia Mint (struck without a mint mark near the lower right corner of the "heads" side, behind George Washington's pigtail). The doubling is visible only on the coin's reverse, and you'll need a magnifying glass to detect it.

• The 1970-D quarter with a doubled reverse.

Double-image reverses turned up in 1970 on quarters from the Denver Mint as well (this time with a D mint mark behind Washington's pigtail). There are quite a few different varieties of this particular error.

• The 1977-D silver-clad quarter.

In 1975 and 1976, the Mint made special part-silver versions of the Washington quarter, Kennedy half dollar, and Eisenhower dollar. These were sold to collectors at a premium. Production of these 40-percent silver coins was discontinued after 1976—or rather, it was *supposed* to have been. But in 1977, a few quarters were made at the Denver Mint (with a D mint mark behind the pigtail) on leftover silver-clad (40-percent silver) coin blanks. These are extremely rare and valuable.

• The 1989 no-P Washington quarter.

The P mint mark went astray again in 1989 on a small number of quarters. (The mint mark should appear behind George Washington's pigtail, near the bottom of the obverse.) And this time the error drew national attention, thanks to a page one story in *The New York Times*.

As with several other important mint errors, this one turned up in the largest quantities in Pennsylvania, especially the Pittsburgh area. An obvious explanation is the fact that the Mint itself is in that state, and these are early stops in the distribution chain. Multiple findings also were reported in North Carolina.

Coin dealer Harry Forman, himself a Pennsylvanian, touted this coin on the television program "Hidden Rewards." A number of lucky viewers who checked their change afterward found "no-P" quarters and shipped them off to Forman to claim their rewards—which were no longer hidden. The longtime Philadelphia dealer has purchased dozens of these coins at prices ranging from $10 to $100 apiece.

- The 1961 half dollar with a doubled reverse.

At first glance, Franklin half dollars seem rather common. These coins, bearing Benjamin Franklin's portrait on one side and the Liberty Bell on the other, had relatively high mintages throughout their short life span, from 1948 through 1963. On closer inspection, however, some have odd features that set them apart. In 1961, for example, some Franklin halves were made with doubling on the reverse, especially in the letters of E PLURIBUS UNUM.

Worth $5,000. *1961 cameo proof Franklin half dollar with doubled lettering on the reverse. (Photo courtesy Heritage Numismatic Auctions, Inc.)*

One of these coins appeared in an auction conducted by Heritage Numismatic Auctions in August 1997. Besides having a doubled reverse, this coin was a cameo proof—a special collector coin with dramatic contrast between its frosty devices (or raised portions) and its mirror-like fields (or background areas). It also was in a very high level of preservation: Proof-67. The winning bidder paid $3,500 for this prize—a princely sum belying the Franklin half dollar's seeming commonness.

- The 1964 half dollar with a doubled obverse.

The Kennedy half dollar drew international attention when it first appeared in 1964, soon after the assassination of President John F. Kennedy. Admirers of the slain president—not only in the United States but all around the world—rushed to obtain examples of the coin as Kennedy mementos. Only sharp-eyed collectors noticed that some of those very first Kennedy half dollars had doubling on the obverse (or "heads" side). You may very well have one sitting in a drawer or cigar box even now!

• The 1964 half dollar with a doubled reverse.

   Some 1964 Kennedy half dollars have doubling on the *reverse*, rather than the obverse. Get out your magnifying glass to look for this variety; it won't jump right out at you. But you'll spot it right away under the glass.

• The 1966 half dollar without the designer's initials FG.

   The Lincoln cent isn't the only coin discovered on occasion without its designer's initials. Eagle-eyed hobbyists have discovered that on some Kennedy half dollars, the letters FG are missing from their designated spot just to the right of the eagle's tail near the base of the coin's reverse. These are the initials of Frank Gasparro, the engraver who designed this side of the coin.

   As in the case of cents without the "V.D.B.," this omission resulted from overzealous polishing of one or more dies (the pieces of metal used to strike the coins).

   This error has been discovered on coins from a number of years and from different mints. Most don't seem to be excessively rare, but the 1966 is one of the scarcest. Relatively few examples are known with this date.

   Half dollars without the designer's initials are not world-class mint errors; some, in fact, might argue that the error is trivial. But don't let that discourage you from looking: If you find one, you can sell it to a small army of dedicated enthusiasts—including Harry Forman—for several dollars.

• The 1972-D half dollar without the designer's initials FG.

   The letters FG are missing on a small number of 1972 Kennedy halves from the Denver Mint (with a D below JFK's neckline on the "heads" side). These 1972-D error coins appear to be much scarcer than later ones.

• The 1973 half dollar without the initials FG.

   Here we go again! While you're checking Kennedy half dollars for Frank Gasparro's initials, make a special point of examining those dated 1973. This is another instance where some were made without them.

• The 1974-D half dollar with a doubled obverse.

   Another double-image error occurred in 1974, this time on Kennedy half dollars from the Denver Mint (with a D below Kennedy's neckline on the "heads" side). The doubling occurs only on the obverse and is plainest on the mottos. This appears to be a rare variety.

- The 1982 Kennedy half dollar without the designer's initials.

    The 1982 half dollar without the letters FG was the first to receive wide-spread publicity. Similar error coins had been known before that, but hadn't really attracted much attention. When the 1982 coins became popular, collectors took a closer look at earlier half dollars and discovered—or rediscovered—several others. At present, the 1982 is worth about $5.

- Wrong-planchet coins.

    On rare occasions, a coin is struck in error on a planchet, or coin blank, intended for a different denomination. A planchet meant for a Washington quarter might be struck, for instance, with dies bearing the image of a Jefferson nickel. Such errors are extremely interesting, very scarce, and usually quite valuable.

    At an auction in August 1997, Heritage Numismatic Auctions offered a Lincoln cent struck on a dime planchet. The error took place in 1968 at the San Francisco Mint—and to make matters even more interesting, this off-metal mistake was struck with highly polished dies meant for special collector coins called "proofs." The coin changed hands at the auction for $1,550.

Worth $1,550. *1968 Lincoln cent struck in error with proof dies on a dime planchet. (Photo courtesy Heritage Numismatic Auctions, Inc.)*

- Coins overstruck with features meant for other coins.

    Every now and then, a coin turns up with extraneous design elements stamped on top of its regular features. In most cases, these will be elements from another coin of the same kind—parts of a Lincoln cent superimposed, for instance, on another Lincoln cent. These errors come about in various ways during the production process. A coin already struck may pass between the dies again, for example, and be stamped in a different position.

    A highly unusual coin of this kind was offered for sale at Heritage's auction in August 1997. It was a Jefferson nickel where the second striking took place not only in a different position but on the opposite side. To heighten the intrigue, the basic coin was a 1973 nickel, but the overstriking was done with

Worth $3,500. *1973 Jefferson nickel overstruck with the design of a 1974 Jefferson nickel. (Photo courtesy Heritage Numismatic Auctions, Inc.)*

a die dated 1974. And the coin was discovered in a government "mint set" of uncirculated coins, where any such error should have been spotted even more readily by inspectors at the Mint. The coin brought $1,650 at the auction, proving again that finding the Mint's mistakes—often "buried" right in full view—can be very profitable for sharp-eyed treasure hunters.

• Any silver coins.

In 1965, with silver rising in price, the U.S. Treasury sought and obtained permission from Congress to change the composition of the coins it was producing in that metal. Under the legislation, new dimes and quarters were made with no silver at all, while the half dollar's silver content was reduced. (In 1971, the last trace of silver was removed from that coin, too.)

As you might expect, the American public responded with a nationwide silver rush, pulling silver coins out of circulation. Within a few years, hardly any remained—and today, a silver coin is an uncommon sight indeed among the copper-nickel dimes, quarters, and halves in our pockets and purses.

But, while seldom seen, silver coins do turn up from time to time—and those who are actively *looking* for these coins are the ones most likely to *see* them. At one time, in the early 1980s, silver was worth about $50 an ounce. Its value has declined considerably since then. But, even so, any silver coin you find in pocket change will bring you a healthy profit. As this is written, silver bullion is valued at approximately $5 an ounce, so any "traditional" silver U.S. coin (with a silver content of 90 percent) will be worth about five times its face value. The value of silver coins, of course, goes up proportionally as silver itself rises in price.

COINS NOT TO LOOK FOR

Some coins that seem unusual when they turn up in pocket change are really not worth your time or trouble. Although they are not encountered every day, they are actually quite common and have little or no premium value as collectibles. These coins may bring a premium in higher Mint State grades, but in lesser condition they're worth very little.

Here are a few coins *not* to look for:

- Susan B. Anthony dollars.

Except for the scarce 1979 variety with the "clear-S" mint mark, Anthony dollars are generally worth no more than face value: one dollar each. It's true that these much disliked coins haven't been produced since 1981. However, the Mint pumped out almost 900 million examples in 1979 and 1980, many of which remain in government vaults.

- Eisenhower dollars.

A few of the Eisenhower dollars minted between 1971 and 1978 are in demand as collector's items. But, with these exceptions, "Ike" dollars are just about as common as the Susan B. Anthony dollars that took their place.

- Kennedy half dollars dated after 1970.

From 1964 to 1970, Kennedy half dollars contained silver. The amount of precious metal was reduced beginning in 1965—but, even so, Kennedy halves from any of these years have bonus value based on the price of silver. Since 1971, virtually all half dollars have been made of a copper-nickel alloy—the same one used to make quarters and dimes. The only exceptions were the special collector's items sold in conjunction with the nation's Bicentennial in 1975–76. These coins may not be encountered very often, but they're certainly worth saving.

- Business-strike Bicentennial coins.

While relatively small quantities of the three Bicentennial coins—the Washington quarter, Kennedy half dollar, and Eisenhower dollar—were struck in silver for sale to collectors at a premium, the vast majority of these coins are regular "business-strike" pieces made of copper-nickel alloy. These may catch your eye when they pop up in change now and then, but they're neither scarce nor valuable.

- "Wheat-ears" Lincoln cents.

As noted earlier, the reverse of the Lincoln cent underwent a design change in 1959. As a consequence, cents with the old design—featuring two simple wheat stalks on the reverse—gradually came to be less common in Americans' pocket change. Today, these "wheat-ears" cents are relatively scarce in circulation. But that doesn't mean they're scarce in an absolute sense: Many millions have been saved by collectors and hoarders. These coins do enjoy a very small premium; you could probably sell a roll of 50 common-date wheat-ears cents for a dollar or two. But that hardly justifies an all-out search for these coins.

• The 1974 aluminum cent.

Another coin you shouldn't bother looking for is the 1974 aluminum cent. In this case, however, it's not because the coin is unduly common: It is, in fact, a rarity which any red-blooded collector would love to own. There are two reasons not to bother looking: First, you almost certainly won't find one; and second, even if you did find one, Uncle Sam would seize it if he found out.

In the early 1970s, a growing shortage of cents—and the rising price of copper—prompted the U.S. Mint to explore alternative metals for our nation's lowest-value coin. It settled upon aluminum as the most likely substitute and actually proceeded with production of considerable quantities—reportedly in the neighborhood of 1 million pieces. But Congress declined to authorize this switch and the Mint was obliged to abandon the idea.

There was just one complication: During the time it was seeking support in Congress for the plan, the Mint sent samples of the new aluminum cents to various senators and congressmen—and some of these coins never found their way back. Even today, some are unaccounted for. However, Mint officials have made it clear that since the aluminum cents were never officially issued, any that might turn up would be subject to confiscation by the U.S. Secret Service.

LESS THAN MINT

Just as there are certain coins you shouldn't waste your time looking for in pocket change, there also are coins you shouldn't waste your money buying. Modern coins and coin sets sold at a premium by government or private mints are high on this list of items to avoid.

In recent years, the U.S. Mint has made and marketed dozens of commemorative coins. These are coins authorized by Congress to honor some special person, place, or event. Typically, they are produced in limited quantities and offered for sale at a premium many times their face value and also well above the value of the metal they contain (generally silver or gold). With few exceptions, these coins have been very poor performers in the resale market. They tend to fall in price after their initial sale by the Mint, and within a few years almost all have market values below their issue price—often well below. In part, this is because the issue prices usually include substantial surcharges earmarked for the benefit of organizations sponsoring these coinage programs. The United States Olympic Committee has been a beneficiary several times, for example.

If your purpose in buying coins is to realize a profit, you would be wise to steer clear of commemoratives when the U.S. Mint offers them for sale. For that matter, new-issue coins and coin sets sold by *any* mint—government or private, domestic or foreign—have amassed a poor track record, by and large, in recent years. The annual proof sets and "mint sets" sold by Uncle Sam are very much in the group of items to avoid. Like U.S. commemorative coins, they have tended to fall in value—often sharply—in the secondary market.

A NEW YORK CITY TREASURE HUNT

In late July 1997, thousands of coin collectors gathered in New York City for the annual midsummer convention of the American Numismatic Association, the world's largest coin club. To help generate interest in the show, rare Lincoln cents worth well over $100 apiece were spent at face value in New York City. Donn Pearlman, a nationally known broadcaster and public relations executive from Chicago, coordinated publicity for the show. The following is his account of how these "coin drops" were conducted.

One of the most successful public awareness campaigns to encourage people to look at their money was conducted in the summer of 1997 by the American Numismatic Association (ANA), Littleton Coin Co. of Littleton, New Hampshire, and House of Collectibles, publisher of this book. The project attracted

Author Scott A. Travers being interviewed by a New York radio reporter after spending a valuable Lincoln cent to help promote interest in a national coin show.

nationwide media coverage for the coin-collecting hobby and prompted people across the country to closely examine their pocket change in hopes of finding valuable pennies.

Four rare coins originally pulled from New York bus and subway fares a half-century ago were deliberately put back into circulation in the Big Apple to publicize the ANA's 106th Anniversary Convention and the so-called World's Fair of Money held in conjunction with it.

The coins, 1914-D Lincoln cents valued at $165 each and part of the nearly 23,000-coin "New York Subway Hoard," were donated to the ANA by Littleton. With radio, TV, and newspaper reporters on hand for the event, the first 1914-D cent was used by Scott A. Travers, the author of this book, to purchase a $1.50 loaf of bread from a street vendor near the New York Coliseum. A rare coin from a famous hoard was back in circulation in New York City for anyone to find and enjoy!

The Subway Hoard coins came from the estates of collector and part-time coin dealer George Shaw of Brooklyn and his brother-in-law, Morris Moscow, who worked for the New York Transit Authority from the 1940s to the 1960s. Moscow and other transit system employees would search through coins used by passengers to pay bus and subway fares, pull out rare pieces and replace them at face value with common coins.

"There were a total of forty-four 1914-D cents in that astounding hoard, many of them housed for decades in New York Transit Authority envelopes," said David M. Sundman, president of Littleton Coin Co. "We deliberately saved a few of these coins to help the ANA publicize its New York convention and encourage the public to carefully look at their pocket change."

Littleton began buying coins from the estates of Shaw and Moscow in 1991 and completed the final purchase in the summer of 1996.

"When we acquired the hoard, many of the coins were grouped by denomination, date, and mint mark in small New York City Transit Authority 'miscellaneous remittances' envelopes with Shaw's handwriting on the outside indicating the types and quantities of coins held inside," Sundman explained.

"Some coins, like the 1914-D cents, were sitting, undisturbed, in those tan-colored envelopes for more than forty years."

Many news stories about the coins described or pictured those envelopes, adding even more flavor to the history of the coins and the excitement of the hunt.

To mark the opening day of the ANA convention, U.S. Treasurer Mary Ellen Withrow spent a 1909-S V.D.B. Lincoln cent valued at $350 to purchase a pretzel from a Times Square street vendor.

The coin drops proved to be a very successful stunt, helping to publicize both the convention and the hobby. CNN broadcast video of the drops for days, and local TV and radio stations and newspapers provided extensive coverage.

Clearly, there is romance and excitement connected with the notion of finding worthwhile coins in your pocket or purse. It's the age-old allure of buried treasure—and in this case it proved to be "buried" in plain sight!

THE 1913 LIBERTY HEAD NICKEL: FAMOUS AND WORTH A FORTUNE

The 1913 Liberty Head nickel has been described as the most famous coin in the world. It's certainly one of the most heavily promoted. And its 15 minutes of fame have stretched into the better part of a century—helped along the way by nationwide treasure hunts that firmly embedded the coin in the public's consciousness.

Jay W. Johnson (l), former director of the United States Mint, points to the Walton family's 1913 Liberty head nickel, while Edward C. Lee points to his newly-acquired $3 million dollar example. Both men attended the American Numismatic Association National World's Fair of Money in August 2003, where all 5 1913 Liberty nickels were on display. (Photo courtesy of the author)

In 1996, a 1913 Liberty nickel became the first coin ever to sell for more than a million dollars at a public auction. In 2003, that same coin changed hands privately for about $3 million. Only five examples are known—and when one of them surfaced in 2003 after being missing for more than 40 years, it was greeted by collectors like a much beloved king returning home from exile.

If it were indeed a king, this coin almost surely would be an illegitimate one. From all indications, it was made surreptitiously and illegally—not by the U.S. Mint, but by a Mint employee after hours. There is no mention of the coin in official government records. As far as Uncle Sam was concerned, the Liberty Head series ended in 1912 and the only five-cent piece issued by the Mint in 1913 was the new Buffalo nickel. But it's easy to see how mischief could have happened.

Anticipating the change in design, the Mint had prepared dies for the 1913 Buffalo nickel. But just in case the transition encountered trouble, the Mint had also made dies for a 1913 coin of the old design. These were locked in a vault at the Philadelphia Mint, to be destroyed once the Buffalo coin went into production. Instead, at least five pieces—all of them proofs—were struck with the Liberty Head dies.

Seven years passed before the coins' existence came to light. Collectors first learned of them through an ad in the December 1919 issue of *The Numismatist*, the official monthly journal of the American Numismatic Association. The advertiser, Samuel W. Brown of North Tonawanda, N.Y., offered to pay "$500 cash" for any 1913 Liberty Head nickel—"in Proof condition, if possible." Soon afterward, Brown disclosed that he had purchased five such coins and sold them all—for $600 each—to Philadelphia coin dealer August Wagner.

Cynics had a field day when they learned that Samuel Brown had worked at the Philadelphia Mint from 1903 to 1913—and that he was thought to have had access to the 1913 Liberty nickel dies. The theory quickly arose—and persists to this day—that Brown himself struck the coins, or had an accomplice make them, and then held them secretly after leaving the Mint. It so happens that 1920, the year when he announced their "discovery," also marked the end of the seven-year statute of limitations for prosecuting anyone who might have struck and removed the coins illegally in 1913.

The Philadelphia dealer who bought the five nickels resold all of them to Col. Edward H.R. Green, son of Hetty Green, the eccentric financier known as the "Witch of Wall Street" and reputed to be the world's richest woman. Green kept them until his death in 1938, after which his collection was dispersed.

Green was a flamboyant collector—but the coins got their greatest exposure and promotion not from him but from B. Max Mehl, a high-profile Texas coin dealer who used the nickels to hype his own business in the 1930s and '40s. Mehl placed nationwide ads—in magazines, Sunday supplements and even match-books—offering to pay $50 each for any and all 1913 Liberty nickels. He knew that none would turn up (besides the original five, which were, of course, already accounted for)—but most people didn't, and so they searched their pocket change, hoping to claim the $50 bounty. The hobby got positive notice, Mehl got new customers and the 1913 nickels got a lasting reputation as really rare coins.

Worth $2.5 million. *1913 Liberty head nickel found at the bottom of a closet (Photo courtesy and copyright American Numismatic Association)*

Over the years, the 1913 Liberty nickels have grown in both stature and value. Despite the legitimate doubts regarding their legitimacy, any one of the five known examples would bring a million dollars or more today. And when all five examples were brought together for a special exhibit at the ANA's National World's Fair of Money in Baltimore in the summer of 2003, it helped make the convention one of the most successful coin shows in history.

Ed Lee of Merrimack, N.H., the coin dealer who paid $3 million to own the finest-known 1913 Liberty nickel, has a unique perspective on his famous acquisition.

"I've been in the coin business since 1958," Lee said, "and this is by far the rarest and most valuable coin I've ever handled. It's the ultimate rarity—truly in a class by itself."

Public interest in the exhibit was stimulated by yet another treasure hunt—this time for the long-missing fifth and final specimen of the 1913 nickel. The coin was in the possession of its owner, North Carolina coin dealer George Walton, when he died in a car crash in 1962, and its whereabouts had been unknown since his death.

MILLION DOLLAR OFFER UNCOVERS CLOSET RARITY

In May 2003, Bowers and Merena Galleries, at that time a Collectors Universe (Nasdaq CLCT) company in Mandeville, La., announced "a reward of at least $1 million" for the discovery and purchase of the "missing, fifth specimen" of the rare nickel. "In fact, we'll pay $10,000 just to be the first to see it," said the company's president, Paul Montgomery. The announcement was coordinated by the exceptionally gifted publicist, Donn Pearlman, president of Minkus & Pearlman in Las Vegas. It received extensive media coverage, including a front-page story in *USA Today*. Pearlman's skillfully executed media campaign sent millions of Americans rummaging through cigar boxes, desk drawers, and sugar bowls in search of the million-dollar coin.

Among those who stopped and took notice were members of George Walton's family. Unlike the other searchers, they found what Paul Montgomery was looking for—in a box at the bottom of a closet.

It turns out that the nickel, along with other coins, had been retrieved from the wreckage of the 1962 crash by Walton's sister, and that she had submitted it to a major New York coin firm, one of America's oldest and largest coin dealers, to check its authenticity. At that time, the family firm had apparently concluded that the coin was not authentic. The woman hadn't sought a second opinion, partly because she knew that her brother frequently carried not only the real 1913 nickel but also an excellent fake.

After the sister's death in 1992, the nickel was handed down to other family members, who set it aside and gave it little thought—until Montgomery's million-dollar offer. Through the years, it had remained in George Walton's original custom-made plastic holder, so it was protected from mishandling. But the sister had placed it in an envelope on which she had made a notation that this was an altered-date coin—so the family thought it had no special value.

The big "reward" had piqued the relatives' interest, and when they learned of the ANA exhibit reuniting the other four 1913 nickels in Baltimore, not far from where they lived in North Carolina, they decided to take their coin for that second opinion—just in case. After all, this was a chance not only to have the coin checked by top experts but also to have it compared with the four nickels acknowledged to be genuine.

The coin arrived in Baltimore literally on the eve of the convention—and soon became the talk of the show. A panel of experts studied the coin carefully, comparing each detail with the other four pieces, and came to the conclusion that this was indeed the missing fifth specimen. "We were like a bunch of schoolboys," Montgomery said, "because we solved the mystery."

The Waltons returned home from Baltimore $10,000 richer—for giving Bowers and Merena the first look at the coin—but with no definite plans for consigning it for sale and thereby claiming the million-dollar reward. Given the prices in recent sales of other 1913 Liberty Head nickels, the coin could bring more than two million dollars—a payoff truly worthy of a nationwide treasure hunt. Collectors Universe later sold the Bowers and Merena firm to Greg Manning Auctions, Inc. (Nasdaq GMAI).

Note: In May 2004, coin dealer Blanchard & Comapny sold the Olsen 1913 Liberty head nickel for $3 million.

UNCONVENTIONAL WISDOM

Serious numismatists—dedicated coin collectors—sometimes make light of "pocket-change rarities." A feeling exists within a certain segment of the hobby that coins found in ordinary pocket change are somehow less significant than beautiful, pristine pieces that never entered everyday circulation. With all due respect to those who hold this view, I feel that on the contrary, coins that have "been around" gain added appeal from having seen actual use.

Most coins (excluding proofs) are made to be spent, so these pieces have served their intended function. And while it's always exciting to own an exceptional coin, there's a special satisfaction—an undeniable thrill—in finding a worthwhile coin in circulation. It's very much like digging up buried treasure.

Pocket-change rarities may not have fancy pedigrees, but many do command fancy prices. And they're definitely out there, waiting to be found. Interesting and valuable coins are turning up in pocket change every day. And more will turn up tomorrow.

So start looking—and happy hunting!

CHAPTER 3

DRAMATIC NEW COINS
FROM UNCLE SAM

Checked your pocket change lately? If so, you've probably noticed some fascinating coins with portraits paying tribute to different states of the Union—perhaps including yours. These special "statehood quarters" are regular twenty-five-cent pieces on the front, with the standard coinage portrait of George Washington, but miniature history books on the back. They're part of a ten-year series that started in 1999, and they've caused a sensation in the coin collecting world and beyond. You can learn a lot from these coins, for each of them conveys a capsule history lesson about the state it honors. You can earn a lot as well, with just a little luck, for some of these coins are selling for very fancy prices as collectibles. Best of all, you can do it without risking one red cent, for premium-value examples can be found in your pocket or purse, or in rolls you buy at a bank for just face value. Think of it as a lottery where you have a chance to win but you simply can't lose. You get great upside potential with zero downside risk.

You also may have come across a brand new kind of coin—just a little larger than the twenty-five-cent piece but golden-brown in color—carrying the portrait of a Native American woman. This is a $1 coin introduced by Uncle Sam at the start of the year 2000. Like the statehood quarters, this so-called "golden dollar" packs a lot of American history in a little bit of space: The woman it depicts is Sacagawea (Sack-uh-juh-WE-uh), the young Shoshone Indian woman who served as a guide and translator for Meriwether Lewis and William Clark on their trailblazing expedition through the newly purchased Louisiana Territory in 1804-06. And like the statehood quarters, the Sacagawea dollar can be your "lottery ticket" to instant winnings.

THE FIFTY-STATE WASHINGTON QUARTERS

For many years, the coins in Americans' pocket change remained pretty much the same. There was very little change in people's "change." Then, at the start of 1999, the United States Mint introduced the first of the new Washington quarters with special designs honoring the nation's fifty states. These statehood quarters added a welcome touch of spice to the bland coinage diet Americans had subsisted on for decades. Almost immediately, people began checking the coins in their pockets or purses for quarters with statehood designs. And one by one, new coins turned up with those designs: a Delaware patriot racing on horseback to a rendezvous with destiny . . . a goddess proclaiming Pennsylvania's pride in American independence . . . a steadfast General George Washington guiding his outmanned troops across the Delaware River to a pivotal battle in New Jersey.

Before long, millions of people were putting together sets of these offbeat new coins—and enterprising companies began manufacturing albums, boards, and other special holders to house these growing sets in an organized way. By the start of the year 2000, collecting statehood quarters had become a national pastime. And the fun and excitement were just getting underway, for the Mint planned to make more of these special quarters—at the rate of five per year— all the way through the year 2008, in the sequence that the states joined the Union.

THE START OF SOMETHING BIG

The fifty-state quarter program was inspired by a popular and highly successful series of coins issued by Canada in 1992 to celebrate a major milestone in that nation's history: the 125th anniversary of Canadian confederation, which united the provinces and territories of our northern neighbor under a central government in 1867. In honor of that anniversary, the Royal Canadian Mint struck twelve special twenty-five-cent pieces in 1992—a different one every month— with distinctive designs honoring the nation's ten provinces and two territories (a third territory, Nunavut, has been established since then). It also minted a $1 coin honoring the country as a whole.

The "Canada 125" coins drew favorable attention in the United States, and perceptive American numismatists began suggesting a similar series here. Among them was prominent coin dealer-author Q. David Bowers, who proposed in a November 1992 interview with *COINage* magazine that the U.S. Mint produce a series of fifty Kennedy half dollars honoring the fifty states of the Union. At the time, it seemed unlikely that the Mint would risk using the Washington quarter, since that coin (unlike the half dollar) plays a vital role in commerce, and special designs might lead to disruptive hoarding.

The Mint had long opposed the use of everyday coins for commemorative purposes, but a new Mint director, Philip N. Diehl, began to rethink the idea in the mid-1990s. Ultimately, Diehl was won over by David L. Ganz who, as president of the American Numismatic Association from 1993 to 1995, served with the Mint director on the Citizens Commemorative Coin Advisory Committee. Ganz convinced him that "circulating commemoratives" would not only promote interest in coin collecting but foster national pride among the American public and generate substantial revenue for the government. Diehl has credited Ganz with being the person most responsible for bringing the fifty-state coin program to fruition.

The notion of statehood coins moved to a faster track following a hearing in the House of Representatives in July 1995. The hearing had been prompted by abuses in U.S. commemorative coinage. One of the witnesses, New York City coin dealer Harvey G. Stack, broached the idea of circulating commemoratives honoring the fifty states and Delaware Congressman Michael Castle, chairman of the House coinage subcommittee, quickly embraced the idea. It didn't hurt that Delaware, the first state to ratify the U.S. Constitution, would likewise be the first state honored on one of the coins. Castle became a key supporter of the proposal, sponsoring it in the House and working hard to achieve legislative approval. His task was made much easier when Diehl gave his blessing to the plan and Treasury Secretary Robert E. Rubin decided that the Treasury wouldn't oppose it.

Congressional approval came in November 1997, and President Clinton signed the bill into law within a matter of days. The legislation provided that in each case, the statehood design would appear on the coin's reverse, with the "heads" side retaining the same coinage portrait of George Washington. To maximize the space available for the special new designs, the Mint got approval from Congress to rearrange the required coinage inscriptions, moving two of them from the back to the front and making Washington's portrait somewhat smaller.

Preparations took place throughout 1998, with the first five states selecting their designs and submitting them to the Treasury and the Mint. Finally, in January 1999, the first statehood quarter burst upon the scene. It came on horseback, featuring a portrait of Delaware patriot Caesar Rodney galloping full-speed to the Continental Congress of 1776, where he would cast a decisive vote in favor of American Independence. It was a fitting start—and it truly was the start of something big.

A NO-LOSE SITUATION

If you've already jumped aboard the bandwagon and started setting aside the statehood coins, you know how intriguing they can be. Even if you're not assembling a set of your own already, you probably know of relatives, friends, coworkers, or other acquaintances who are searching for these coins and saving them in holders for themselves, their children, or their grandchildren. But if you haven't joined this nationwide treasure hunt yet, what are you waiting for? You have nothing at all to lose, and plenty of potential to be a winner.

Unlike most commemorative coins produced by Uncle Sam in years gone by, the statehood quarters are circulating issues—coins intended for use in everyday commerce. And they're available everywhere Americans spend and get money—banks, restaurants, supermarkets, convenience stores, and other retail establishments—for just face value, or twenty-five cents apiece. It's true you could spend ten or twenty dollars for a holder to house and display a set of these coins. But if you simply pulled one statehood quarter of each different design from your pocket change over the course of the ten-year program, your outlay would be a paltry $12.50. If you saved one example of all fifty coins from each of the two Mints producing statehood quarters every year for circulation (the main Mint in Philadelphia and the branch Mint in Denver), you'd still have only $25 tied up, and you could spend them anytime without losing a cent of your "investment."

On the other hand, there's a chance that a small amount of money spent on statehood quarters, or a modest amount of time spent looking for them in change, could net you a nice return—even a real bonanza—with little or no risk if you found a scarce variety. At the very least, you'd probably derive a great deal of pleasure and satisfaction. And unlike state lotteries, where eager anticipation gives way all too often to predictable disappointment, there are no losing tickets to discard in this pocket-change game. Even if you don't hit the jackpot, you still get to keep your ante—the money you "bet" in the first place. In fact, you end up with a great consolation prize: a very appealing collection of interesting, attractive, and educational coins.

MINTING MISTAKES

One of the fastest ways to make money from statehood quarter dollars—or, for that matter, any newly struck modern coins—is to find what are known as "mint errors." These are coins that deviate from the norm in some readily perceptible way. The more obvious and dramatic the error, the more valuable a coin is likely to be. Among the mint errors you have a reasonable chance of finding, and that often fetch significant premiums, are "clips" (coins with part of the metal missing along the rim); off-center coins, where part of the design is missing; and double-struck coins, where part of the metal protrudes beyond the rim. Many such errors occurred in the early years of the 50-state quarter program—partly because the huge mintages forced the Mint to compromise on quality control. The proliferation of errors embarrassed Mint officials and caused them to implement major production changes. These, combined with much more manageable mintage levels, drastically reduced the number of errors occurring on subsequent state quarters. Since 2002, there have been relatively few with major mistakes—and for that reason, the ones that do turn up command impressive premiums.

OTHER TIDY DIVIDENDS

Finding mint errors isn't the only way to turn a nice profit on statehood quarters. Another potential approach involves coins at the opposite end of the spectrum—coins distinguished not by minting defects, but by the absence of such flaws. Discriminating collectors have reaped handsome profits by cherry-picking exceptionally well-struck, attractive specimens of state quarters from uncirculated rolls and submitting those coins to major certification services, such as the Professional Coin Grading Service (PCGS) and the Numismatic Guaranty Corporation of America (NGC). When these companies certify such coins with the very highest grades of Mint State-70 and Mint State-69, they can bring premiums of many hundreds of dollars. The standard certification fee is only about $20, so the downside risk is nominal, compared with the upside potential—but anyone attempting this approach should first gain a basic knowledge of the fundamental elements of grading, so he or she can judge when a coin may qualify for a top grade.

In the early stage of the state quarter program, even normal examples of certain quarters provided their owners with unexpected profits, enabling some to sell the coins in roll and bag quantities for four times or more their original cost. This unforeseen windfall resulted from a major miscalculation on the part of the U.S. Mint, as well as most coin dealers and collectors, regarding the popularity of the program. At the outset of the series, the Mint announced plans to produce approximately 750 million examples of each statehood quarter. With five different quarters being issued every year, that translated into a total annual mintage of 3.5 billion coins, roughly twice the number of regular Washington quarters the Mint had been producing up to that time. It was generally agreed that this would be enough to accommodate demand for the new coins from collectors, and from noncollectors saving them because they were unusual, while still meeting the needs of the nation's commerce. But it quickly became apparent that this figure would be woefully inadequate. With TV, print, and direct-mail advertisements deluging the public with offers of statehood quarter sets and the public responding enthusiastically, supplies of the early issues all but dried up within a matter of months. By February 2000, Mint-sewn bags of the Delaware and Pennsylvania quarters, the first two coins in the series, were being snapped up by product-starved promoters for $4,000, $5,000, and sometimes even more—four or five times the $1,000 face value of the 4,000 Washington quarters each bag contained. In other words, these buyers were paying a dollar apiece, or even $1.25, for each twenty-five-cent piece in those bags. And these were new coins produced by the hundreds of millions within just the previous year.

By the end of 1999, the Mint had revised its production plans sharply upward. After making only about 662 million examples of the New Jersey quarter, the third in the series, the Mint cranked out 939 million of the next one, honoring Georgia, and more than 1.3 billion of the first year's final quarter, which showcased Connecticut. Mintages remained over a billion for the next seven coins in the series, peaking at nearly 1.6 billion for the Virginia quarter in 2000. After that, however, demand began to decline—and so did production, dipping below a billion with the 2001 Rhode Island quarter and continuing a generally downward trend thereafter. All five coins issued in 2003 had mintages less than 500,000, bottoming out with that year's Maine quarter at under 449,000. Rather than reflecting a loss of interest in the series, this seemed to indicate that many people were simply saving fewer of the coins—perhaps one or two examples of each, rather than one or two rolls. In fact, as the program progressed, the Mint estimated that the number of individuals saving the state quarters was actually growing, rather than shrinking. By the program's midway point at the end of 2003, the Mint placed that number at close to 130 million Americans—nearly half the population of the nation.

Clearly, the intensity of market demand for the 50-state quarters was greatest in the beginning, when the program was still a novelty. The series has shown great staying power, though, and seems certain to continue holding Americans' interest right through the closing weeks of 2008, when the last coin is scheduled to honor Hawaii, the 50th and final state to join the Union. (Congress is considering a one-year extension of the program to add coins for the District of Columbia and five U.S. territories.) Indeed, the interest picks up added momentum each time a new state is showcased and people in that state who hadn't done so before begin to look for the quarters and set them aside. Obviously, those already on the bandwagon have an advantage—for the sooner they (and you) start exploring the statehood quarters, the sooner they (and you) can start finding valuable mint errors or, as an alternative, submitting exceptional specimens for possible certification in very high grades.

VALUABLE MINT ERRORS

Make no mistake, error coins can be worth their weight in gold—and sometimes a whole lot more. As I noted in Chapter 2, "mistakes" are often many times more valuable than perfect, error-free coins. That's because they're much scarcer, and also because mint-error collecting has grown by leaps and bounds in recent years, to the point where it is now one of the rare coin hobby's most active specialty areas. Thousands of collectors aggressively pursue imperfect coins, and when they find an error that's exceptionally dramatic in a dealer's display case, they gladly pay a very strong premium to obtain it.

Mint errors have occurred on the statehood Washington quarters to about the same extent they occur on other current U.S. coinage. And when such errors show up on one of the statehood quarters, they're doubly intriguing, because these coins are different from the norm to begin with. The appeal of these errors is further enhanced by the fact that each statehood quarter is a one-time-only coin—a coin that is produced in only one year, with just one date. Indeed, each one is minted for only a ten-week portion of that year. Many collectors are trying to put together sets of mint-error statehood coins. Some, for example, are seeking off-center examples of all the different quarters—pieces on which the design isn't perfectly centered. Others are saving sets of statehood quarters struck on clipped planchets—coin blanks that look as if someone had bitten off a piece, or even several pieces. Still others are pursuing even more esoteric mint mistakes. Demand for such errors is strong, and they frequently change hands for hundreds—even thousands—of dollars. In fact, statehood quarter errors have been bringing several times as much as similar mint mistakes on the regular Washington quarters from 1998 and before, reflecting the enormous interest in these coins not only from collectors but also from the American public at large.

Let's take a closer look at some of the mint errors you might find on statehood quarters—possibly including the very coins you're carrying in your pocket or purse even now. The market values given here were furnished by Fred Weinberg, a coin dealer from Encino, California, who maintains one of the country's largest inventories of such coins, and they reflect retail prices as of February 2004. Weinberg is past president of the Professional Numismatists Guild, a prestigious organization whose membership includes many of the nation's most prominent and influential dealers in rare coins. He also is the primary authenticator of mint-error coins for the Professional Coin Grading Service (PCGS).

- An ***off-center coin*** occurs when a planchet (or coin blank) isn't aligned perfectly between the two dies during the striking process. Normally, the planchet is confined within a collar when the dies (one for the obverse, the other for the reverse) converge on the metal to stamp it with the design. But if part of the planchet is outside the collar, the coin will emerge with just part of the design, and that portion will be off-center.

Worth $450. *1999 New Jersey quarter struck 65 percent off-center. (Photo courtesy PCGS; coin courtesy Fred Weinberg & Co.)*

With statehood quarters, as with other coins, the value of an off-center coin depends, in large measure, on how off-center it is—in other words, how much of the design is still visible. As noted previously, the more dramatic the error, the more valuable the coin. At this writing, dealers are charging about $300 for an early statehood quarter that is off-center 10 to 20 percent and between $600 and $675 for one that is off-center 40 to 70 percent. The prices are significantly higher for similar error quarters struck since 2002.

Worth $450. *1999-D Pennsylvania quarter struck 60 percent off-center. (Photo courtesy PCGS; coin courtesy Fred Weinberg & Co.)*

Worth $150. *1999-P Pennsylvania quarter with a 15 percent clipped planchet. (Photo courtesy PCGS; coin courtesy Fred Weinberg & Co.)*

• A *clipped planchet* occurs because of a malfunction during the preparation of coin blanks. It is common minting procedure today to punch many planchets at one time from large sheets of metal that are fed into a blanking press. As each group of blanks is punched out, the sheet moves forward. Occasionally, however, if a sheet fails to advance far enough, the next series of punches may overlap some or all of the previous ones, much like cookie cutters slicing through existing round designs cut out of dough. When this happens, coin blanks emerge with part of the metal missing—and the coins that are struck on these blanks look as if someone had taken a bite out of them, or even several bites. With clipped-planchet errors, size matters—and so does the number of clips. On average, a pre-2002 statehood quarter with a single clip is worth about $75 to $90. It would be worth $125 to $150 with a double clip, $150 to $225 with a triple clip. A coin with particularly dramatic clips, or with more than three clips, could be worth even more. Conversely, a coin

Worth $150. *1999-D Delaware quarter with a 15 percent clipped planchet. (Photo courtesy PCGS; coin courtesy Fred Weinberg & Co.)*

Worth $750. *1999 New Jersey quarter that is double-struck—second strike 85 percent off-center. (Photo courtesy PCGS; coin courtesy Fred Weinberg & Co.)*

with relatively small clips could be worth substantially less. The location of the clip (or clips) isn't a major factor in determining the value of such a mint error. It's a matter of interest to error-coin specialists, but secondary to size. Again, the values are dramatically higher for quarters from 2002 and later.

- A ***double strike*** occurs when the coining press fails to eject a newly minted coin completely from the striking area, and it then receives a second blow from the dies while partially outside the collar. From the standpoint of appearance, this is the flip side of a clipped-planchet error—for a double-struck coin seems to have more metal than it should, rather than less. This is an illusion, for the typical double strike started out as a normal planchet; the extra strike simply spread the metal outward. Just as a single clipped-planchet coin can have more than one clip, multiple-strike coins can receive more than one extra strike.

Worth $600. *1999 Connecticut quarter with a second strike 75 percent off-center. (Photo courtesy PCGS; coin courtesy Fred Weinberg & Co.)*

Worth $2,500. *1999 P Mint state quarter double-struck capped die. (Photo courtesy PCGS; coin courtesy Fred Weinberg & Co.)*

Each double strike is unique, and eye appeal plays a significant part in determining the value of any given piece. However, this type of error is not encountered nearly as often as off-center coins and clips, and this scarcity is reflected in higher market values: Most double-struck early state quarters are worth between $900 and $1,200 apiece.

Worth $500. *1999 Georgia quarter with a 40 percent brockage obverse. A brockage is an incuse impression from a previously struck coin. (Photo courtesy PCGS; coin courtesy Fred Weinberg & Co.)*

• A ***clad-layer split-off*** occurs when one of the outer layers of metal in a copper-nickel clad U.S. coin isn't bonded properly to the core and peels off during or after the minting process. Like all Washington quarters produced for circulation since 1965, the statehood quarters consist of two outer layers of copper-nickel alloy bonded to a core of pure copper—a composition that gives the coins the electromagnetic properties needed for use in vending machines. The outer layers and core are bonded together before the metal is rolled to the proper thick-

Worth $2,750. *2001-P New York quarter with a dramatic second strike and the date fully formed and visible in 2 places on the reverse. (Photo courtesy Scott Travers Rare Coin Galleries, LLC; coin courtesy Fred Weinberg & Co.)*

ness. If this bonding process is faulty, one of the outer layers may break away—and, when that happens, the coin that emerges will have the design on that side stamped on the copper core.

Clad-layer split-off statehood quarters are quite scarce and unusual looking; seeing the design in copper, rather than the silvery-looking copper-nickel alloy, is extremely eye-catching—especially if it appears on the reverse, which features the special statehood design in each case. An error coin of this type is worth about $375 if the reverse outer layer is missing and about $300 if the missing side is the obverse (the side with George Washington's portrait).

• A **wrong-planchet** error occurs when a coin of one denomination is struck on a blank meant for a different coin. An off-metal coin occurs when such a coin is struck on a planchet made of a different metal. These mistakes result when incorrect planchets are fed accidentally into a coining press. There are several types of errors under this general heading, and they range in degree from relatively subtle to spectacular. A not-too-obvious error coin could have the right diameter and the proper metallic composition but the wrong weight and thickness. This might happen, for instance, if metal strip for dimes was run through a blanking press set up to produce statehood quarter planchets. Both coins have the same color and composition, but thinner strip is used for dimes, so quarter planchets punched from that strip would be the thickness of dimes, rather than quarters. The coins then struck on those planchets might not be discernible as mint errors except upon closer inspection. On the other hand, off-metal errors often can be spotted at a glance, and often are spotted and removed from the pipeline before they leave the Mint—which helps account for their rarity. Their visual appeal heightens their attractiveness as collectibles.

Off-metal statehood quarters are far less common than the errors mentioned previously, and far more valuable. In January 2000, for example, at the Florida United Numismatists (FUN) show in Orlando, Fred Weinberg handled a Georgia quarter that had been struck on a cent planchet. It was the same size and weight as a Lincoln cent, but carried the design—or rather, a portion of the design—from the Georgia quarter. Weinberg sold this coin, which he described as a "gem red, brilliant uncirculated" specimen, for $3,500—quite a pretty penny, or rather a pretty quarter! And barely three years later, the coin was worth about $5,000. Weinberg believes that only a handful of off-metal statehood quarters have been produced—perhaps no more than two or three for any given coin. He's reasonably sure that other such coins are out there, however, waiting to be discovered by lucky pocket-change treasure hunters. And obviously, the treasure is well worth the hunt.

• Yet another rare and valuable type of mint mistake found on statehood quarters, and handled by Fred Weinberg, is the ***double-denomination error.*** This occurs when a coin of one denomination is overstruck with the design of a different denomination. Typically, it happens when the original coin remains undetected in a tote bin of newly struck coins after the bin is emptied by workmen at the Mint, and the same bin later is used to deliver planchets for a different coin to the coining press—where the coin is then overstruck with the second coin's design.

At the FUN show in January 2000, Fred Weinberg handled a double-denomination New Jersey statehood quarter which had been struck on a 1999 Roosevelt dime. It was the size and weight of the dime, but had part of the design from the New Jersey quarter, with the dime's design visible underneath. Weinberg sold this coin for $5,000—the highest price he was aware of, up to that time, paid for any statehood quarter. Three years later, its value had climbed to $7,500.

Finding a $5,000 mint-error statehood quarter in ordinary pocket change, or in a roll of quarters you buy for face value at the bank, isn't something that's likely to happen, it's true. But neither is winning $5,000 in the lottery. People do win the lottery, though—and people do find valuable coins in circulation. The difference is, most people waste a lot of money trying to win the lottery, while searching for scarce statehood quarters doesn't have to cost a single cent. And though you may never find a coin worth $5,000, you might easily find some worth $5, $50—or even $500. You'll probably have a great deal of fun, as well. When was the last time you had any fun examining your losing lottery tickets?

REALLY SPECTACULAR ERRORS

The start of the state quarter program coincided with a rash of major mint errors—some of them never before seen on U.S. coins. The unprecedented production levels forced the Mint to operate virtually around the clock, straining both the equipment and the work force and requiring the addition of many new and inexperienced employees. This caused a natural loss of quality control. It also set the stage for theft and fraud by a few Mint workers who saw the potential profit to be gained from the sale of such errors. These factors combined to spawn a sudden outpouring of dramatic—and valuable—error coins.

The single most jaw-dropping mint error was a **double-denomination "mule"**—the first ever seen in the history of the Mint—bearing the obverse (or "heads" side) of a statehood Washington quarter and the reverse of a Sacagawea dollar, struck on a coin blank meant for the new dollar. In time, 10 examples of this coin came to light, and most have been sold for strong five-figure prices. The first one reportedly was received from a bank in the spring of 2000 by an Arkansas man, who sold it soon afterward for close to $30,000. More turned up in the months that followed, and several changed hands for even higher prices. Subsequently, however, the federal government charged that two employees at the Philadelphia Mint had illegally sold five of the "mules" to dealers and collectors, raising questions about how the coins were made and how they got out of the Mint. As of February 2003, no action had been taken to confiscate these coins from their owners, and it was unclear whether such action might be taken. A government official did say that at least two of the 10 error coins had entered circulation through normal channels, apparently making these less likely to be subject to seizure.

The dollar/quarter mule wasn't unique for long. Within weeks, hobbyists learned of a second double-denomination coin—a mint error struck on a cent planchet with the obverse of a 1999 Lincoln cent and the reverse of a Roosevelt dime. Other remarkable error coins followed in quick succession. Among them were a 2000 Maryland state quarter struck on a "golden dollar" planchet; a 1999 George Washington commemorative $5 gold piece struck on a dime blank; and several 1999 Susan B. Anthony dollars struck on planchets meant for the Sacagawea dollar. All of these sold for thousands of dollars.

Outgoing Mint Director Jay W. Johnson implemented corrective measures before leaving his post in August 2001 and his successor, Henrietta Holsman Fore, added further safeguards. Among other things, workers were assigned to inspect early strikes every time dies were changed; drum-like "scrap" containers used for disposal of defective coins were replaced with locked boxes; new

German-made Schuler presses drastically reduced the number of error coins made in the first place; and sorting and counting procedures were improved through the installation of new "riddling" equipment that weeds out misshapen coins and the use of very large sealed bins, rather than mint-sewn bags, to transport coins. These precautions stemmed the tide of errors so effectively that on a percentage basis, the output of these coins was at a historic low by the start of 2003, creating pent-up demand and much higher prices for the limited supply reaching the collector marketplace.

SPECIAL GOVERNMENT SETS

Besides making statehood quarters for use in the nation's commerce, the U.S. Mint also has been producing proof versions of the coins for sale at a premium as collectibles. Proofs are special coins struck on pristine planchets with highly polished dies. They receive multiple strikes in order to make the design razor-sharp, and on current U.S. proofs there is typically a cameo contrast between the raised design elements (or devices), which tend to have attractive frosted surfaces, and the plain background areas (or fields), which normally have a mirror-like appearance. These coins are highly appealing to collectors and also have captured the interest of non-collectors who have seen them while visiting coin shops to purchase statehood quarters or fifty-state coin boards.

Unlike the statehood quarters made for commercial use, proofs must be purchased—either from the Mint at the time of their original release or after that from dealers or collectors. In the first five years of the program, the Mint offered proof statehood quarters in three different kinds of sets:

- A nine- or 10-coin set containing base-metal copper-nickel "clad" examples of all five statehood quarters from a given year, plus one proof example of every other coin from that year. This set had an issue price of $19.95. In 1999, the set contained only nine coins: the five quarters plus the cent, nickel, dime, and half dollar. In 2000, the Mint added the Sacagawea dollar to the set without raising the issue price, and this coin also was included in subsequent sets.

- A similar nine- or 10-coin set, but with all five quarters plus the dime and half dollar being made of 90-percent silver, the same alloy used in those three denominations prior to 1965. This set had an issue price of $31.95.

- A five-coin set containing just the statehood quarters, struck in copper-nickel clad. This set had an issue price of $13.95.

In 1999, the Mint also offered an 18-piece uncirculated coin set (or mint set) containing two business-strike clad examples (the kind used in commerce) of each quarter—one from each of the two Mints (Philadelphia and Denver) that produced the coins for daily use. This set, which also included two examples apiece of the cent, nickel, dime, and half dollar, had an issue price of $14.95. In 2000 and subsequent years, the Mint also included two business-strike specimens of the Sacagawea dollar, again without raising the issue price.

All of these sets come in attractive packaging that serves to both protect and showcase the coins. They make nice gifts and they're also a convenient way to obtain and preserve high-quality specimens of the quarters. At the same time, as you can see, they cost considerably more than face value. They have the potential to increase in value as collectibles in years to come, as more and more people begin saving statehood quarters and added demand is created for the limited supply of sets from previous years. In fact, at this writing in February 2003, the 1999 silver proof set is selling for upwards of $200—more than six times its issue price—and the 2001 and 2002 silver proof sets are bringing strong premiums, too. Still, this is not a can't-lose situation—the kind you enjoy when you set aside statehood quarters obtained at face value. You have upside potential, but also downside risk. On the plus side, proofs are the very finest way to acquire statehood quarters, and that will reinforce their appeal and market value as time goes by.

Once the original ordering period ends, and proof sets and uncirculated coin sets no longer are available directly from the Mint, the only way to acquire them is in what is known as the "secondary market"—primarily from dealers who bought the sets in large quantities from the government or purchased them from collectors. In this resale market, prices are determined by the law of supply and demand. If there is a large supply of a given set and not too much demand, it may very well carry a price tag below its original issue price. On the other hand, if demand exceeds supply, you'll probably have to pay a premium above the issue price—possibly a large one.

HIGH-GRADE CERTIFIED COINS

Just as error-coin specialists seek out statehood quarters with imperfections, there also are collectors looking for examples that are perfect—or as close to perfection as they can find. And there are dealers who cater to this demand by searching systematically for the most pristine examples in rolls and bags of uncirculated coins and, especially, government sets. After locating such coins, these dealers then submit them to a third-party certification service, where they are graded and encapsulated in hard plastic holders. The dealers sell these certified coins at prices well above face value—perhaps hundreds or even thousands of times face value, if the grade awarded by the certification service is unusually high.

Michael Keith Ruben of Hilton Head Island, South Carolina, is a major dealer in high-grade modern U.S. coins. He reports that demand for certified statehood quarters in the very highest levels of preservation has been "insatiable . . . unfillable." Ruben has been dealing almost exclusively in proofs, rather than business strikes (the kind meant for use in circulation), because exceptional business strikes of copper-nickel clad coins, including statehood quarters, are too few and far between, he said, to justify the investment of time and effort. Proofs, on the other hand, are by their nature coins of superior quality. Dealers such as Ruben go one step further and pick out the crème de la crème from among these upper-end coins.

Even among proofs, there is considerable variation in the quality of the early statehood quarters, according to Ruben. The first two coins in the series—those paying tribute to Delaware and Pennsylvania—are far more elusive in very high grades, he said, than those that followed. He estimated that out of a typical group of 1,000 proof Connecticut quarters, the last ones issued in the series' first year, two-hundred coins would be certified as Proof-70 Deep Cameo, the highest grade attainable—while in a similar group of 1,000 proof Delaware or Pennsylvania quarters, possibly only thirty would make that grade. This greater relative scarcity is reflected in the prices of these coins: As this book went to press, Ruben was charging about $75 apiece for Proof-70 Deep Cameo specimens of the Connecticut quarter and up to $180 for similar examples of the Delaware and Pennsylvania coins. The other two first-year statehood quarters, those honoring New Jersey and Georgia, fell in the middle, Ruben reported. He said he made an effort initially to find pristine business strikes as well, but abandoned it after becoming convinced that these were "unobtainable" in grades above Mint State-67 on the standard grading scale of 1 to 70.

Seeking superb examples of statehood Washington quarters is an excellent idea; these may very well enjoy significant premium value in years to come, and a set of fifty matched "gem" specimens will surely be a marvelous memento once the series is complete. The chance of future profit will be limited severely, though, if you pay the premiums dealers are charging today for these super-grade coins. Instead, you might consider conducting a search of your own through rolls of brand new quarters or proof sets you buy from the Mint. You may not end up with the ultimate set, or coins that are sheer perfection, but your outlay will be modest—even minimal—and you will have fun, derive satisfaction, and pick up a great deal of knowledge along the way.

THE SEQUENCE OF THE FIFTY STATEHOOD QUARTERS

The U.S. Mint is issuing the fifty statehood quarters at the rate of five per year, starting with the thirteen original states in the order that they ratified the U.S. Constitution and, following that, with the thirty-seven remaining states in the sequence that they joined the Union. The series began with Delaware, which proudly proclaims itself "The First State," in January 1999 and will conclude with Hawaii, the fiftieth state, toward the end of 2008. The set is coming together just as the nation itself did—starting with the states that hug the Eastern Seaboard, then rolling inexorably westward like a majestic wave until it reaches and ultimately leapfrogs the shores of the Pacific. Along the way, it is helping millions of Americans learn more about their states, and helping additional millions learn more about other people's states. And as each new coin comes out, and another state joins the roster, the series is gaining ever greater momentum and recruiting an ever-growing army of enthusiastic collectors.

Following is a list of the fifty states showing when their coins will be (or have been) issued, plus the date that each state either ratified the Constitution or, in subsequent instances, joined the Union. Within each year, the states are listed in the order in which their coins will be minted and distributed. As a general guideline, the coin corresponding to the state listed first will enter circulation in January of that year, with the others coming out in March, May, July, and October, respectively.

1999:

    Delaware—Dec. 7, 1787
    Pennsylvania—Dec. 12, 1787
    New Jersey—Dec. 18, 1787
    Georgia—Jan. 2, 1788
    Connecticut—Jan. 9, 1788

2000:

    Massachusetts—Feb. 6, 1788
    Maryland—April 28, 1788
    South Carolina—May 23, 1788
    New Hampshire—June 21, 1788
    Virginia—June 25, 1788

2001:

  New York—July 26, 1788
  North Carolina—Nov. 21, 1789
  Rhode Island—May 29, 1790
  Vermont—March 4, 1791
  Kentucky—June 1, 1792

2002:

  Tennessee—June 1, 1796
  Ohio—Feb. 19, 1803
  Louisiana—April 30, 1812
  Indiana—Dec. 11, 1816
  Mississippi—Dec. 10, 1817

2003:

  Illinois—Dec. 3, 1818
  Alabama—Dec. 14, 1819
  Maine—March 15, 1820
  Missouri—Aug. 10, 1821
  Arkansas—June 15, 1836

2004:

  Michigan—Jan. 26, 1837
  Florida—March 3, 1845
  Texas—Dec. 29, 1845
  Iowa—Dec. 28, 1846
  Wisconsin—May 29, 1848

2005:

  California—Sept. 9, 1850
  Minnesota—May 11, 1858
  Oregon—Feb. 14, 1859
  Kansas—Jan. 29, 1861
  West Virginia—June 20, 1863

2006:

  Nevada—Oct. 31, 1864
  Nebraska—March 1, 1867
  Colorado—Aug. 1, 1876
  North Dakota—Nov. 2, 1889
  South Dakota—Nov. 2, 1889

2007:

   Montana—Nov. 8, 1889
   Washington—Nov. 11, 1889
   Idaho—July 3, 1890
   Wyoming—July 10, 1890
   Utah—Jan. 4, 1896

2008:

   Oklahoma—Nov. 16, 1907
   New Mexico—Jan. 6, 1912
   Arizona—Feb. 14, 1912
   Alaska—Jan. 3, 1959
   Hawaii—Aug. 21, 1959

THE SACAGAWEA DOLLAR

The statehood quarters aren't the only new coins in Americans' pockets and purses these days. At the start of the year 2000, they were joined by the Sacagawea dollar, a coin that is new in both design and composition—and dramatically different in appearance—from all of the other "small change" that Americans are using at the dawn of the new millennium. Like the statehood quarters, this intriguing new dollar offers chances for you to find something interesting and valuable in the coins that pass through your hands. In fact, it represents a golden opportunity—even though it doesn't contain any gold.

The Sacagawea dollar was conceived as a replacement for the ill-fated Susan B. Anthony dollar, a coin that had been introduced in 1979 to fill a perceived need for a small-size but high-value coin in the nation's vending machines, pay phones, tollbooths, and other such mechanical devices. The Anthony dollar encountered immediate public resistance, primarily because it was too close in size and appearance to the quarter—a confusion that resulted in costly mistakes. As a result, its production was suspended in 1981 and hundreds of millions of "Susies" languished in federal vaults for more than a decade. In the mid-1990s, this stockpile started to shrink as toll road, tunnel, and bridge authorities set up their equipment to accept the "mini-dollar" coin—and especially when the U.S. Postal Service began to accept the coin and give it out in change, in its stamp-vending machines. By 1999, in fact, the supply on government shelves was all but exhausted, causing the Mint to produce a batch of new Anthony dollars. By then, however, the Treasury and the Mint already had come up with a replacement.

The Anthony dollar fiasco in 1979 sent Uncle Sam, quite literally, back to the drawing board. Advocates remained convinced that a small dollar coin would be useful in everyday commerce and that, over time, it would save the government money (since the coin would have a much longer useful life than the corresponding piece of paper money). It was obvious, however, that a new kind of coin would be needed—one that not only looked different from the Anthony dollar but felt different, too, so it could be distinguished at a glance and at a touch from other U.S. coins, particularly the quarter.

At length, the Mint came up with a coin that has the same size, weight, and diameter as the previous mini-dollar but a different edge, new metallic composition, and distinctive golden color. The new coin's edge is smooth—not reeded, like the edges of the Anthony dollar and the current half dollar, quarter, and dime. And whereas the old dollar was made of the same copper-nickel clad alloy as those other three coins, the new one is a very different kind of metallic "sandwich": It consists of two outer layers of 77 percent copper, 12 percent zinc, 7 percent manganese, and 4 percent nickel bonded to a core of pure copper. This alloy was chosen not only for the color it produces, but also for its compatibility with coin-operated machines.

THE COLOR OF OUR NEW MONEY

From early indications, the public has embraced the new dollar coin. Reaction to the portrait of Sacagawea, carrying her infant son on her back, has been generally positive and the golden color has blunted any concerns about confusion. At the same time, however, it seems apparent already that the "golden dollar"— as it is called by the Mint—won't remain golden very long once it enters circulation. Early examples appeared to darken quickly to a deeper brownish hue. In addition, many dealers and collectors were reporting a high percentage of Sacagawea dollars with extensive spotting.

Toning of the new coin wasn't unexpected; Lincoln cents, after all, also turn from red to brown after a short time in circulation. The spotting is a matter of greater concern, and some have suggested that it may point to a problem with the manganese in the alloy. Though useful for its electromagnetic properties, which help make the coin acceptable in vending machines, manganese is relatively unstable and tended to separate from the other component metals in its only previous U.S. coinage use—in the wartime Jefferson nickels issued from 1942 to 1945. As a result, many "war nickels" became unsightly and greasy-feeling after extensive use. Mint officials have offered assurances that no similar manganese-related problems will occur this time, but the spotting has focused new attention on the subject.

Whatever the cause of the early surface changes in the new dollar coin, and the frequent blemishes, their existence suggests that problem-free examples— mint-fresh pieces in pristine condition, with a truly golden color still intact— may be scarce even now, and may command a premium in the future if they are preserved in that condition. These coins are available today at face value, so the only investment you really need to make is one of time. If they prove to be quite scarce and do go up in value, you can then redeem your coinage "lottery tickets" and claim your winnings. If they don't, you can simply spend them.

SACAGAWEA DOLLAR ERRORS

Like the statehood quarters, Sacagawea dollars have started turning up with major minting mistakes. The numbers were relatively modest initially, but dealer Fred Weinberg expressed confidence that many more would emerge as greater quantities of the new coin entered circulation. The overview provided here, and the retail market values, were furnished by Weinberg.

Among the oddities seen to date are coin blanks that are, quite literally, blank. These Sacagawea planchets, readily identifiable by their golden color (one not found on any other current U.S. coins), somehow escaped from one of the mints without being stamped with the dollar's design. They are worth about $100 apiece in the error-coin marketplace.

Worth $500. *2000-P Sacagawea dollar. Large broadstrike on a Type I (no-rim) planchet. A broadly struck coin is one that does not fit into the collar, but instead stays on top of the collar when struck. (Photo courtesy PCGS; coin courtesy Fred Weinberg & Co.)*

Worth $3,500. *2000-P Sacagawea dollar struck 30 percent off-center. (Photo courtesy PCGS; coin courtesy Fred Weinberg & Co.)*

Off-center Sacagawea dollars range in value from $350, for a coin that is off center by 10 percent, to $600 for one that is off by 30 percent.

Worth $1,750. *2000-P Sacagawea dollar struck 25 percemt off-center on a 30 percent straight-end clip. A straight-end clip is from a blank punched from the side of the planchet strip. (Photo courtesy PCGS; coin courtesy Fred Weinberg & Co.)*

Golden dollars struck on clipped planchets are worth from $50 to several hundred dollars, depending upon the number of clips and their size.

Double strikes would be worth between $1,500 and $2,500, depending upon the degree of the mistake and how dramatic it looked.

One widely publicized multiple-strike specimen of the new dollar, certified as Mint State-64 by the Numismatic Guaranty Corporation of America, was struck at least fifteen times, according to NGC error-coin specialist Dave Camire. He estimated that the entire process probably occurred in less than two seconds, although it was a mystery why the striking mechanism failed to eject the coin. The owner of this coin reportedly was asking $8,500 for it.

Worth $300. *2000-P Sacagawea dollar. Large 30 percent clipped planchet. (Photo courtesy PCGS; coin courtesy Fred Weinberg & Co.)*

Another valuable error combines the new mini-dollar with the old one. It's a 1999 Susan B. Anthony dollar struck on a planchet intended for the Sacagawea coin. At least two examples of this "golden oldie" have surfaced. Weinberg sold one for slightly more than $10,000, and a subsequent find reportedly changed hands for $15,000.

Worth $9,000 or more. *2000-P Sacagawea dollar struck on aluminum and certified as Mint State-64 by PCGS.*

Worth $75,000. *States quarter and Sacagawea dollar "mule" double denomination error. The U.S. Mint's first double-denomination mule error has the obverse of a Washington quarter and the reverse of a Sacagawea dollar. Although initially believed to be unique, other examples have surfaced. (Photo courtesy Auctions by Bowers and Merena, Inc.)*

I can speak from personal experience about how fascinating—and valuable—mint-error Sacagawea dollars can be. Recently, on behalf of a client, my firm, Scott Travers Rare Coin Galleries, Inc., brokered a "golden dollar"—or, more precisely, *part* of a golden dollar—that actually was made of aluminum. This mint error, which has been authenticated by PCGS, apparently was struck on an elongated aluminum trial planchet. Experts theorize that the planchet shattered upon striking and most of the pieces were retrieved and melted. But one piece containing much of the design remained intact and somehow escaped the melting pot. We sold the coin for an undisclosed sum, but its new owner values it at more than $7,500.

For further reading on the state quarters: *The Official Guidebook to America's State Quarters,* by David L. Ganz (Random House/House of Collectibles, paperback, scheduled date of publication Nov. 2000).

CHAPTER 4

MAKING MONEY
WITH COINS

Treasure doesn't always come in a massive oak chest buried by pirates on a lush tropical island. It can also be found in an ordinary cigar box tucked away in a corner of your attic.

If you find such a box and it's filled with old coins, it may very well be worth a small fortune—and possibly even a big one.

I'll give you an example.

One day in the late 1970s a man walked into a Boston coin store. The man had inherited a group of old coins from his father, and he didn't have the foggiest notion what they were or how much they were worth. These coins had been stored in the attic for thirty or forty years, in little cardboard boxes stuffed with cotton.

They turned out to be original sets of proof coins, purchased from the U.S. Mint in the late 1800s and early 1900s by the father, who had been a collector. And they proved to be a bonanza for the son.

"These coins had a face value of probably seventy or eighty dollars, and the man had no idea they were worth any more than that," said Jim Halperin, then the chief executive of that Boston coin firm. "Upon my recommendation, he consigned them to one of our auctions and they realized nearly half a million dollars."

This story is not unique. Rare coins have brought handsome profits to many millions of people who found or bought the coins themselves or acquired them from family members or friends. These lucky individuals have included people from every stratum of society—rich and poor, young and old, the powerful and famous, and the ordinary man and woman in the street.

Everyday people reap windfalls from coins all the time, and often they obtain those coins in unpredictable ways.

Steve Ivy, now a business partner of Halperin's in the hugely successful Heritage Rare Coin Galleries of Dallas, tells of a man who bought an old silver dollar from a drinking companion in a bar in Eureka, California. Neither knew the value of the coin; both considered it just a conversation piece. So the friend sold the coin to the man for just a dollar. A while later, the buyer received some literature from Heritage; his name had wound up on a mailing list used by the firm. He got in touch with the company and asked about his coin.

His $1 purchase turned out to be a great rarity—a silver dollar minted in 1870 in San Francisco. He placed it in one of Ivy's auctions and it realized more than $30,000.

PRICE PERFORMANCE

Coin prices tend to follow a boom-and-bust cycle, rising in value sharply, then going down in price almost as sharply, sometimes within a period of just a couple of months. Over the long term, however, many truly rare coins have enjoyed phenomenal price growth—and sustained it.

Coins are popular not only because sometimes they might appreciate in value, but also because they can be appreciated for what they are: timeless works of hand-held art that mirror the history of man. People like to look at them, admire their beauty, and ponder the role they played in the drama of civilization.

Truly rare coins sometimes go up in value even during periods when the coin market as a whole is in a slump. Dramatic evidence came in October 1993 when a 1913 Liberty Head nickel—one of five known examples of this great U.S. rarity—changed hands at a New York City auction for $962,500. The seller, prominent Texas numismatist Reed Hawn, had bought the coin in 1985 for $385,000. Thus, he more than doubled his money in less than a decade, even though he sold the coin in a hostile market environment.

Coin prices got an artificial boost in the late 1980s when major Wall Street brokerage firms pumped millions of dollars in new investment money into rare coins. Merrill Lynch and Kidder, Peabody both established limited partnerships tied to investments in coins, and together these funds injected tens of millions of dollars into the coin market—including significant sums from people who had never bought coins before. The new money, combined with anticipation of even more, sent coin prices soaring; in the spring of 1989, many were at or near all-time highs.

Unfortunately, the timing was bad. Like much of the U.S. economy, the coin market soured during the recession of the early 1990s. Making matters worse, the Federal Trade Commission—drawn by Wall Street's involvement—found and publicized evidence of wrongdoing by certain unscrupulous elements in the coin market, and this frightened many investors away. The brokerage firms retreated as well, leaving longer-established coin buyers and sellers with only bittersweet memories of this whirlwind courtship and leaving the rare coin marketplace itself in disarray. Eventually, well-known California entrepreneur Bruce McNall pleaded guilty to fraud in connection with his role as manager of Merrill Lynch's Athena II rare-coin fund. Those who invested in that fund fared better, however: The brokerage agreed to compensate them in full for their losses. One of the law firms litigating the case against Merrill Lynch hired me as an expert numismatic consultant, so I had the satisfaction of helping these people recover their money.

In the eyes of many outsiders, this whole unhappy episode dimmed rare coins' luster as an investment vehicle. But those with longer perspectives and closer ties to the coin market know that this affair was an aberration. Rare coins should not be viewed as shooting stars; they are steady, solid stores of value, and if they are purchased wisely, treated well, and held for the longer term, they might well bring their owner a profit. They may not perform as spectacularly as they did in the 1980s, when outside influences drove their prices up unrealistically, but their long-range track record has been excellent. In fact, it was that record—documented in annual reports issued by the Salomon Brothers investment firm—that caught Wall Street's attention in the first place. Those reports showed that, over a twenty-year period beginning in the late 1960s, rare coins had outperformed all other investment vehicles measured by the firm, including stocks and bonds.

Many savvy investors considered rare coins a good buy in the late 1980s. Events proved them wrong in the short term. But if those shrewd buyers liked the investment potential of coins priced at $5,000 apiece, it certainly seems reasonable to look upon those coins as even better values today, now that they're available for just a fraction of that. Wall Street's marriage with the rare coin market ended in a quickie divorce, but rare coins were doing fine long before Wall Street came into their life, and we hope that they'll prosper once again now that they're on their own.

THE CERTIFIED ADVANTAGE

If you find any Mint State or proof examples of coins no longer seen in circulation, I advise you to have them certified by a reputable, independent third-party grading service. As this book is being written, the leading services are the Numismatic Guaranty Corporation of America (NGC), the Professional Coin Grading Service (PCGS), ANACS, and the Independent Coin Grading Company (ICG). Having your coins certified will not only enhance their marketability, but also provide them with tamper-resistant holders.

In years gone by, a number of people who purchased or found rare coins ended up selling them for less than their fair market value. They would go to a dealer and offer their coins for sale and the dealer would tell them, "This coin is fairly common; I'll give you five dollars for it." And the dealer would then turn around and sell the coin for hundreds—or even thousands—of dollars.

Today, we have organizations that help protect collectors, and the populace at large, against such abuse.

A coin encapsulated by the Professional Coin Grading Service. (Photo courtesy PCGS)

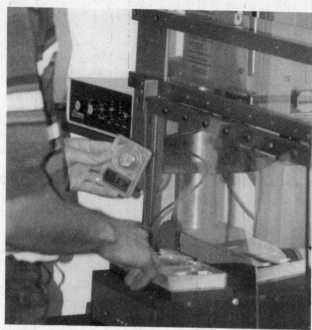

Coin holder being sonically sealed in the PCGS's encapsulation room. (Photo courtesy PCGS)

They're known as independent coin-grading services, and they serve in a real sense as watchdogs for the coin-collecting public. For a modest fee, these services examine coins that are sent to them for review, then render expert judgments concerning the grade of each coin—its level of preservation—on a 1 to 70 scale. This, in turn, gives the consumer a good idea of how much her coin is worth, since grade is a key determinant of price. Each coin is returned in a sonically sealed, hard plastic holder, along with a paper tab stating its grade.

These grading organizations have no vested interest in the coins they are examining. Thus, the consumer can have the utmost confidence in their judgments.

Consumers with coins that appear on the list at the end of this chapter should give serious consideration to having these coins certified. I would urge without hesitation that any such coins be independently certified before being offered for sale.

Most coin dealers are knowledgeable and reliable, and will pay fair value for any coins offered to them for sale. However, there's always a chance that you may be unlucky and end up dealing with someone less fair and honest. Having your coins certified will help protect you against that possibility.

Certification also provides you with a safe holder in which to store your coin. If you choose not to have your coins certified, I'll give you some tips at the end of this chapter on how to safely hold and house your coins.

COINS TO LOOK FOR

By now, perhaps you've tracked down some old coins in a desk or dresser drawer, or maybe in that cigar box in the attic. Naturally, you're curious to know whether any of these are valuable—and, if so, how much they're worth.

I don't propose to offer you a comprehensive list of every U.S. coin ever minted. Rather, I've selected the scarcest and most valuable coins from each series and shown the market value for each of these coins—coins, with few exceptions, which have a realistic chance of turning up in that long-forgotten cigar box.

Some U.S. coins of extraordinary value don't appear on this list, primarily because there's little or no chance of finding them. Many other coins with modest premium value are likewise omitted. I know you're not really interested in whether your coins are worth 10 or 25 cents—or even a dollar or two—more than their face value. You want to know whether you've hit it big.

First-year-of-issue coins have always been widely saved, so these are quite likely to turn up in your holdings. People tend to set aside examples of new coins in the year they first appear; consequently, such coins are often found years later in very high levels of preservation. But this doesn't mean that first-year-of-issue coins can't be scarce and valuable. Take the 1909-S V.D.B. Lincoln cent, for example. This is a first-year coin, yet a Mint State example can be worth $2,500—and you may very well find just such a coin in your personal treasure trove.

Treat this list as a guide. If you find you have several coins that appear in this compilation, chances are good that what you actually have is a carefully assembled collection—one that may be worth a lot of money. If so, I advise you to seek more information from a professional. In fact, if you have *many* of the rare-date coins that are listed here, feel free to contact the author directly: Scott Travers Rare Coin Galleries, LLC, F.D.R. Box 1711, New York, NY 10150.

For more detailed pricing information on U.S. coinage as a whole, and additional historical details, there are four yearly price-guide books that many find helpful: my own book, *The Insider's Guide to U.S. Coin Values* (Bantam Dell, yearly); *The Official Blackbook Price Guide of United States Coins* by Marc Hudgeons (House of Collectibles, yearly); *A Guide Book of United States Coins* by R.S. Yeoman, edited by Kenneth Bressett (Whitman Publishing LLC, yearly); and the *Coin World Guide to U.S. Coins, Prices & Value Trends*, written by the staff of *Coin World* (Signet New American Library).

The values given here are for average circulated examples—coins that have passed from hand to hand and display significant wear. These prices correspond to coins that would be graded Fine-12. For further information about grading, turn to Chapter Seven.

These are *fair market values*—the prices that would be paid in a retail transaction by a buyer with reasonable knowledge of the market, and the prices that would be charged by a seller under no undue duress to consummate the sale.

You won't necessarily be able to walk into your neighborhood shop and buy any of the coins listed here at these values—or be able, on the other hand, to sell any of the coins listed here at these values. This market is a volatile one, and the prices listed here could change substantially between the date of preparation of this list and the time you actually read this compilation.

Liberty Cap Half Cents (1793–1797)
*(Coins valued at $4,250 or more
in average circulated condition)*

1793 with head facing left	$ 5,000
1796 with pole behind Miss Liberty	15,000
1796 without pole	45,000
1797 with lettered edge	4,250

Draped Bust Half Cents (1800–1808)
*(Coins valued at $2,200 or more
in average circulated condition)*

1802/0 Draped Bust half cent, with the reverse design of 1800. (Photo courtesy American Numismatic Rarities, LLC)

1802/0 with the 2 engraved over a 0	$ 2,200
1802/0 with the reverse design of 1800	40,000
1805 with a small 5 and stars	3,000

Flowing Hair Large Cents (1793)
(All are valuable)

1793 Flowing Hair cent with chain reverse	$ 12,500
1793 Flowing Hair cent (either plain or lettered edge) with wreath reverse	4,500
1793 Flowing Hair cent with wreath reverse and strawberry leaves above the date	500,000

Liberty Cap Large Cents (1793–1796)
(Coins valued at $4,000 or more in average circulated condition)

1793	$ 10,000
1794 with the head of 1793	4,000
1794 with starred reverse	30,000
1795 with Jefferson head and plain edge	25,000

Draped Bust Large Cents (1796–1807)
(Coins valued at $2,000 or more in average circulated condition)

1799	$ 10,000
1799/8 with the 9 engraved over an 8	8,000
1803 with large date and small fraction 1/100	20,000
1804	2,000
1807/6 with the 7 engraved over a 6 (with a small 7)	8,000

Classic Head Large Cents (1808–1814)
(Coins valued at $375 or more in average circulated condition)

1809	$ 600
1811	375
1811/0 with the second 1 engraved over a 0	450

Coronet Large Cents (1816–1857)
(These coins are much more common than earlier large cents. The following coins are valued at $150 or more in average circulated condition.)

1821	$ 200
1823	375
1823/2 with the 3 engraved over a 2	400
1824/2 with the 4 engraved over a 2	150

1826/5 with the 6 engraved over a 5	225
1834 with large 8 and stars and medium letters	300
1839/6 with the 9 engraved over a 6	1,200

Flying Eagle Cents (1856–1858)

1856 Flying Eagle cent, Mint State. (Photo courtesy American Numismatic Rarities, LLC)

1856	$ 7,000
1857	40
1858, both small-letters and large-letters varieties	40
1858 with the second 8 struck over a 7	225

Indian Head Cents (1859–1909)
(Coins valued at $60 or more in average circulated condition)

1864-L Indian Head cent, Proof. (Photo courtesy American Numismatic Rarities, LLC)

1864 with the designer's initial L visible on the headdress	$ 100
1866	75
1867	75
1868	75
1869	200
1869 with the last 9 recut (over another 9)	275
1870	200
1871	250
1872	250
1873 with the 3 closed	75
1873 with the word LIBERTY doubled	1,000
1876	60
1877	1,500
1878	75
1908-S with an S below the wreath	90
1909-S	400

Lincoln Cents (1909–present)
(Coins valued at $75 or more in average circulated condition)

1909-S V.D.B. Lincoln cent, Mint State. (Photo courtesy American Numismatic Rarities, LLC)

1909-S V.D.B. with an S below the date and V.D.B. at the base of the reverse	$ 600
1909-S without the V.D.B.	90
1914-D with a D below the date	300
1922 Plain without the D below the date	725
1931-S	75
1944-D/S with a D engraved over the S below the date	85
1955 doubled die with doubling on the lettering on the front of the coin	900
1972 doubled die with doubling on the lettering on the front of the coin	100

Two-Cent Pieces (1864–1873)
(Coins valued at $150 or more in average circulated condition)

1864 with small motto IN GOD WE TRUST	$ 150
1869/8 with the 9 engraved over an 8	1,100
1872	500

Copper-Nickel Three-Cent Pieces (1865–1889)
(Coins valued at $50 or more in average circulated condition)

1885 Copper-nickel three-cent piece, Proof. (Photo courtesy Auctions by Bowers and Merena, Inc.)

1876	$ 50
1879	75

1880	150
1882	150
1883	300
1884	450
1885	500
1887	225
1888	80
1889	100

Silver Three-Cent Pieces (1851–1873)
(Coins valued at $30 or more in
average circulated condition)

1851-O (with an O to the right of the Roman numeral III on the reverse)	$ 50
1854	30
1855	100
1856	50
1857	50
1858	50
1859	50
1860	50
1861	50
1862/1 with the 2 engraved over a 1	60
1862	50

Flowing Hair Half Dimes (1792–1795)
(Coins valued at $1,000 or more in
average circulated condition)

1794 Flowing Hair half dime. (Photo enlargement courtesy Auctions by Bowers and Merena, Inc.)

1792 half dime	$ 35,000
1794	1,200
1795	1,000

Draped Bust/Small Eagle Half Dimes (1796–1797)
(Coins valued at $2,200 or more in average circulated condition)

1796/5 Draped Bust half dime. (Photo enlargement courtesy Auctions by Bowers and Merena, Inc.)

1796/5 with the 6 engraved over a 5	$ 3,000
1796	2,200
1796 with LIBERTY spelled LIKERTY	2,200
1797 with 15 stars	2,200
1797 with 16 stars	2,200
1797 with 13 stars	2,500

Draped Bust/Heraldic Eagle Half Dimes (1800–1805)
(Coins valued at $40,000 or more in average circulated condition)

1802 Draped Bust half dime. (Photo enlargement courtesy Auctions by Bowers and Merena, Inc.)

1802	$ 40,000

Seated Liberty Half Dimes (1837–1873)
(Coins valued at $200 or more in average circulated condition)

1863 Seated Liberty half dime, Mint State. (Photo courtesy Auctions by Bowers and Merena, Inc.)

1838-O with no stars (with an O below the wreath
   on the reverse) $ 350
1839-O with a large O   1,000
1844-O   200
1846   600
1853-O with no arrows beside the date   500
1863   250
1864   500
1865   500
1866   500
1867   700

Shield Nickels (1866–1883)
*(Coins valued at $50 or more in
average circulated condition)*

1867 Shield nickel, Proof. (Photo courtesy Scott Travers Rare Coin Galleries, Inc.)

1867 with rays $ 75
1871   100
1873 with the 3 closed   50
1877   1,600
1878   600
1879   475
1880   500
1881   400
1883/2 with the 3 engraved over a 2   200

(Most common dates are worth $25 in Fine-12.)

Liberty Head Nickels (1883–1912)
(Coins valued at more than $250 in Fine-12 condition)

1885 $ 800
1886   500

1886 Liberty Head nickel, Proof. (Photo courtesy Scott Travers Rare Coin Galleries, Inc.)

1912-S with an S below the dot to the left of the word CENTS on the reverse	300
1913 (not an official mint issue; only 5 known)	2,500,000

Buffalo Nickels (1913–1938)
(Coins valued at $100 or more in average circulated condition)

1913-D Variety 2 with the buffalo on flat ground and a D below the words FIVE CENTS	$ 200
1913-S Variety 2 with the buffalo on flat ground and an S below the words FIVE CENTS	400
1914-D	150
1915-S	100
1916 with doubling visible	7,700
1918/17-D with the 8 engraved over a 7	2,500
1921-S	150
1937-D with only three legs on the buffalo	700

(Most common dates are worth $2 in Fine-12.)

Jefferson Nickels (1938–present)
(Coins valued at $25 or more in average circulated condition)

1943-Over-2 Jefferson Nickel. Worth $30. (Photo courtesy Coin World)

1939 doubled die with doubling in the words
  MONTICELLO and FIVE CENTS $ 50

1943/2 with the 3 engraved over a 2   50

1943-P doubled die with a large P over the dome
  of Monticello on the reverse   25

1949-D/S with the D mint mark, to the right
  of Monticello, engraved over an S   25

1994-P with matte finish   40

1997-P with matte finish   75

Draped Bust/Small Eagle Dimes (1796–1797)
(Coins valued at $2,800 or more in
average circulated condition)

1797 Draped Bust/Small Eagle dime, with 13 stars. (Photo courtesy American Numismatic Rarities, LLC)

1796 with small eagle $ 3,000

1797 with 16 stars   2,800

1797 with 13 stars   2,800

Draped Bust/Heraldic Eagle Dimes (1798–1807)
(Coins valued at $2,000 or more in
average circulated condition)

1798/7 with 13 stars (with the 8 engraved
  over a 7) $ 2,000

1802   2,000

1804   2,000

Capped Bust Dimes (1809–1837)
(Coins valued at $150 or more in
average circulated condition)

1809 $ 300

1811/9 with the final 1 engraved over a 9   300

1814 small date   150

1822	1,000
1829 with a curl-base 2	12,000

Seated Liberty Dimes (1837–1891)
(Coins valued at $150 or more in
average circulated condition)

1874-CC Seated Liberty dime, with arrows beside the date, Mint State. (Photo courtesy Auctions by Bowers and Merena, Inc.)

1839-O with the reverse of 1838 (with an O below the wreath on the reverse)	$ 300
1843-O	150
1846	190
1858-S with an S below the wreath	300
1860-O	1,000
1863	500
1864	500
1865	500
1866	500
1867	800
1871-CC with the letters CC below the wreath	3,000
1872-CC	1,000
1873-CC with arrows beside the date	3,000
1874-CC with arrows beside the date	6,000
1879	500
1880	500
1881	500
1885-S	1,100

Barber Dimes (1892–1916)
(Coins valued at $100 or more in average circulated condition)

1894-S Barber dime, Proof. (Photo courtesy Auctions by Bowers and Merena, Inc.)

1892-S with an S below the wreath
1893-O with an O below the wreath
1894
1894-O
1894-S (unauthorized; 24 manufactured
   by the Mint) $ 50,000
1895   400
1895-O   800
1895-S   150
1896-S   300
1897-O   300
1901-S   300
1903-S   400
1904-S   200
1913-S   100

Winged Liberty Head (or "Mercury") Dime (1916–1945)
(Coins valued at $100 or more in average circulated condition)

1916-D Mercury dime, Mint State. (Photo courtesy Auctions by Bowers and Merena, Inc.)

1916-D with a D to the right of ONE on the reverse $ 2,500
1921   100
1921-D   200
1942/1 with the 2 engraved over a 1   700
1942/1-D with the 2 engraved over a 1 and a D to
   the right of ONE on the reverse $ 700

Twenty-Cent Pieces (1875–1878)
(Coins valued at $150 or more in Fine-12 condition)

1875 $ 250
1875-CC with the letters CC below the eagle   250
1875-S   150
1876   400
1876-CC only 12 to 15 known   40,000

(The 1877 and 1878 twenty-cent pieces are proof-only issues, generally
worth several thousand dollars or more.)

Early Quarters (1796–1807)

1796 with small eagle	$ 15,000
1804 with heraldic eagle	5,000
1805	700
1806/5 with the 6 engraved over a 5	750
1806	700
1807	700

Capped Bust Quarters (1815–1837)

(Every coin in this series is worth $75 or more in Fine-12 condition. The following coins are worth $150 or more.)

1815	$ 150
1818/5 with the second 8 engraved over a 5	150
1818	150
1822	175
1824/2 with the 4 engraved over a 2	300
1825/2 with the 5 engraved over a 2	350

Seated Liberty Quarters (1838–1891)

(Every coin in this series is worth $25 or more in Fine-12 condition. The following dates are worth $200 or more.)

1842 large date	$ 250
1842 small date	7,500
1843-O with a large O below the eagle on the reverse	$ 250
1849-O	1,500
1851-O	600
1852-O	600
1853 over 53, with a recut date	600
1854-O with a huge O	2,000
1857-S	300
1858-S	250
1859-S	350
1860-S	700
1861-S	300
1865-S	200
1866 with the motto IN GOD WE TRUST	1,000
1866-S	700
1867	550
1867-S	600

1868-S	300
1869-S	300
1871-CC	7,000
1871-S	500
1872-CC	1,800
1872-S	1,500
1873 with a closed 3	500
1873-CC with arrows beside the date	6,000

1873-CC Seated Liberty quarter, with arrows beside the date, Mint State. (Photo courtesy Auctions by Bowers and Merena, Inc.)

1875-CC	$ 250
1878-S	300
1879	200
1880	200
1881	250
1882	250
1883	250
1884	500
1885	250
1886	500
1887	500
1888	500
1889	400
1891-O	450

Barber Quarters (1892–1916)

(Coins valued at $20 or more in average circulated condition)

1901-S Barber quarter. (Photo courtesy Auctions by Bowers and Merena, Inc.)

1892-S with an S below the eagle	$ 75
1896-S	1,200
1897-S	200
1901-O with an O below the eagle	100
1901-S	7,250
1909-O	100
1913	85
1913-S	4,000
1914-S	150

Standing Liberty Quarters (1916–1930)
(Coins valued at $50 or more in
average circulated condition)

1916 Standing Liberty quarter, Mint State. (Photo courtesy American Numismatic Rarities, LLC)

1916	$ 5,000
1917-D Type 1 with bare breast on Liberty and a D	
to the left of the date	50
1917-D Type 2 with mailed breast on Liberty	75
1917-S Type 2 with mailed breast on Liberty and an S	
to the left of the date	75
1918-D	50
1918/17-S with the 8 engraved over a 7	2,000
1919	50
1919-D	150
1919-S	150
1920-D	50
1920-S	50
1921	200
1923-S	300
1924-D	75
1927-S	75

Washington Quarters (1932–present)
(Coins valued at $50 or more in
average circulated condition)

1932-D with a D below the eagle	$ 150
1932-S with an S below the eagle	100
1943-S doubled die (with doubling on the lettering on the front of the coin)	125
1950-D/S with the D engraved over an S	50
1950-S/D with the S engraved over a D	50

Flowing Hair Half Dollars (1794–1795)
(All dates are valuable)

1794	$ 7,500
1795	1,000
1795 with three leaves under each wing of the eagle	3,000

Draped Bust/Small Eagle Half Dollars (1796–1797)
(All dates are valuable)

1796 with 15 stars on the front	$ 28,000
1796 with 16 stars on the front	30,000
1797 with 15 stars on the front	25,000

Draped Bust/Heraldic Eagle Half Dollars (1801–1807)
(Coins valued at $500 or more in
average circulated condition)

1801	$ 500
1805/4 with the 5 engraved over a 4	550

Capped Bust Half Dollars (1807–1839)
(Coins valued at $100 or more in
average circulated condition)

1807 with small stars on the front	$ 150
1807 with large stars on the front	100
1812/1 large date with the 2 engraved over a 1 and a large 8 in the date	2,800

1815/2 with the 5 engraved over a 2	1,200
1836 with reeded edge and 50 CENTS	800

Seated Liberty Half Dollars (1839–1891)
(Coins valued at $150 or more in
average circulated condition)

1840 with medium letters	$ 175
1842-O small date with an O below the eagle on the reverse	1,200
1844-O doubled date	1,000
1846 with a horizontal 6	250
1846-O tall date	350
1847/6 with the 7 engraved over a 6	2,800
1850	350
1851	400
1855/54 with the last 5 engraved over a 4	200
1855-S with arrows beside the date and an S below the eagle	750
1857-S	150
1866-S without IN GOD WE TRUST	200
1870-CC with the letters CC below the eagle	2,500
1871-CC	400
1872-CC	200
1873-CC without arrows beside the date	300
1873-CC with arrows beside the date	300
1874-CC	900
1878-S	20,000

Barber Half Dollars (1892–1915)
(Coins valued at $75 or more in
average circulated condition)

1892-O with an O below the eagle	$ 300
1892-S with an S below the eagle	300
1894-O	75
1896-O	125
1896-S	150
1897-O	300
1897-S	300
1914	200

Walking Liberty Half Dollars (1916–1947)

(Coins valued at $30 or more in
average circulated condition)

1916	$ 50
1916-D with a D below IN GOD WE TRUST	50
1916-S with an S below IN GOD WE TRUST	150
1917-D with the D below IN GOD WE TRUST	40
1917-S with the S below IN GOD WE TRUST	50
1919	40
1919-D with a D on the reverse, above and to the left of HALF DOLLAR	40
1919-S with an S on the reverse, above and to the left of HALF DOLLAR	40
1920-D with the D on the reverse	30
1921	200
1921-D with the D on the reverse	300
1921-S with the S on the reverse	250
1938-D with the D on the reverse	60

Flowing Hair Silver Dollars (1794–1795)

(Both dates are valuable)

1794	$ 35,000
1795, type of 1794	3,000

Draped Bust/Small Eagle Silver Dollars (1795–1798)

(All dates are valuable)

1795	$ 2,000
1796	2,000
1797 with 9 stars left, 7 stars right, and small letters	3,000
1797 with 9 stars left, 7 stars right, and large letters	3,000
1797 with 10 stars left, 6 stars right	2,000
1798 with 13 stars	2,000
1798 with 15 stars	2,500

Draped Bust/Heraldic Eagle Silver Dollars (1798–1804)

(All dates from 1798 to 1803 are valued at approximately $1,000 in average
circulated condition; the 1804 is a great rarity worth upwards
of $950,000 in average condition)

Gobrecht Silver Dollars (1836–1839)
(Coins valued at $6,000 or more in
average circulated condition)

1836	$ 6,000
1836 with new, slightly reduced weight	6,250
1839	7,500

Seated Liberty Silver Dollars (1840–1873)
(Coins valued at $500 or more in
average circulated condition)

1850	$ 500
1854	1,200
1855	1,200
1861	750
1870-S with an S below the eagle (7 to 12 known)	40,000
1871-CC with the letters CC below the eagle	2,650
1872-CC	1,200
1873-CC	4,000

Trade Dollars (1873–1885)
(Coins valued at $100 or more in
average circulated condition)

1878-CC Trade dollar, Mint State. (Photo courtesy American Numismatic Rarities, LLC)

1873	$ 100
1873-CC with the CC mint mark above the D of DOLLAR on the reverse	150
1873-S with an S above the D of DOLLAR on the reverse	150
1874	100
1875	250

1875-S/CC with the S mint mark engraved over
the letters CC   200
1877-CC   140
1878-CC   500

Morgan Silver Dollars (1878–1921)
(Coins valued at $100 or more in average circulated condition)

1881-S Morgan dollar, Mint State. (Photo courtesy American Numismatic Rarities, LLC)

1879-CC with the letters CC below the wreath $ 100
1879-CC with a large CC engraved over a small CC   100
1880-CC with the reverse of 1878   150
1880-CC   150
1881-CC   300
1883-CC   100
1884-CC   100
1889-CC   1,300
1890-CC   100
1891-CC   100
1892-CC   100
1893   100
1893-CC   200
1893-O with an O below the wreath   100
1893-S with an S below the wreath   2,000
1894   600
1895-O   175
1895-S   250
1903-O   200

Peace Dollars (1921–1935)
*(Coins valued at $100 or more in
average circulated condition)*

1921 $ 100
1928   300

GOLD COINS

All gold coins have significant value because gold itself is so valuable. As this is written, the price of gold is approximately $300 per ounce. Since the largest regular-issue U.S. gold coin—the Double Eagle (or $20 gold piece)—contains very close to an ounce of gold, each and every example of this coin is worth several hundred dollars just as metal. Smaller gold coins are worth proportionally less as bullion, but even very small ones have respectable metal value. Many gold coins are worth a great deal more as collectibles, but the metal value of gold establishes a floor for even the commonest gold coins and those with substantial wear.

Following are values for some of the rarer and more collectible U.S. gold coins. As with all the previous coins in this compilation, the prices shown here are current retail values as of July 2004 for pieces in Fine-12, or average circulated condition.

Gold Dollars (1849–1889)
(Coins valued at $1,600 or more in
average circulated condition)

1855-D with a D below the wreath on the reverse	$ 2,000
1856-D with large head	3,000
1860-D	1,800
1861-D	5,000
1875	1,600

Capped Bust $2.50 Gold Pieces (1796–1807)
(All dates are valuable)

1796 with no stars	$ 20,000
1796 with stars	20,000
1797	20,000
1798	6,000
1802/1 with the 2 engraved over a 1	6,000
1804 with 14 stars	5,000
1804 with 13 stars	22,500
1805	5,000
1806/4 with the 6 engraved over a 4	5,000
1806/5 with the 6 engraved over a 5	8,500
1807	4,500

Capped Draped Bust $2.50 Gold Pieces (1808)

1808	$ 35,000

Capped Head $2.50 Gold Pieces (1821–1834)
(All dates are valuable)

1821	$ 5,000
1824/1 with the 4 engraved over a 1	5,000
1825	5,000
1826	5,000
1827	5,000
1829 struck on a small planchet, or coin blank	4,000
1830	4,000
1831	4,000
1832	4,000
1833	4,000
1834	8,500

Coronet $2.50 Gold Pieces (1840–1907)
(Coins valued at $2,000 or more in average circulated condition)

1854-D with a D below the eagle on the reverse	$ 2,000
1854-S with an S below the eagle on the reverse	50,000
1855-D	2,000
1856-D	4,000

Three-Dollar Gold Pieces (1854–1889)
(Coins valued at $2,000 or more in average circulated condition)

1854-D Three-dollar gold piece. (Photo courtesy American Numismatic Rarities, LLC)

1854-D with a D below the wreath on the reverse	$ 5,000
1870-S with an S below the wreath	750,000
1873 with a closed 3	2,000

Capped Bust/Small Eagle $5 Gold Pieces (1795–1798)
(All dates are valuable)

1797 Capped Bust/Small Eagle $5 gold piece, with 16 stars. (Photo courtesy Auctions by Bowers and Merena, Inc.)

1795	$ 8,000
1796/5 with the 6 engraved over a 5	10,000
1797 with 15 stars	12,000
1797 with 16 stars	12,000
1798	100,000

Capped Bust/Heraldic Eagle $5 Gold Pieces (1795–1807)
(Coins valued at $7,000 or more in average circulated condition)

1797/5 with the final 7 engraved over a 5	$ 7,000
1797 with 16 stars	20,000

Capped Head $5 Gold Pieces (1813–1834)
(Coins valued at $3,500 or more in average circulated condition)

1821	$ 8,000
1825/1 with the 5 engraved over a 1	4,000
1826	3,500
1830 with small 5 D	12,000
1830 with large 5 D	12,000
1831 with small 5 D	12,000
1831 with large 5 D	14,000
1832 with square 2 and 13 stars	12,000
1833	10,000
1834 with plain 4	12,000
1834 with crosslet 4	12,000

Coronet $5 Gold Pieces (1839–1908)
*(Coins valued at $1,500 or more in
average circulated condition)*

1864-S Coronet $5 gold piece, Mint State. (Photo courtesy Auctions by Bowers and Merena, Inc.)

1842-C small date with a C below the eagle on the reverse	$ 4,500
1854-S with an S below the eagle on the reverse	100,000
1861-D with a D below the eagle on the reverse	2,500
1864-S	2,000
1870-CC with the letters CC below the eagle on the reverse	1,500
1878-CC	1,500

Capped Bust/Small Eagle $10 Gold Pieces (1795–1797)
(All dates are valuable)

1795 with 13 leaves	$ 15,000
1795 with 9 leaves	25,000
1796	15,000
1797	20,000

Capped Bust/Heraldic Eagle $10 Gold Pieces (1797–1804)
(All dates are valuable)

1798/7 Capped Bust/Heraldic Eagle $10 gold piece, with 7 stars left, 6 stars right. (Photo courtesy Auctions by Bowers and Merena, Inc.)

1797	$ 6,000
1798/7 with 9 stars left, 4 stars right (with the 8 engraved over a 7)	10,000
1798/7 with 7 stars left, 6 stars right	20,000
1799	7,000
1800	7,000
1801	7,000
1803 with small stars	7,500
1803 with large stars	7,500
1804	7,500

Coronet $10 Gold Pieces (1838–1907)
*(Coins valued at $12,000 or more in
average circulated condition)*

1870-CC Coronet $10 gold piece. (Photo courtesy Auctions by Bowers and Merena, Inc.)

1864-S with an S below the eagle on the reverse	$ 3,000
1870-CC with CC below the eagle	4,000
1878-CC	2,000
1879-CC	4,000
1883-O with an O below the eagle	1,200

Liberty Head $20 Gold Pieces (1850–1907)
*(Coins valued at $1,500 or more in
average circulated condition)*

1855-O with an O below the eagle on the reverse	$ 2,000
1859-O	3,000
1860-O	3,000
1870-CC with the letters CC below the eagle	30,000
1871-CC	2,500
1879-O	2,000
1881	2,500
1885	4,000

| 1885-CC | 1,500 |
| 1891-CC | 2,000 |

Saint-Gaudens $20 Gold Pieces (1907–1933)
(Coins valued at $1,000 or more in
average circulated condition)

1924 Saint-Gaudens $20 gold piece. (Photo courtesy Scott Travers Rare Coin Galleries, Inc.)

1907 with high relief, Roman numerals, and a wire rim	$ 4,000
1907 with high relief, Roman numerals, and a flat rim	4,000
1920-S with an S above the date	10,000
1921	11,000
1927-D with a D above the date	80,000
1927-S	2,000
1929	2,000
1930-S	9,000
1931	7,800
1931-D	7,800
1932	8,500

PROOF SET PRICES

Proof sets aren't pocket-change rarities; in fact, they're not intended to circulate at all. These annual government sets of specimen-quality coins are normally acquired through purchase, rather than chance discovery. Nonetheless, they often turn up in old accumulations or in organized collections that someone in the family passes along. For that reason, I'm including them in this review of the fair market value of U.S. coins you're likely to encounter.

In recent years, late-date U.S. proof sets haven't kept pace with the rest of the coin market; their price performance hasn't been as spectacular as that of many other U.S. coins. This is not to say that proof sets aren't desirable; some are worth thousands of dollars—and almost all have great aesthetic appeal. However, for the most part, the beauty of these coins hasn't been matched by similarly beautiful escalation in value.

A generation ago, quite the opposite was true. Back in the 1950s and 1960s, many Americans made substantial profits every year by ordering proof sets from the Mint, then selling them to coin dealers for considerably more than what they had paid. At that time, the Mint was charging only $2.10 per set, and people who purchased these sets directly from the government were routinely able to sell them for 50 percent or 100 percent more than that—and sometimes even more.

In 1968, the Mint raised the price to $5 per set. To help justify this very sizable increase, it also introduced an attractive—but bulky—new holder. Up to then, the Mint had packaged proof sets in slender Pliofilm sleeves just about the size of a small letter-size envelope; in fact, it had mailed each set in an envelope just that size.

The new kind of holder introduced in 1968 offered greater protection for the coins; it was made of hard plastic that not only enhanced security but also was suitable for use in displaying the set. However, many people found this packaging inconvenient, since it took up so much space and thus made storage more difficult.

With this bulky plastic holder, people had three options:

1. They could display their proof sets around the house in these beautiful new holders.
2. They could store these bulky holders in their safety deposit boxes. But it didn't take many sets to fill an entire box, and safety deposit space was becoming more expensive.
3. They could put their rare coin investment dollars into other areas and forget about buying new proof sets every year.

Many people chose Option 3, reducing demand for new sets. Demand was further weakened by subsequent price increases. As this is written, the Mint is charging $19.95 apiece for new proof sets—nearly ten times the issue price of pre-1965 sets—and unlike those, the standard sets today contain no silver coins. The Mint does offer silver sets as an option, but those now cost $31.95. On the plus side, the current sets do include nine coins, rather than five, since the Mint is preparing them with proof examples of five different statehood Washington quarters.

If you're buying coins for investment, you're better off with other kinds of coins that appear to have greater potential for appreciation. Some of the proof sets made in recent years are available today for less than the Mint's original issue price. These sets really haven't recovered from the setback the market suffered when the government raised the price and introduced the hard plastic holders. The big exception to this applies to many modern mint products, which has increased in value phenomenally as a result of interest in America's state quarters and related issues. A typical example of this type of price appreciation is the 1997-S silver proof set: from $30 to $160 in a year.

Many of the scarce and rare coins listed earlier in this chapter would be well worth keeping, rather than selling, if you found them. These coins have excellent prospects for going up in value even more—so if you don't need the money right now, it could be well worthwhile to hold them as investments. With proof sets, on the other hand, you should seriously consider selling any extras you may have, or any that you may find in a stash or a collection that comes your way.

Proofs are certainly beautiful to behold—but the later ones, at least, aren't likely to add any similar luster to your bank account. If some of the sets you're holding have sentimental value, by all means hang on to them. Just remember that while they may be worth a million dollars in a sentimental sense, their actual value is almost surely a great deal less than that—and it probably isn't rising very fast.

The U.S. Mint began making proof coins in the early nineteenth century; some U.S. coins produced even earlier are regarded as proofs by coinage experts. Sale of these coins to the general public began in the 1850s and—with occasional interruptions—has continued ever since.

The following list, however, is limited to proof sets produced by the U.S. Mint since 1936. These are the ones you're most likely to encounter in family collections or old accumulations you may find. Proofs made prior to 1936 all have significant value unless they are impaired in some way.

Proof Sets

Date	Value	Date	Value
1936	6,000	1976-S three-piece 40-percent silver set	20
1937	3,500	1976-S regular six-piece copper-nickel set	10
1938	1,900	1977-S	10
1939	1,700	1978-S	10
1940	1,475	1979-S	10
1941	1,200	1979-S Type 2	130
1942	1,200	1980-S	10
1942 Type 2	1,400	1981-S	10
1950	600	1981-S Type 2	300
1951	600	1982-S	6
1952	350	1983-S	8
1953	350	1983-S with no-S dime	1,000
1954	225	1983-S prestige set	85
1955	150	1984-S	12
1955 flat pack	175	1984-S prestige set	20
1956	75	1985-S	9
1957	40	1986-S	20
1958	80	1986-S prestige set	35
1959	30	1987-S	8
1960	25	1987-S prestige set	20
1960 small date	60	1988-S	10
1961	12	1988-S prestige set	25
1962	12	1989-S	9
1963	15	1989-S prestige set	30
1964	10	1990-S	10
1968-S	7	1990-S with no-S cent	7,000
1968-S with no-S dime	8,900	1990-S prestige set	25
1969-S	7	1991-S	18
1970-S	15	1991-S prestige set	70
1970-S small date	100	1992-S	10
1970-S with no-S dime	1,300	1992-S prestige set	45
1971-S	8	1992-S silver	20
1971-S with no-S nickel	1,300	1992-S silver premier set	15
1972-S	7	1993-S	15
1973-S	13	1993-S prestige set	40
1974-S	13	1993-S silver	30
1975-S	13		
1975-S with no-S dime	40,000		

Date	Value	Date	Value
1993-S silver premier set	35	1998-S	30
1994-S	20	1998-S silver	35
1994-S prestige set	50	1999-S nine-coin set*	70
1994-S silver	40	1999-S five-coin set*	40
1994-S silver premier set	40	1999-S silver nine-coin set*	75
1995-S	70	2000-S ten-coin set	20
1995-S prestige set	200	2000-S silver	30
1995-S silver	90	2000-S Quarters	20
1995-S silver premier set	90	2001-S	50
1996-S	15	2001-S Silver	80
1996-S prestige set	350	2001-S Quarters	32
1996-S silver	40	2002-S	25
1996-S silver premier set	40	2002-S Silver	60
1997-S	45	2002-S Quarters	15
1997-S prestige set	150	2003-S	19
1997-S silver	75	2003-S Silver	30
1997-S silver premier set	70	2003-S Quarters	12

*Containing all five 1999 statehood quarters

PROOF COINS

There are also a number of individual proof coins with mint errors that can add considerably to their value. Here are some to look for:

• The 1983 no-S proof Roosevelt dime.

I mentioned this variety earlier in the chapter. It won't turn up in pocket change, but if you or someone you know has any 1983 proof sets, take a close look at the dime. The mint mark was missing on some proof dimes that year, and these coins are worth up to $350.

• The 1974-S proof quarter with a double S.

The S mint mark on this coin has obvious doubling. Look for the S on the obverse (or "heads" side) of the coin, just behind Washington's pigtail.

• The 1973-S silver-clad proof Eisenhower dollar.

Most Eisenhower dollars are made from a copper-nickel alloy, rather than silver. But from 1971 to 1976, the Mint did produce special "Ike" dollars with limited silver content (40 percent, versus 90 percent in "traditional" silver dollars). These were made in both proof and uncirculated (business-strike) versions.

Of all the "silver Ikes," the scarcest and most valuable is the proof version minted in 1973. Only about a million of these were made—not very many, by modern minting standards—and, at one point, these were worth nearly $150 apiece, or 15 times their $10 issue price.

Strictly speaking, this isn't a "pocket-change rarity." Like all proofs, it's unlikely to turn up in ordinary change. Still, there's an excellent chance that you, or someone you know, may find one stuck away in a desk or cabinet. If so, you have a coin worth upwards of $30—and with the potential to rise in value substantially.

• The 1979-S clear-S Anthony dollar.

If you were around in 1979, you certainly remember the hullabaloo surrounding the Susan B. Anthony dollar. This "mini-dollar" coin—considerably smaller than its predecessors—was supposed to save the government enormous sums of money. In fact, it was intended as a permanent replacement for the $1 bill. The theory was that while this coin was somewhat more expensive to produce than a paper dollar, it would last many times longer, so production costs would be sharply curtailed in the long run.

The only problem was, people disliked the coin and refused to use it. Many complained that because it wasn't much bigger than a 25-cent piece, they confused the new coin with the quarter and made expensive mistakes. In 1981, the Mint conceded defeat and suspended further production of Anthony dollars. But, by then, more than 800 million examples had been produced.

The public may have hated the coin, but hobbyists fell in love with at least one Anthony dollar: the "clear-S" or "Type 2" version of 1979.

Like most proof coins made by the U.S. Mint since 1968, Anthony dollar proofs were produced in San Francisco (with an "S" on the obverse just above Susan B. Anthony's right shoulder). On most proof dollars of 1979, the "S" looks like a blob. On some, however, the mint mark is clear and sharp. Being relatively scarce, these "clear-S" coins command a premium. The Type 1 proof set of 1979 (with a clogged "S" mint mark) costs about $10 at this writing, while the Type 2 set brings $65. All six coins in the set (the cent, nickel, dime, quarter, half dollar, and dollar) are either clear or clogged, as a rule, but the dollar is easily the most valuable. So check those desk and dresser drawers today!

HOLDING AND HOUSING YOUR COINS

It's very important to hold your coins properly. If you don't, they may suffer damage that will seriously compromise their value.

By now, perhaps you've gathered together a number of coins that you would like to set aside and store safely. Here, then, are some tips on how to care for your coins.

Always hold a coin tightly by the edges between your thumb and forefinger. Never take a finger and rub it over a coin; if you do, you may leave a mark that cannot be removed and will lower the coin's value significantly. Your hand contains natural oils which can cause irreparable damage to a Mint State coin (one that's in brand new condition), even reducing the grade of that coin from Mint State to lightly circulated. A single fingerprint across the face of a coin can decrease its value by tens of thousands of dollars.

You owe it to future generations of collectors to preserve your coins in the same condition you found them. What's more, you owe it to yourself: If you *don't* take care of your coins, you stand to lose a great deal of money when you sell them.

Proper storage of coins is also extremely important. Many people house their coins in folders, albums, or 2-by-2 cardboard holders. Doing so is better than not using any holder at all, and may be perfectly adequate for circulated coins. But these holders may not be good enough for coins in mint condition—those that have never passed from hand to hand.

Many coin albums have acetate inserts that are meant to protect the coins but which, in fact, can *harm* the coins when these inserts are pulled out or put back in. In sliding over the surfaces of Mint State coins, they can impart scratches or cause minute wear on the highest points. This kind of damage can never be repaired.

CLEANING AND POLISHING COINS

In general, you should never clean your coins. However, there's a difference between abrasive cleaning, where you penetrate the metal of the coin, and nonabrasive cleaning, which is restorative. Abrasive cleaning can ruin a coin's collectibility and destroy its premium value. But experts often use nonabrasive cleaning to restore a coin. For example, if a coin has a small piece of gum stuck to it, removal of the gum without penetrating the metal of the coin is deemed to be a restorative process.

Valuable coins should never be polished. Polishing a coin means cleaning it abrasively, and in doing so you remove the top layer of metal from the coin. That, in turn, removes details of the design from the surface—details which the designer and the Mint intended the coin to have when it was manufactured. By removing this detail, which can never be restored, you actually lower the grade of the coin.

There's also another problem: When you clean a coin abrasively, you penetrate its surface and activate the metal from which the coin is made. That sets in motion chemical reactions which often leave the coin far more unattractive than it was before you cleaned it, sometimes leaving the coin with unsightly blotches.

Before being placed in long-term storage, coins are frequently degreased using denatured alcohol. This helps protect them against unwanted chemical reactions that otherwise might occur with impurities in the environment. The alcohol doesn't damage the coins and doesn't penetrate their surface. But even the use of denatured alcohol should be left to the experts. And, if you use it, you should do so in a well-ventilated area.

STORING YOUR COINS

Coins should be stored in airtight containers, away from freely circulating air. Airborne particulate matter—particles you can't see—can lower a coin's value significantly.

Coins should also be stored in a stable environment, where the temperature is relatively moderate and constant. And if possible, they should be stored in the presence of a vapor-phase inhibitor—a chemical that changes the molecular composition of the surrounding air to help keep the coins from deteriorating due to environmental factors. A corrosion inhibitor marketed under the brand name Metal Safe is available from E&T Cointainer Company, P.O. Box 103, Sidney, OH 45365.

As this is written in August 2000, a new product about to be introduced by longtime professional numismatist John Albanese appears to offer an even better way to protect coins from deteriorating while in storage. This product, called Intercept Technology, represents an improvement over vapor-phase inhibitors. Rather than producing a chemical change in the air, it reacts with—and neutralizes—substances that pose a potential danger.

Intercept Technology was developed by Lucent Bell Labs for a purpose totally unrelated to coin preservation. The company needed a way to prevent corrosive reactions that were damaging solid-state elements of its equipment. Lucent claims that when this product is stored with its equipment, it keeps the environment stable and safe for ten years. And unlike corrosion inhibitors, it leaves no residue on the surfaces of the material it is protecting—including stored coins.

Albanese, who founded NGC in 1987 but has since sold his interest in that company, plans to introduce Intercept Technology commercially in a number of different sizes and forms. He says these will include a strip that can be placed inside a plastic holder (or "slab") by grading services to enhance the protection of the coins they have graded and certified. He also plans to market the product to dealers and collectors on an individual basis, in a variety of convenient sizes and at nominal cost.

Coins should be stored in a dry environment. If you store your coins in a safety deposit box at your local bank, check to make sure that the bank doesn't have an ozone-purification or air-control system that regularly humidifies the air. Moisture is the enemy of coin preservation. From this standpoint, no-frills banks are often better repositories for rare coin collections, since they're less likely to have such elaborate air-purification devices.

The banks that have such systems are looking out for the interests of people who store documents in their safety deposit boxes. When paper gets dry, it turns yellow—so moisturizing the air helps preserve such documents. But as far as coins are concerned, dry and stable air is the perfect environment.

Speaking of paper, coins should be kept away from direct contact with paper. Paper contains sulfur, and sulfur causes coins to tarnish.

Take care of your coins and they will retain their beauty, and their value, for many years to come.

TONING OR CORROSION?

Some experts have questioned whether toning is merely a form of corrosion which can be likened to rust on a car. The process that causes silver coins to tone or tarnish, however, is different from the one that causes iron to rust.

My father, Harvey C. Travers, is a chemical engineer with a master's degree from the Massachusetts Institute of Technology, and he has carried out extensive studies on this subject. Some of his opinions are:

- When moisture reacts with iron, there is *an all-out destructive attack*—corrosion—of the metal. Iron spalls or loses metal when it rusts.

- Silver is relatively inactive and does not react with oxygen in the air, even at high temperatures. It reacts with certain chemical compounds, notably those containing sulfur, if a catalyst is present—moisture, for example. The reaction, however, stops short of being an all-out destructive attack. In the case of silver coins, the sulfur causes a protective coating to form on the surface of the metal.

- When silver tones or tarnishes, it is not eaten away—corroded—by this limited chemical reaction, and there is no loss of metal.

CHAPTER 5

ANSWERS TO THE
MOST-ASKED COIN QUESTIONS

I'm called upon frequently to discuss rare coins on television talk shows and radio call-in programs. During these appearances, I get a lot of questions from the hosts of these shows, members of the studio audience, and viewers and listeners around the country.

Many of these questions come up again and again. This suggests to me that many of the people reading this book may have the same interests and concerns.

Here, then, are the questions most frequently asked of me, plus my answers.

What's the most valuable U.S. coin?

On July 30, 2002, two leading auction firms jointly conducted a public auction for sale of the fabled 1933 Saint-Gaudens double eagle. Pre-sale estimates were in the $4-million to $6-million range. The coin sold for an astounding $7,590,020. This now stands as the highest price ever paid at auction—and the highest price confirmed to have been paid publicly—for a single U.S. coin.

In August 1999, an 1804 silver dollar changed hands at a New York City auction for $4,140,000. That figure included a hammer price of $3,600,000 plus a 15-percent buyer's fee of $540,000. The August 1999 sale stood as the highest price ever paid at auction—and the highest price confirmed to have been paid publicly—for a single U.S. coin—prior to the sale of the 1933 Saint-Gaudens double eagle in 2002In fact, it was more than double the previous record of $1,815,000, which was achieved by a different specimen of the same coin in April 1997 Both silver dollar coins were sold by Bowers and Merena Galleries of Wolfeboro, New Hampshire.

The 1804 dollar is not the rarest coin ever made by Uncle Sam; in fact, a number of others have lower mintages. However, it may be the most highly publicized—and romanticized—of all U.S. coins. Just 15 specimens are known, and all of them were minted many years after 1804. Eight are so-called "original" examples struck in the mid-1830s for inclusion in presentation sets prepared by the U.S. Mint as gifts from President Andrew Jackson to rulers in the Far and Middle East—monarchs with whom the U.S. government was seeking to establish trade relations at the time. The other seven coins are restrikes minted in the late 1850s.

The piece that brought the first record price on Aug. 30, 1999,] was an original (or Class I) example considered to be the finest of all the known 1804 silver dollars. It came from a collection formed over several generations by the Childs family of Vermont and had been purchased in 1945 by Charles Frederick Childs for a mere $5,000. Originally, the coin had been part of a presentation set given by U.S. envoy Edmund Roberts to the Sultan of Muscat, a Middle East nation now known as Oman.

I was an eyewitness to that first historic sale at the Park Lane Hotel in midtown Manhattan. In fact, I was a serious bidder for the coin: My firm, Scott Travers Rare Coin Galleries, Inc., represented a client who was willing to pay significantly more than the previous auction record. The bidding exceeded his limit, but I did have the satisfaction of calling out the bid that shattered the old record: My offer of $1,750,000, when augmented by the 15-percent buyer's fee, officially put the Childs coin over the top.

A 1913 Liberty head nickel, one of five known, sold for $1,485,000 in May 1996. This specimen was from the collection of Louis E. Eliasberg, Sr., and sold at public auction by Bowers and Merena. It was purchased by well-known dealer Jay Parrino of Missouri.

I have a collection of medallions struck by The Franklin Mint. They're attractive silver pieces portraying various U.S. presidents. I understand that very few were struck, and I have certificates from The Franklin Mint which guarantee they're made of sterling silver.
Are these medallions valuable?

Chances are, the items you have are worth no more than "melt value"—the value of the silver they contain. Thousands of Franklin Mint issues were struck and sold for substantial premiums, but a significant resale market never materialized. Your "medallions" may be beautiful, but they're not negotiable; you can't spend them. And since there isn't a strong secondary market for these pieces as collectibles, the only real value they have is their precious metal.

Remember, three factors determine the value of a coin or medallion: (1) the level of preservation, which these medallions probably have in their favor because they are undoubtedly well preserved; (2) the number struck, and many Franklin Mint items have relatively low mintages; and (3) the collector base.

I visited several countries in Europe a few years ago and picked up coins everywhere I went during my travels. Are they worth anything?

Probably not. These coins are probably worth no more than their face value in the countries where you obtained them. Even if by chance you got some unusual variety, it still isn't likely that these coins would command much of a premium. There's simply not much of a market for modern foreign coins.

The rare coin market in the United States is an easy-entry, easy-exit field; there is little regulation governing sellers of coins. Consequently, many of the people dealing in coins in this country are freewheeling entrepreneurs who don't have extensive backgrounds in areas of numismatics that are, quite literally, foreign. Most of these people don't speak foreign languages and don't really know much about foreign coins. They stick with the subject they're comfortable with—United States coins. Similarly, the overwhelming majority of coin collectors and coin investors in this country limit their purchases to U.S. issues.

Modern foreign coins do turn up in coin shops and at coin shows—but often they're in boxes containing common material that dealers sell by the pound for nominal sums. The foreign coins you acquired in your travels might very well be found in such a box.

My grandmother left me an old Buffalo nickel, but I can't see the date. Is it worth anything, and is there any way to restore the date?

That Buffalo nickel could be worth a million dollars—in sentimental value. But if you try to cash that in, you won't get more than a nickel.

Dateless Buffalo nickels are so worn that they're barely identifiable as to type. These coins don't have any collector value. Chemical date restorers are available—but while these might enable you to determine the date of the coin, they won't do a thing to enhance its collector value.

*I just received a telephone call from someone
I've never heard of, trying to sell me rare coins.
What should I do?*

Hang up the phone! Selling coins over the telephone is never a cost-effective proposition. Consequently, just about anyone who sells coins over the phone—via telemarketing—marks up their prices tremendously, in some cases several hundred percent. I'm sure there must be reputable telemarketers somewhere, but they're few and far between.

I've heard chilling horror stories about the abuses perpetrated by telemarketers. However, these go far beyond the scope of this response. Suffice it to say that if you're ever called on the phone by someone selling coins, someone you don't know, you should hang up the phone. Don't be polite. And never, under any circumstances, give your credit-card number over the telephone to someone that you have not called.

*I talked to a coin-collector friend about selling some mint
errors I found in change, but my friend said the coins
I found weren't really "errors." Is he right?*

There are many coins that deviate from the norm. Some are off-center and others exhibit doubled letters, to cite a couple. These coins were once lumped together as "mint errors." Now certain specialists argue that these coins should be classified under "minting varieties."

Author Alan Herbert is one of these experts. In Herbert's view, not every unusual coin is an "error." The coin may have been manufactured that way, perhaps because the mint was using worn dies to save money. Herbert differentiates between these *intentionally* different-looking coins and those that come out different *by mistake*. Only the latter, he argues, are really errors, but both come under the heading "minting varieties."

An excellent listing of minting varieties can be found in *Walter Breen's Complete Encyclopedia of U.S. and Colonial Coins* (Doubleday, 1988).

*Last year, after reading a financial publication, I decided to invest
$5,000 with a very good company that sells bullion and coins. I got several $20 gold pieces. They looked pretty and I put them away for a
while. Last week, I decided to show them to a local coin dealer. He
looked at them and said they're not worth anything. What should I do?*

One thing you shouldn't do is accept the opinion of your local coin dealer without checking further. Any dealer to whom you bring coins for an appraisal has a vested interest in the outcome of the discussion. If you ask a dealer to render an opinion on coins that you purchased from a competitor, you really can't expect him to be objective. Human nature being what it is, that dealer isn't going to say: "You got a wonderful deal. You shouldn't buy coins from me; you should buy all your coins from my competitor." He's much more likely to say: "You got a terrible deal. These are horrible coins. You should return them and buy all your coins from me."

In buying coins and in getting coins appraised, you should always seek the protection of independent third-party grading. Buy only coins that have been certified by leading independent grading services. And before having coins appraised, submit them for certification by one of these firms. These organizations will encapsulate your coins in tamper-resistant, sonically sealed holders with inserts stating their grade. That way, you'll know what your coins are worth—or what they aren't worth.

I understand that coins are graded on a 1 through 70 scale. How can I tell the difference between a coin which grades 65 and is worth $5,000 and a similar coin which grades 64 and is worth only $1,000?

Don't expect to be able to tell the difference. Only trained experts can do this. But do apply a little common sense. If you have a portrait coin with a likeness of Miss Liberty, for example, look at the portrait. Her cheek is what is known as a grade-sensitive area. If you see nicks, marks, scratches, gouges, or other imperfections on that cheek, common sense should tell you that this particular coin probably won't qualify for a grade of Mint State-65.

There's a greater ethical burden on the coin dealer's shoulders than on someone who is selling a uniform commodity. Suppose you go out and buy yourself a television set—a brand-name 19-inch television set. As long as it comes in a factory-sealed box and has a U.S.A. warranty, you can be reasonably certain that you're getting what you're paying for. But if you buy coins which haven't been independently certified, you have no reasonable certainty as to what you're getting. If you don't know your coins, know your dealer. If you don't know either, get your coins independently certified. In fact, play it safe: Always get your coins certified by NGC, PCGS, ANACS, or ICG.

I've heard about independent certification, and I have some coins I might want to have certified. Lots of certification services are reliable, and how do I get my coins certified by them?

As this is written, four organizations which have reputations for strict, consistent grading—and whose coins enjoy great acceptance in sight-unseen trading—are the Professional Coin Grading Service (PCGS), the Numismatic Guaranty Corporation of America (NGC), ANACS, and the Independent Coin Grading Company (ICG). You can write for a list of authorized dealers, or submit coins, as follows:

- Professional Coin Grading Service, P.O. Box 9458, Newport Beach, CA 92658

- Numismatic Guaranty Corporation, P.O. Box 4776, Sarasota, FL 34230

- ANACS, P.O. Box 18214, Columbus, OH 43218-2141

- Independent Coin Grading Company, 7901 East Belleview Ave., Suite 50, Englewood, CO 80111

> *I see that the price of common-date Mint State-65 Morgan dollars is about $75 apiece. I saw an advertisement for coins that were independently certified as Mint State-65 by the Numismatic Certification Institute (NCI), and these were priced at $40 per coin. How can this be?*

The Numismatic Certification Institute (NCI) is a wholly owned subsidiary of Heritage Capital Corporation of Dallas, the world's largest rare coin dealer. As of this writing, NCI is not actively grading coins; however, many NCI-graded coins remain on the market. NCI standards—by Heritage's own admission—are from three-quarters of a point to a point-and-a-half more liberal than the standards set forth by NGC and PCGS. Thus, a coin graded Mint State-65 by NCI and priced at $50 might in actuality be the equivalent of only a Mint State-64 coin from either NGC or PCGS.

Whenever you buy coins, make certain you know which set of standards is being used to describe the coins' grade. There is no Santa Claus in numismatics—and if you're not careful, you could end up doing business with a Scrooge.

> *I found one of those 1989 Congress silver dollars with a rotated reverse. I told my local dealer that it's worth $600, and he thought I was nuts. Who would actually pay this price?*

Anthony J. Swiatek, P.O. Box 218, Manhasset, NY 11030, says that he will pay $300 in cash as this book goes to press. However, this price is subject to change.

Swiatek invites calls on the matter at 1-516-365-4120, and will take collect calls from people who have such coins to sell.

Where can I sell some of these other pocket-change rarities?

Perhaps the leading market-maker in off-metal U.S. coins is Fred Weinberg & Co., Inc., 16311 Ventura Blvd., Encino, CA 91436. Be sure to call and confirm the arrangements before sending any coins (the number is 1-818-986-3733). For information about doubled-die coins and other mint errors, contact the Combined Organizations of Numismatic Error Collectors of America (CONECA) in care of Mike Ellis, Rt. 2, Box HI-504, Donalson, GA 31745-0504.

I'm a young collector and I don't have very much money, but I'd like to get more involved in the hobby. I'd also like to learn more about it. What should I do?

The American Numismatic Association has set up a wonderful participatory educational program for young people. There's no charge to join or participate, and the program provides not only numismatic activities but also a social outlet. For further information, contact Lawrence J. Gentile Sr., 542 Webster Ave., New Rochelle, NY 10801, or call him at 1-914-632-5259.

Larry Gentile's programs include free seminars, free coins, free books, and a wealth of information that youngsters find helpful. To be placed on the Young Numismatist mailing list, you need only send to Larry a postcard with your name, address, and age. Please include your telephone number as well.

With certification of coins being so important, is there any book I can buy that would explain in clear and understandable terms exactly what standards are used by these various certification organizations?

At press time, August 2004, the only independent grading service that has issued an authoritative book defining its grading standards is PCGS. Its award-winning, 432-page profusely illustrated book, *The Official Guide to Coin Grading and Counterfeit Detection, Second Edition* (House of Collectibles/ Random House, Inc., $19.95), will help you understand what's involved in the grading of coins and what factors are taken into consideration when assigning numerical grades. The grading standards are authored by the book's exceptionally-skilled text author, John W. Dannreuther. I am proud and honored to be the book's editor and applaud PCGS and Random House for this colossal effort.

I have some silver dimes, quarters, and half dollars. All of them are common-date coins, and all are well worn from having circulated. I assume they're worth just their bullion or metal value. How can I determine what they're worth?

The rule of thumb is that for every $1 of circulated silver U.S. coins, the value is approximately 70 to 75 percent of the price of a troy ounce of silver on that day. If you have five silver dimes and one silver half dollar—or any other combination adding up to $1—and the price of silver that day is $4 an ounce, you'd probably be able to cash in those coins for $2.80.

Of course, different equations are used for different coins. The formula given here applies only to traditional U.S. silver coins with a silver content of 90 percent. These include the dimes, quarters, and half dollars made before 1965. Kennedy half dollars minted between 1965 and 1970 also contain silver—but only 40 percent. You'll get less money for these. Jefferson nickels made during World War II also contain silver, but in an altogether different composition.

I have about $500 to spend and I want to get involved in buying coins. Where should I start?

High-grade coins—those with grades of at least Mint State-65 or Proof-65—performed very well in the market's last big boom—and although their prices have fallen since then, they still hold great appeal. People want coins in the very highest grades they can obtain, or at least in the highest grades they can afford.

Demand in the coin market moves horizontally, not vertically. If someone is collecting a certain kind of coin—Morgan silver dollars, for example—in high Mint State grades and the prices for these coins go up dramatically, that buyer may find it difficult to purchase more Morgan dollars in those grades. But rather than lowering his sights and buying Morgan dollars in lower grades, he'll probably turn instead to a different kind of coin that's substantially less expensive—and then collect that series in the same high grades to which he was accustomed with Morgan dollars.

As this is written, one good starting place would be Mint State-66 or Mint State-67 Mercury dimes. Another would be Mint State-66 Walking Liberty half dollars. A third would be Franklin half dollars graded Mint State-66 or even Mint State-67. All of these coins are affordable, all of them have good potential, and all of them are quite scarce in extremely high grades.

With Mercury dimes, for example, there are certain dates for which only five or six specimens have been certified in Mint State-67. Yet some of these coins can be purchased for less than $1,000—sometimes substantially less—in Mint State-67. That's a tremendous value; you really can't get hurt when you buy a coin like this.

Is there any one coin that you recommend as the best to buy?

My favorite U.S. coin of all time is the Liberty Seated quarter. Buy the highest grade you can afford. I like both proof and business-strike examples (the coins the Mint intended people to spend) in grades 65 and above on the 1 through 70 grading scale. Different styles or "varieties" of Liberty Seated quarters were struck from 1838 through 1891.

A "type" coin is a representative example of a particular coin series, but not one of the rarest and most valuable specimens from that series. Experienced collectors and investors have found certain type coins to be the biggest winners. I extend my highest recommendation—in high grades only—to the following: Liberty Seated dimes, quarters, halves, and dollars; Barber dimes, quarters, and halves; Bust dimes, quarters, halves, and dollars; Trade dollars; and nonmodern proof gold coinage. These coins are the blue chips, not the "sleepers," and have formed the backbone of the market for U.S. coins. But most importantly, these coins are beautiful.

How much can a dealer mark up coins sold for investment without getting in trouble with the government?

If you're selling something that's not an investment, you can charge whatever the market will bear. For example, if you buy a painting for $500 and sell it for $50,000, that's not illegal in itself. But if you represent that painting as a good investment, you'll surely have the watchdogs from the Federal Trade Commission sniffing down your neck, because the market value of that painting would have to go up spectacularly in a relatively short time to come even close to the $50,000 that your buyer was foolish enough to pay for it.

Barry J. Cutler, former director of the FTC's Bureau of Consumer Protection, says that when he was working for the commission, dealers selling items for investment tended to invite government scrutiny when they exceeded a markup of 100 percent, but that a 50-percent or even 75-percent markup (though this can be pushing it, he says) usually would escape the FTC's scrutiny. This doesn't mean that in private litigation in a civil court, a judge is going to give a dealer his or her blessing for a 75-percent markup—but based on the FTC's apparent yardstick, a dealer charging 50 percent or even 75 percent is probably free and clear.

Dealer representations can be very important in this area. Often, a dealer will claim to be charging a commission of only 2 or 3 percent when in fact he or she is charging 50 percent—in which case that person is committing fraud. By the way, Barry Cutler is now an attorney at McCutcheon, Doyle, Brown, and Enersen in Washington, D.C.

Why do I sometimes have to pay a lot more than the price-guide price for certain coins?

Coin market analyst Maurice H. Rosen of Plainview, New York, editor and publisher of the prize-winning *Rosen Numismatic Advisory*, several years ago came up with the term "market premium factor," or MPF to cover such situations. When you're purchasing coins, MPF refers to the percentage you're sometimes required to pay above published price-guide values.

Price guides are reflective of the marketplace, but the marketplace is not necessarily reflective of price guides. If a price guide says a coin is worth $1,000, but that coin is booming in the marketplace, suddenly you might have to pay $1,400, $1,500, or $1,600 to acquire it, even though the previous week's price guide indicated a market value of $1,000. So if you're at a coin convention and there's a particular coin you want, and the market for that coin is hot, just because your week-old pocket price guide says it's worth $1,000 doesn't mean you can write out a check for $1,000 to any dealer who has that coin and walk away with it.

If the market is hot, you need to use your intuition—your "market smarts"—in deciding what would be a fair market price for that coin. If the market is really booming, you might even have to pay upwards of $2,000 for that sought-after numismatic treasure.

CHAPTER 6

MARKETPLACE PSYCHOLOGY

To buy and sell coins advantageously you need to understand what makes the market tick.

People who buy and sell coins are really no different from buyers and sellers in most other fields. They base their decisions on a number of different factors, both practical and emotional—and marketplace psychology plays an important part in determining what they buy or sell, and when they buy or sell it.

I've developed a three-step system to help you understand the psychology of the coin market—three easy steps by which you can determine how hot (or how cold) the coin investment environment may be at a given time by using the thermometer of market psychology.

These three basic steps are as follows:

- First, identify the prevailing psychological trend.

- Second, learn how *you* can benefit.

- Third, determine the proper way to buy and sell in this environment, taking into consideration the types of people you're dealing with and how much *more* than the price-guide price—or how much *less*—you'll have to pay when buying, or have to take when selling.

First, let's consider the question of psychological trends.

In the coin market as in many other markets, including the stock market, herd mentality governs most people's behavior. People feel very uncomfortable doing something alone.

People have a tendency to do things which are socially acceptable, and society encourages conformity. We can see this in the way young people are educated, not only in America but throughout the world. Conformity is encouraged: Those who are conformists are rewarded; those who are risk-takers are punished. Consequently, the vast majority of people do things to conform. They do things so they won't be viewed as outcasts.

This has quite a bit to do with psychological trends in the coin market. When the market has achieved a good deal of momentum and prices are higher than they've ever been before, this tendency to conform gives people a false sense of security. It makes them feel comfortable, and they continue to buy when, in actuality, they may very well be buying at the absolute height of the market.

Conversely, this predisposition to conformity makes people reluctant to buy when the market is weak. Since few other people are buying, they don't want to be nonconformist. Yet this may be the best time of all to buy. With the market at the bottom, there's very little "downside risk," as money experts like to call it— very little likelihood of losing money. In fact, there may be great "upside potential"—a strong possibility that prices will go up. But because of their reluctance to stand out from the crowd, many people won't take the plunge at such a time—even though the water may be perfect for investment.

Many of the world's greatest capitalists have been nonconformists—people who had no compunctions about deviating from the norm. These people have achieved remarkable success by disregarding the herd and following their own intuition—doing what their training and experience told them to do. They really haven't cared what was socially acceptable—or, for that matter, what they may have learned at some of our great institutions of learning. Keep in mind that even some of our finest business schools instill an overriding sense of conformity in their students. Thus, when they enter the marketplace, many graduates of these institutions—with all their knowledge and savvy—still find it difficult to buy when things seem bleak and others are sitting on the sidelines, even though their technical training would tell them to do otherwise.

In measuring the temperature of the marketplace, and thereby learning how to take full advantage of the thermometer of market psychology, you need to understand the distinction between a *bear* market and a *bull* market.

Whether in coins or any other field, a bear market is a period when people are selling things off—when the outlook seems grim and there isn't much hope on the horizon. In a bear market, you often see prices go down on a regular basis.

A bull market is just the opposite. People are extraordinarily enthusiastic— often falling all over each other in their headlong rush to buy coins.

In between a bull market and a bear market is a compromise situation called a *business-as-usual market*.

To simplify comparisons, let's calibrate our thermometer of market psychology from 1 to 10, with 1 being the coldest point and 10 being the hottest. (If you'd be more comfortable using some other type of scale, you're free to do so.)

On a 1 to 10 scale, it's prudent to sell when the marketplace reaches a heat level of 8 or above, and it's prudent to buy at levels no higher than 6 or 7.

Let's say the market is gathering momentum; the increases have begun and the psychological level has moved up from 5 to 6. What you should do at this point is compare the current price of a given coin to its "book value"—how it has performed in the past—and try to determine where a reasonable person might expect it to go in the future. If the current price doesn't seem exaggerated by these standards, you can feel reasonably confident buying it, even at levels 6 or 7, with the goal of taking some short-term profits as it moves up from there toward 10.

Not too long ago, this type of thinking would have been looked upon as heresy. The conventional wisdom was to buy coins and hold them as long-term investments. The buy-and-hold philosophy isn't nearly as popular today. Experience has shown that it has some serious shortcomings, especially in regard to commoditized coins—those which change hands routinely on a sight-unseen basis like stocks and bonds. (We'll discuss these coins in greater detail in a later chapter.)

As part of your assessment of the market's overall temperature, you need to determine what's hot and what's not—what's the hottest area of the marketplace and what's the coldest.

You can trace the recent performance of various kinds of coins by following the price charts in major periodicals that cater to buyers and sellers in this field. Coins that are hot are probably showing phenomenal increases in these charts, possibly reflected by plus signs. Coins that are cold may have dropped in value sharply and may have minus signs. Keep in mind that very few coin advisory services recommend when to *sell* coins. Their emphasis is on *buying*. Thus, it is difficult to know when to sell unless you monitor market levels yourself.

Pricing information is featured regularly in all of the following publications, some of which are readily available on newsstands:

- The *Coin Dealer Newsletter*, P.O. Box 11099, Torrance, CA 90510 ($54 for 26 weekly issues, $98 for 52 issues, plus free monthly supplements). This publication, known as the "Greysheet," gives authoritative values for "raw" coins (those not certified by one of the grading services).

- The *Certified Coin Dealer Newsletter*, P.O. Box 11099, Torrance, CA 90510 ($65 for 26 weekly issues, $117 for 52 issues). This publication, known as the "Bluesheet," gives widely accepted values for certified coins.

- *Coin World*, P.O. Box 150, Sidney, OH 45365 ($29.95 per year in the United States; add $40 outside the U.S.; weekly newspaper). Prices are featured in the weekly Trends Value listings by Stuart Segan.

- *Numismatic News*, 700 East State Street, Iola, WI 54990 ($32 in the United States, $105 outside the U.S.; weekly newspaper). Prices are featured in the Coin Market listings by Joel T. Edler.

- *COINage*, 250 Maple Court Suite 232, Ventura, CA 93003-3517 ($24 per year in the United States; $33 outside the U.S.; monthly magazine). Price trends are shown in *The COINage Price Guide*.

- *Coins*, 700 East State Street, Iola, WI 54990 ($25.98 per year in the United States; $36.98 outside the U.S.; monthly magazine). Prices are featured in the Coin Value Guide, edited by Joel T. Edler.

COINage and *Coins* are both available on newsstands just about everywhere. To obtain the other publications, you may have to take out subscriptions.

In determining what's hot and what's not, you won't find every decision cut and dried. Sometimes, certain coins are just lukewarm. Other times, given items may remain out of favor for extended lengths of time, and thus may stay at the bottom, rather than moving up in a cyclical way. With this in mind, it's not a good idea to assume that just because something is cold, it's bound to turn warmer sometime soon.

THE THEORY OF MARKET CYCLES

One of the most respected experts in the coin field, professional numismatist Q. David Bowers of Wolfeboro, New Hampshire, has expounded a theory of market cycles. This theory can be applied to the marketplace as a whole or to just one specific type of coin.

Bowers contends that "each cycle seems to take place on a succeedingly higher plateau." Suppose the price of a given coin bottoms out at Point A, rises to a high at Point B, drops to another low at Point C, then rises again to a second high at Point D. Under Bowers' theory, Point C won't be as low as Point A, and Point D will be higher than Point B. Basically, such a scenario indicates a steady and growing marketplace.

This is sometimes true with *rare* coins—very low-mintage coins costing hundreds or thousands of dollars. However, we've seen some notable exceptions in the more commoditized items such as Morgan silver dollars, Peace dollars, and Walking Liberty half dollars. We saw lows in 1990 which were lower than the lows of five years earlier—and in some cases lower than the lows of *seven* years earlier. These coins are really not all that rare; some of them, in fact, are relatively common. At the time of this writing, there just aren't as many buyers as there are coins of some issues. As discussed in the previous chapter, these common coins often need economic justification (such as anticipation of inflation) for a value increase.

The theory is sound, but it doesn't work for every series and every situation, as Bowers himself concedes. If there is a variable which causes buyer disinterest, it might take two hundred years for a coin that's very cold to get very hot, and no one wants to base investment decisions on cycles that require two hundred years for a coin's new high to be higher than its previous high.

HEALTHY, GROWING MARKETS

One of the keys to making a solid purchase, in coins or in anything else, is to stick with an item that conforms to Q. David Bowers' theory of market cycles— in other words, an investment whose lows are higher than the previous lows, and whose highs are higher than the previous highs.

If we were to formulate a graph based upon a rare coin investment meeting these criteria, what we would see is a gradual but continuous upward line. This, in turn, would indicate a healthy, thriving, and growing area of the market. The theory of market cycles may be hypothetical, and may be better suited to a textbook than it is to the workaday world of buyers and sellers, but many coins do indeed enjoy steady upward movement, and this can be quite impressive when it is expressed in graphic form.

Consider Figure 1, for example. This is a graphic depiction of the marketplace performance of Type 2 Indian Head gold dollars (U.S. $1 gold pieces minted from 1854 to 1856) in Mint State-65 condition. It covers the period from 1986 to 1990. The low value was $22,000; the high value was $46,700. And although there are many lows and many highs, and this coin's performance illustrates the new volatility of the rare coin marketplace, the general trend when we look at the graph is upward. These coins are climbing in value consistently—and in fact dramatically.

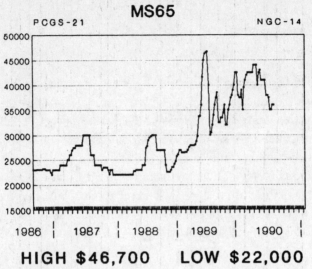

HIGH $46,700   LOW $22,000

Figure 1. *Indian Head gold dollars, Type 2 (Graph courtesy of Richard Nachbar, c/o Richard Nachbar Rare Coins, 5820 Main Street, Suite 601, Williamsville, NY 14221)*

Figure 2 charts the market performance of Mint State-65 Trade dollars during the same period. (Trade dollars are large silver U.S. coins similar in size and shape to silver dollars, which were used in foreign commerce during the latter part of the nineteenth century.) From 1986 to 1990, the low value of these coins was $4,500 and the high was $22,000. And while the chart shows some spiked highs and volatile lows, the general trend is upward.

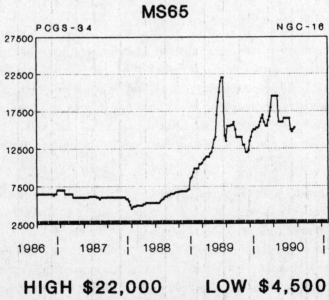

HIGH $22,000   LOW $4,500

Figure 2. *Trade dollars (Graph courtesy of Richard Nachbar)*

Figure 3 tracks the performance of Mint State-65 Liberty Seated silver dollars bearing the motto *IN GOD WE TRUST* (this motto appeared only during the final few years of the series). From 1986 to 1990, these coins moved between a low value of $7,300 and a high of $52,000—and, once again, the general trend was upward.

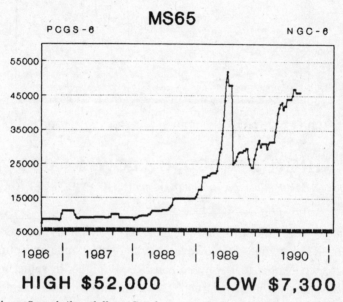

Figure 3. *Liberty Seated silver dollars (Graph courtesy Richard Nachbar)*

The graph of the Liberty Seated dollar shows us that whenever a coin increases in value dramatically within a very short period, it then will come crashing down. This is an artificial high—and as the graph demonstrates, this was the time to sell. Even so, the general trend of this coin was consistent, reassuring— and upward. The only exception is the time when it surged dramatically in a very short period, then fell right back. And, even then, after falling to that low, it gradually climbed again almost to the previous high.

Figure 4 depicts the upward movement of yet another coin that fits the Bowers theory of market cycles. This time, the coin is the Liberty Seated half dollar without the motto *IN GOD WE TRUST*, again in the grade of Mint State-65. Between 1986 and mid-1990, the market range of this coin extended from a low of $4,000 to a high of $17,000. Again, we see one time in 1989 when the coin escalated in value at a frenzying pace and fell to almost the point where it had been before. Thereafter, it climbed, but not quite to the high it experienced in 1989. But, in 1990, it still was considerably higher than it had been in 1986 and the overall growth pattern once more appeared consistent and reassuring.

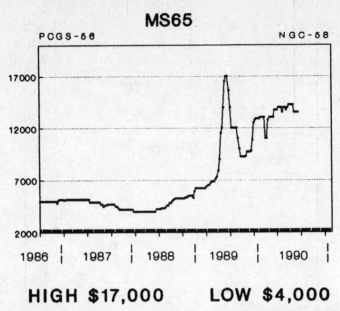

MS65

PCGS-65   NGC-65

HIGH $17,000   LOW $4,000

Figure 4. *Liberty Seated half dollars, without the motto* IN GOD WE TRUST *(Graph courtesy Richard Nachbar)*

There are many coins like this. In fact, most rare coins had this reassuring upward pattern in years gone by. However, there are also some exceptions to this pattern of growth. Rather than moving consistently higher in value, some coins display a consistently *downward* trend. I've gone into considerable depth about some of these types of coins.

You can still make money trading these coins—but the trick is to *trade* them, not hold them over a long-term period. Over the long term, unless there's economic justification for these coins to increase in value, they're simply not going to perform all that well.

Let's go back to the continuum I wrote about in Chapter 1. As you may recall, I showed the collector at the left of this continuum and the investor at the far right. It's primarily the investor, on the far right, who buys generic Mint State coins (those that exist in significant quantities). But when there's no economic justification for a solid investor to buy such coins—when we don't see rampant inflation in the national economy, for example, or when people don't perceive some other sort of economic crisis—investors feel no need to buy these coins in quantity. And, in the absence of such purchases, these coins tend to languish at relatively low price levels.

A case in point would be Mint State-63 and Mint State-64 Saint-Gaudens double eagles (see Figures 5 and 6). The Mint State-63 graph shows steady and consistent downward adjustments. Whereas the previous graphs provided reas-

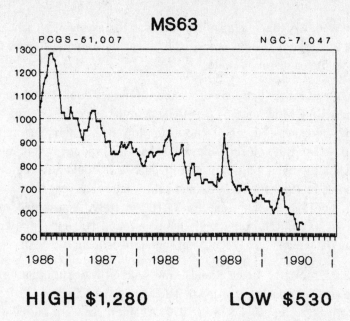

Figure 5. *Saint-Gaudens $20 gold pieces (Graph courtesy Richard Nachbar)*

surance to prospective coin buyers, this one can only cause concern. The high for this coin was $1,280 and the low was $530—but the high occurred in 1986 and the low came in 1990, and the coin decreased in value consistently during the period. The Mint State-64 Saint-Gaudens double eagle fluctuated between a high of $2,400 in 1986 and a low of $810 in 1990, and again we see a steady

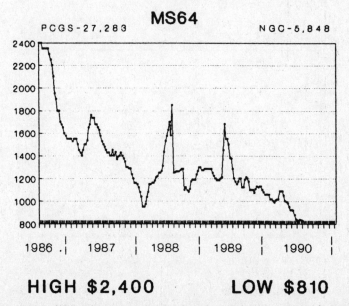

Figure 6. *Saint-Gaudens $20 gold pieces (Graph courtesy Richard Nachbar)*

downward trend. A major reason for this was the availability, since 1986, of American Eagle gold bullion coins, which bear the same design as the Saint-Gaudens double eagle on one side.

As we can see in Figure 6, tremendous sums of money could have been made by buying and selling Mint State-64 Saint-Gaudens double eagles during the period covered by the chart—buying at one of the low points, then selling when the market moved up. But you certainly would have lost money if you bought these coins and held them as long-term investments. You could have purchased one of these coins in 1988 for $1,000, then sold it later that year for $1,800; similarly, you could have bought one for $1,200 in 1989, then turned around and sold it for $1,700. But, if you bought that coin for $1,000 and simply held on to it, you would have lost nearly half your initial investment by 1990.

The graphs for Mint State-63 and Mint State-64 Morgan dollars (Figures 7 and 8) are similar: consistently down. The Mint State-63 coins fell from a high of $100 in 1986 to a low of $28 in 1990. Again, there were rallies which presented some dramatic money-making opportunities. But, on the whole, the graph shows most people cashing out of these coins. The Mint State-64 Morgan dollars plunged from a high of $260 in 1986 to a low of $58 in 1990.

The lesson to be learned is quite apparent: If some investment adviser comes to you and says you should be buying these coins for long-term investment, rather than trading them actively, think again—and think for yourself. No matter how

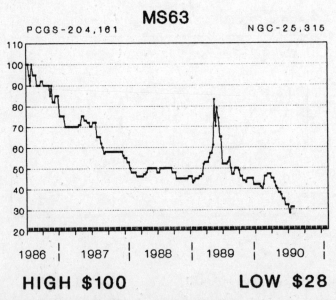

Figure 7. *Morgan silver dollars (Graph courtesy Richard Nachbar)*

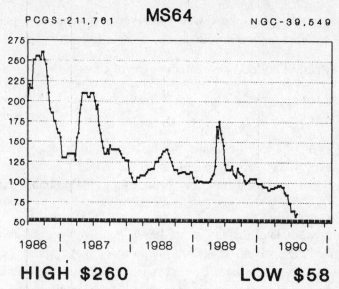

Figure 8. *Morgan silver dollars (Graph courtesy Richard Nachbar)*

well-intentioned he may be, he's dead wrong. These coins are wildly volatile, but have netted many short-term speculators 50 or 60 percent quickly and easily. This is a gambler's game, so be careful. *Under no circumstances should you buy these coins and hold them with the goal of gaining long-term appreciation.*

USING THE MARKET SCALE

On our 1 to 10 temperature scale, the range from 1 to 3 corresponds to a time when the coin market is quite cold and people are pessimistic about the outlook. By 4 and 5, the market is fundamentally healthy and getting stronger. And by 6 and 7, we see many more participants entering the arena.

By 10, we're seeing amazing levels of overvaluation—levels that may be higher than they've ever been before and higher than can reasonably be expected. Even if they aren't record highs, it shouldn't be difficult to spot them as representing the apex of the current market cycle. If the prices seem unreasonably high and the people buying the items seem more like speculators than shrewd investors, chances are good that the market is at its peak and the prices are going to decline very sharply and very soon.

In assessing the price potential of a given coin or series of coins, it's important to consider three factors:

- The grade of the coin—how well preserved it is and how many nicks, scratches, or other flaws it has on it.

- How many people collect that particular type of coin.

- The number of examples of that coin that are available.

If you see a coin, or a series of coins, that has tens of thousands of pieces available and it seems to be enjoying popularity at the moment, but it doesn't have a solid base of dedicated collectors, stay away from it. It's probably a fad, and its current market value is probably exaggerated.

We saw an example of this in the late 1980s—not with coins, but rather with a series of one-ounce silver medals bearing portraits of Walt Disney characters. Initially, these were offered at prices not much higher than the value of the silver they contained. Within a couple of months, as dealers promoted them, they were being sold for hundreds of dollars apiece. It was clear that there wasn't a very strong collector base for these medals; what's more, a single company controlled the number available—which, in relative terms, was rather high.

Predictably enough, this turned out to be a fad that died away. A lot of the values have dropped rather sharply, and as this is written the medals can be obtained for just a small fraction of their highs.

As this example illustrates, you really need to use your intuition and common sense and not simply follow the crowd.

Besides being able to identify the prevailing psychological trend, you should also have the ability at this point to judge the market objectively and rationally, standing at an arm's-length distance from the people in the arena who are either too excited or too pessimistic. *You* now know the market's tendencies and understand how coin buyers think and act. This should give you a tremendous advantage over the herd, and over buyers and sellers who are blindly and unthinkingly following that herd—if not to the slaughter, then at least to a substantial financial bath.

ROTATIONAL LEADERSHIP

Another factor you have to keep in mind in assessing the coin market's psychology is the issue of *rotational leadership*. This sounds like a complicated concept, but its meaning is really quite simple: In a rip-roaring bull market, different coins often take turns increasing in value.

One week, commemorative coins may jump in price. Another week, silver dollars may go up. The next week, the big winner may be Liberty Seated quarters or Barber half dollars. Some coins may level off while others are taking a turn. Thus, in a sense, the baton is passed around so that different kinds of coins lead the advances.

Rotational leadership also can occur in a marketplace retreat. In a declining marketplace, you might see silver dollars decreasing in value one week, type coins (representative coins of a particular series which are not rare dates of that series) might be the biggest losers the next week, and yet another series—commemoratives, perhaps—might then take a hit the week after that.

Rotational leadership should be taken into account when assessing the strength or weakness of any particular area of the market. Before deciding just how bullish or bearish Morgan silver dollars are, for example, you also need to look at other major areas of the market. Check your price guides to see how commemoratives or Walking Liberty half dollars are doing; while you're at it, take a look at type coins. The market is a mosaic, and every piece has bearing on every other one.

BENEFITING FROM MARKET PSYCHOLOGY

Now that you understand the thermometer of market psychology, you can learn very quickly and easily how to benefit from its use. This brings us to the second of our three basic steps in understanding and using marketplace psychology.

Before going any farther, it's worth recalling an old expression often heard on Wall Street, but equally true with rare coins: "Bulls make money, bears make money, but pigs lose out." Keep in mind, too, that there's a name for people who always buy low and sell high. They're called liars. Suffice it to say that one of the primary ways to benefit from market psychology is not to be a pig—not to try to squeeze every last dime out of every deal.

Let's say you've bought a coin at level 6 or level 7 on our market-cycle scale of 1 to 10. As the market then climbs closer to the top, you'll start to notice shudders—chinks in the market's armor, if you will. But, while there may be some small disappointments, the feeling will persist that there's no place to go but up. It's sort of like a boxing match where one of the boxers absorbs a couple of whacks but stays on his feet and seems to be going strong. Then comes the knockout punch—a 10-count for the boxer but a knockdown for the coin market all the way from 10 back to 1.

You have to be on your guard. A hot market is persuasive; it mesmerizes you and lures you in. The time to sell that coin you bought at level 6 is really level 7 or level 8; if you wait for level 10, you'll probably end up owning it back at level 1.

Contrary to what you may have been told, the coin market is not a standard financial market. It's a supplement to traditional modes of investment. And, at the time of this writing, it's a totally unregulated marketplace, in no way subject to the jurisdiction of either the Securities and Exchange Commission (SEC) or the Commodity Futures Trading Commission (CFTC). The only government activity now taking place in this industry is the limited involvement of the Federal Trade Commission (FTC), which has charged a number of coin dealers with false, deceptive, and misleading practices in trade and in commerce. These dealers have signed consent decrees with the commission and this has served to clean up the industry.

Because of the absence of government controls, the coin market may react differently from standard financial markets. Thus, when the coin market shudders, prices may continue to escalate—go right through the stop sign, so to speak. In large part, that's because there isn't a federal "policeman" sitting behind a billboard at the corner. This is expected to change shortly.

Under the circumstances, you have to be able to recognize the stop signs and police your own buy-and-sell activities. Otherwise, you may end up being one of the victims when the market crashes.

For one thing, you should watch for signs of rotational leadership. If you see several different areas of the market experiencing declines in value in a relatively short period, the market may be sending you a signal: It may be saying the boom-and-bust theory is absolutely true and that bulls and bears make money while pigs—those who are too greedy—just make bacon and ham.

ACTUAL BUYING AND SELLING

The third and final step in understanding and using market psychology involves the actual buying and selling of coins.

For all practical purposes, you'll have to deal with a dealer in buying coins. Rare coins are viewed as a credence good. In other words, you—as a non-dealer—are not expected to be able to tell the difference between a coin grading Mint State-64 and its counterpart grading Mint State-65. The burden is on the dealer or, in a sense, on the grading service whose product you are buying.

Leading coin-grading services have somewhat solved the grading problem for you. You don't have to know how to grade coins; you don't have to be able to tell the difference between a 65 and a 56. As I explained earlier, these expert services have achieved outstanding records for accuracy and consistency, and you can rely on their judgments. Nevertheless, still use your common sense. If a coin looks ugly to you, don't buy it.

What you *do* need to know about is pricing.

You can work out commissions with your dealer. But you should be aware that many dealers have earned commissions of 75 percent—or even 100 percent—and yet haven't been viewed as overcharging their clients. Substantial legal precedent exists on this point: The Federal Trade Commission, for example, has allowed some coin merchants to charge upwards of 90 percent as a commission or markup.

You're entitled to ask your dealer how much of a markup he's charging—and you should. And you should make every effort to limit this premium, especially when you're buying certified coins. Because of their liquidity, these normally carry much more modest markups than "raw" coins—those that haven't been certified.

In a very hot market, or even just a moderately hot market (one that might rate a 7 on the 1 to 10 scale), you'll probably have to pay a premium over the values published in the price guides.

Let's say prices are increasing at frequent intervals and let's say you're purchasing a Liberty Seated quarter whose wholesale price-guide value (the typical cost to a dealer) is $5,000. In order for a dealer to buy that coin in a rising market, chances are he'll have to pay $5,500 or $5,800. Newsletter writer Maurice Rosen calls this the "market premium factor." Obviously, the dealer will then have to charge *you* more, as well.

In a business-as-usual market (5 on the 1 to 10 thermometer) or a cold market (1, 2, 3, or 4), you can buy coins very close to the levels in the wholesale price guides. In fact, in such markets, dealers sometimes get nominal discounts off the wholesale prices. These discounts are not tremendous; they might amount to 3 to 5 percent. Still, they represent savings that the dealer can then pass along. In a rip-roaring bull market, by contrast, a dealer might have to pay 10 percent more than the level in current price guides.

This is really an anticipatory factor. It's based on what the market is expected to do in the very near future. If the market is in the 7 position, for example, you may have to pay $6,500 for that Liberty Seated quarter that shows up on the wholesale price list at $5,000. That's because with prices trending higher, short-term profits can be made, and these are being anticipated each time the coin changes hands.

Does this mean your dealer is pocketing a profit of $1,500? Not necessarily. In fact, there's an excellent chance that he's making a good deal less—say, $500 or so.

There you have it: the way to understand the psychological makeup of the rare-coin marketplace and use the thermometer to your advantage.

The coin market, like the weather, can be changeable. At times, it can be as hot as the Sahara and at other times as cold as a barren tundra. But if you equip yourself with the tools in this chapter, you'll find that you can prosper in any kind of weather from 1 to 10.

REGISTRY SETS

Statehood Washington quarters are far from the only modern coins that dealers and collectors are seeking in very high grades. Lincoln cents, Jefferson nickels, Roosevelt dimes, Franklin half dollars—these and other late-date coins also have become the objects of a nationwide search for the very best pieces available. This quest gained new impetus in 1997, when the Professional Coin Grading Service introduced its Set Registry™ program, and really took off in 2001, when PCGS expanded this program to the Internet. The concept of the "registry" program is simplicity itself: Collectors who own coins certified by PCGS form those coins into sets, then "register" these sets with the grading service by entering their serial numbers on the company's Web site. At that point, PCGS uses special software to assign a rating to each set, based upon the rarity of the coins—not just in absolute terms but also in the grades at which they were certified. A particular modern coin may have a relatively high mintage and thus may not be rare in absolute terms, but may have had only one example, or just a few examples, certified as perfect (Proof- or Mint State-70) or virtually so (Proof- or Mint State-69). As registry sets grew in popularity, collectors began pursuing such coins in an effort to obtain higher ratings for their sets—since the sets are listed sequentially on the Web site, from the highest rating down, and the top-rated sets in various categories are singled out for special recognition. This competition boosted demand to white-hot levels in certain series, such as Lincoln cents—and since the supply of pristine, high-grade coins is surprisingly small for certain dates in these series, prices went through the roof. In some cases, in fact, they went all the way to the Moon. Coins that normally sell for just a few dollars in average mint condition—say, Mint State-63—were bringing thousands of dollars in ultra-high grades, and many collectors were shaking their heads in amazement.

The poster boy for registry set coins was a 1963 Lincoln cent graded Proof-70 Deep Cameo by PCGS. This coin changed hands in a January 2003 auction at the FUN (Florida United Numismatists) show for an incredible $39,100. It was said to be the only proof cent of that date ever to receive a perfect grade from either PCGS or the Numismatic Guaranty Corporation of America (NGC), which also has a registry program now. Still, the price seemed inexplicably high to many hobby observers, especially considering that the coin seemed to have toned and perhaps even deteriorated slightly in its holder, after being certified and encapsulated. Following the sale, I learned that special circumstances involving a child's coin collection had motivated the buyer, and that money was no object in this purchase. It was clear to me, however, that $39,100 was not a fair market price—the amount that a willing buyer pays to a willing seller when neither is under any special compulsion or compunction to complete a transaction. The whole episode was closed a year later when PCGS bought the coin back after it was consigned to the 2004 FUN auction. Both FUN auctions were conducted by Heritage Numismatic Auctions, which has been a major player in the sale of registry-set coins. David Hall, president of PCGS, said his company purchased the coin "to take it off the market since it had turned in the holder and was no longer PR70." Still, deterioration notwithstanding, there were still bidders willing to pay a pretty penny for that less-than-pretty penny, simply because of the "perfect" grade.

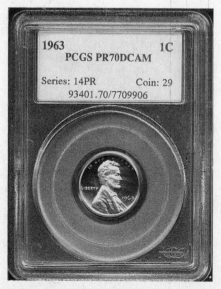

"Perfect" 1963 Lincoln cent, now the poster boy for registry sets, sold at auction for a pretty penny—$39,100. (Photo courtesy Heritage)

I have been an active participant in the registry set phenomenon. On behalf of my company, Scott Travers Rare Coin Galleries, I have brokered the sale of many millions of dollars worth of coins intended for inclusion in these sets, and I have assembled the most important Number One registry sets ever formed. There is nothing inherently wrong with this approach to collecting coins; in fact, it has provided a major boost to the hobby by stimulating interest and healthy competition. I do advise caution, though, in paying very high prices for coins that ordinarily are considered quite common. Grading-service population and census reports may be misleading when they show very few examples of certain modern coins being certified in the very highest grades. It may simply be that not very many examples have been submitted for certification. When a coin has a mintage of many millions, there's always a possibility that hoards of pristine examples may exist. Modern proofs, in particular, aren't truly rare in extremely high grades, because they were made so well in the first place. If the notion of forming a registry set appeals to you, by all means join the chase and have some fun. But think twice before you pay an exorbitant price for a coin that may not be worth it.

CHAPTER 7

GRADING IN FIVE
EASY STEPS

The value of a coin varies—often dramatically—in accordance with its "grade," or level of preservation. As a coin passes from hand to hand (or "circulates"), it becomes increasingly worn and loses detail which can never be regained. This, in turn, erodes its value as well. By determining the *grade* of a coin, you go far toward determining its *value*.

The grade assigned to a coin is really a kind of shorthand used by knowledgeable "numismatists," or coin collectors, to tell each other what the coin looks like. Many coins are purchased through the mail, and when buying in this manner it is helpful to know beforehand how they look. The grade used by the seller to describe such a coin, or assigned by a grading service, tells a great deal about the coin's appearance and thereby lets you gauge how much you should pay.

Numismatists use a 1 through 70 scale to communicate information regarding coins' level of preservation, or grade. The number assigned to each coin depends on a number of factors: how much wear it has suffered, how many scratches or nicks or dents or other imperfections it may have, and basically how appealing—or, for that matter, how *unappealing*—it may be.

The number 1 denotes a coin which is barely identifiable as to its type—a cent on which Abraham Lincoln's portrait is barely discernible, for example. At the other end of the grading spectrum, 70 denotes a coin which is perfect—one which has no nicks, no flaws, no scratches, and no imperfections of any kind.

In practice, the number 70 is rarely used. For all practical purposes, from the moment they are minted most coins have flaws which preclude their designation as "perfect."

The 11 numbers from 60 through 70 are set aside for "Mint State" coins—coins which have never entered circulation. A coin graded anywhere from 60 to 70 has never passed from hand to hand and thus has no friction on its high points. It is said to be "uncirculated."

Mint State coins are highly prized, and you should take great care of any coin you may possess which merits a grade from 60 to 70. The slightest touch from your fingers can lower the grade of a Mint State coin considerably. Suppose you owned a coin that was graded 65—Mint State-65—on a scale from 1 to 70. If you were to take your perspiration-soaked thumb and rub it over the coin, that single touch might lower the coin's value by several thousand dollars. That's why it's important to hold a coin only by its edge and never touch it directly on the front ("obverse") or back ("reverse").

For grading purposes, there are two basic categories of coins you need to know about. Each will be discussed in this chapter, and after you finish reading about them you will be much more expert at grading coins. It's all here, it's fun, it's easy—and, most important of all, once you've read this chapter and mastered its principles and lessons, you will find it to be extraordinarily profitable.

The first category you need to know about is *Mint State* coins. The second is *proofs*. Learn the grading principles involved with these two basic categories and you will master the process of coin grading—and with it coin pricing.

MINT STATE COINS

Coins which are "Mint State" have no friction on their very highest points, have not passed from hand to hand, and are not circulated.

Learning how to grade Mint State coins, or at least understand what numismatists look at when grading these coins, is vital to your success as a buyer or seller. The reason is basic economics: A coin graded Mint State-67 can be worth thousands of dollars—even tens of thousands of dollars—more than a similar coin graded Mint State-65.

No nonprofessional can be expected to master the grading of Mint State coins with 100 percent consistency. For that reason, it's important to have an independent grading service examine these coins for you. The four leading services as this is written are the Professional Coin Grading Service (PCGS) of Newport Beach, California; the Numismatic Guaranty Corporation of America (NGC), of Parsippany, New Jersey; ANACS of Columbus, Ohio; and the Independent Coin Grading Company (ICG) of Englewood, Colorado.

Even professionals have to work long and hard to perfect their skills at grading Mint State coins. John Albanese, founder of NGC, has told me that it took him four years to be able to tell the difference consistently between Mint State coins grading 64 and Mint State coins grading 65.

The grading of Mint State coins is a five-step process; when you grade these coins, just say to yourself: "1-2-3-4-5." That will help you recall the five easy steps you need to consider: surfaces, luster, toning, strike, and eye appeal. Remember: "1-2-3-4-5 . . . surfaces, luster, toning, strike, and eye appeal."

Surfaces   When we speak about the "surfaces" of a coin as an element of grading, we're referring to the number of scratches, gouges, or other imperfections the coin may have. Even Mint State coins have such imperfections; however, the more they have, the lower their grade will be.

With rare coins as in few other fields, beauty is truly skin-deep, and the surfaces are of supreme importance.

Let's start by considering coins graded Mint State-65 (or MS-65). This is not the highest grade; in fact, it's in the exact center of the 60 to 70 Mint State grading range. But MS-65 is a benchmark grade—a point of reference used in determining other Mint State grades that are higher and lower. It's also at the top of the "normal" Mint State range; anything higher than Mint State-65 is viewed as a "supergrade" coin—one with exceptional appeal and a correspondingly exceptional price tag.

MS-65 coins can have a few scattered marks, but nothing too heavy or noticeable. A similar coin with a few additional marks, or with marks in more obvious locations, would probably be downgraded to MS-64 if all other factors were equal. Similarly, a coin with fewer marks might merit a grade of MS-66.

Mint State-60 (or MS-60) is another benchmark grade. MS-60 coins barely qualify as uncirculated; they are the least desirable of the Mint State coins. Generally speaking, an MS-60 coin is not especially attractive; it may have heavy bag marks, abrasions, or other imperfections and these may be easily discernible with the naked eye. On large coins such as silver dollars or $20 gold pieces, there may be an especially obvious gash or other mark in a high, exposed area of the design. Nonetheless, an MS-60 coin will betray no evidence of wear—or having passed from hand to hand—and thus will be technically uncirculated.

The final two benchmark grades within the Mint State range are Mint State-63 (or MS-63) and Mint State-67 (or MS-67). Like the other basic MS grades (MS-65 and MS-60), these serve as reference points for grades above and below them. One professional grader puts it this way: "These benchmark grades are the automatics; when a Mint State coin doesn't quite fit one of these four categories, you have to embellish and fill in the grades in between."

Coins graded MS-63 are seen at independent grading services more often than any other kind. These are attractive coins, but less so than those graded MS-65 and MS-64. They can—and probably do—have marks that attest to handling or possibly stacking. However, these marks must be light. They would be much less apparent than the surface imperfections on a coin graded MS-60.

MS-67 coins are truly premium pieces. They can have one or two very small detracting surface marks—"faint faults," as one grader puts it, but these must be visible only under a 5-power magnifying glass. Looking at an MS-67 coin, it's easy to see why collectors and investors alike find such coins so appealing and are willing to pay big premiums to obtain them.

Mint State-69 (or MS-69) coins are very nearly perfect. In practice, this is probably the highest grade you'll ever see assigned to a certified coin, since MS-70—the ultimate grade—has come to be regarded as all but unattainable.

Don't expect to see too many coins graded MS-69, either. A coin doesn't have to be perfect to merit this grade, but it has to be so close that very few coins pass the test. An MS-69 coin must have no visible imperfections, even under 10-power magnification. One or two rim flaws may appear, but they must be almost imperceptible even under the glass.

Mint State-68 (or MS-68) coins aren't far behind. These, too, look nearly perfect to the unaided eye and betray only very minor flaws under a 10-power glass.

MS-69 and MS-68 coins are "wonder coins" in the finest sense of the term. As one coin enthusiast I know comments: "They practically glow in the dark, they're so beautiful."

The number of scratches and other detracting marks visible on a Mint State coin are key indicators of its grade. A coin that looks as if a city bus ran over it, or looks as if your mother-in-law threw it out the window—a coin with nicks, marks, scratches, gouges, and other abrasions all over it—cannot be in a high grade, no matter what anyone says, even if that someone is a coin-grading service. So use your common sense when you look at any coin. If it's nicked, marked, gouged, or severely dented, don't buy the coin, no matter what any dealer or grading service says.

Luster   In our 1-2-3-4-5 process of grading, luster is the second consideration for Mint State coins. *Luster* is the manner in which a coin reflects light.

Take a flashlight. Hold it up to a mirror and see how the mirror reflects the light. A proof coin—one with chromium-like surfaces—will often reflect the light the way the mirror did. Now envision the ocean. An ocean always reflects light, no matter what angle you look at it from, because of the many crevices and ridges on the surface of the water. No matter how you look at the ocean, it always reflects light. A Mint State coin reflects light in the same way, because that coin is manufactured with thousands of small striations which can't be seen with the naked eye. These tiny striations are called "flow lines," and they help give a Mint State coin its natural vibrant luster.

Go to the bank and get a shiny new penny. Chances are, it still has its original mint luster. That coin hasn't been spent, hasn't passed from hand to hand, and radiates the same original brilliance—the same appealing mint luster—it possessed the very day it was manufactured. But any coin, at any given time, is really in an intermediate stage between being completely brilliant and turning completely black. And this is especially true of Mint State coins.

Even if you took a coin on the day it was struck, carefully put it away, and meticulously preserved it, that coin would still progress from complete brilliance to total blackness. But the quality of that coin's mint brilliance, or luster—the manner in which it reflects light—would be an important determinant of its grade.

Some coins are said to be "toned," and this quality can be quite appealing. Keep in mind, however, that there's a very big difference between toning and tarnish.

Tarnish is the quick and irregular process by which a coin deteriorates over a short period of time. A copper coin stored in a moist environment could develop spots, for instance, in a matter of just a few days or even hours.

Toning is the slow and natural process by which a coin develops a patina over a period of months or years. If you took that same copper coin—the one that broke out in spots after being stored in a moist environment—and stored it instead in a dry environment, it could develop a beautiful protective patina over a period of many years.

Toning is actually an intermediate stage between complete brilliance—the way a coin looks right after being struck at the Mint—and complete blackness.

Many veteran collectors find toning extremely attractive. Novices, on the other hand, tend to think all coins should be bright and shiny—and, with that in mind, they often clean them. This is not just a bad idea; it's a *terrible* idea. It makes as much sense as lighting a match near spilled gasoline. Never, never, *never* clean your coins. If you were to take a brush and clean your coins, you would wear down the metal on their surfaces, and those coins would lose detail which could never be regained. This would be easily recognizable by numismatists, and would cause your coins' value to drop precipitously. What's more, the cleaning would activate the coins' surfaces chemically, causing them to deteriorate rapidly.

What *is* acceptable is a preservation process, but this should be left to experts. This process consists not of cleaning coins, but of neutralizing them for long-term storage. Consult your coin dealer for details.

Here are some guidelines regarding the impact of *luster* on grade:

- A coin can be designated Mint State-69 only if it has full and vibrant luster.

- A Mint State-67 coin has intense luster, emanating usually from surfaces that are immaculate.

- A Mint State-65 coin cannot be lackluster.

- A coin with the surfaces of an MS-67 coin but the mint luster of an MS-65 might be deserving of the grade between those two: Mint State-66.

- A Mint State-63 coin may have toning that is not universally appealing.

- A Mint State-60 coin *can* be lackluster or dull.

In summary, if you have a coin that reflects mint luster when you tilt and rotate it under a halogen lamp, and that coin reflects light in the same way the ocean does, it is probably a true Mint State specimen. To determine its grade more precisely, you should use the criteria outlined here.

Toning   As I have explained, toning is the color to which a coin turns through sulfide reaction over the years. Certain types of toning are universally attractive to numismatists and certain other types are universally viewed as being ugly.

Concentric-circle toning can be exceedingly beautiful. On a silver coin, for instance, you might see ocean blue or rose red toning around the periphery fading into a sunset-golden center. Such a coin would have universal appeal because the toning is beautiful and original and gives the coin a distinctive personality.

By contrast, a coin which is black—which looks as if it has been exposed to the air for a long time—isn't nearly as attractive. In fact, many numismatists might consider it to be downright ugly.

Many new collectors think brilliance is best, but most experienced hobbyists actually prefer coins with attractive toning. Toning gives a coin its overall aesthetic appeal—its eye appeal.

Artificial Toning

Since toning is so desirable, certain unscrupulous people have devised ways of treating coins to give them the appearance of being naturally toned. The colors imparted to these coins by "artificial toning" may fool the uninitiated, but experienced individuals can spot it readily. Grading services will not certify coins with artificial toning.

To determine whether a coin has been artificially toned, study the coin's surfaces and underlying mint luster. In many instances, artificial toning is applied not only in an effort to simulate natural toning, but also to cover up an imperfection. On a Morgan silver dollar, for example, artificial toning may be used to divert attention from a large scrape on Miss Liberty's cheek. It also may be used to conceal the fact that a coin has been cleaned. This is another reason you should always examine a purportedly Mint State coin under a pinpoint light source such as a halogen lamp. If the coin has been cleaned, it won't reflect mint luster or reflect light properly when you tilt and rotate it under the lamp. That would be a good indication that the coin has been toned artificially.

Professional numismatists are adept at detecting artificial toning. Using their book knowledge, practical experience, and intuitive feel, they can often spot it a mile away. Obviously, that degree of skill can't be developed overnight. But, with a little practice, you too can become quite skillful. The key is to look beyond and beneath the toning. Look closely at the surfaces to see if you can find any imperfections, or see if there's a lack of mint luster. Follow these simple steps and before long you should be able to spot artificial toning with almost as much consistency as the pros.

Two prominent coin dealers, Maurice Rosen and Bob Campbell, have been in the forefront of efforts to expose artificial toning and those who engage in this dishonest practice. Details of their work appeared in the award-winning *Rosen Numismatic Advisory*, where Rosen interviewed Campbell on the subject. The article created controversy within the coin industry, but represented a valuable public service.

To obtain a copy of the newsletter, write to Rosen Numismatic Advisory, P.O. Box 38, Plainview, NY 11803. Campbell is the proprietor of All About Coins, 1123 E. 2100 S, Salt Lake City, UT 84106.

Strike   is the amount of detail a coin receives at the time of its manufacture by the Mint. Some coins become worn through being passed from hand to hand as people spend them, but others exhibit a worn appearance from the very moment they are made. Simply stated, all coins are not created equal; some are manufactured without all the detail they're supposed to have. If a Mint State coin is not fully struck, and therefore lacks details it was meant to have, that coin will be assigned a lower grade.

Here are some points to remember with regard to *strike*:

• A Mint State-70 coin would have to be fully struck, since anything less than an absolutely full strike would render its appeal less than perfect. By extension, Mint State-68 and Mint State-69 coins also would require a full strike.

• A Mint State-65 coin cannot be weakly struck, although it can have a few areas which are not extremely sharply defined.

• A Mint State-64 coin *can* display some weakness of strike in key areas.

• A Mint State-63 coin doesn't necessarily have to be fully struck.

Logically, any coin grading higher than Mint State-65 would have to be well struck. On the other hand, any coin grading lower than Mint State-63 would not have to exhibit a sharp strike.

Eye Appeal   is the fifth and final element in our five-step grading process. This term refers to the overall appearance of a coin. Certain types of coins—coins with colorful, attractive toning, for example—are universally appealing to the eye. Others—coins with large nicks, gashes, or scratches or unattractive toning—are universally *unappealing*.

The concept of "eye appeal" applies not only to Mint State coins and proofs (see the following section), but also to circulated coins.

Circulated coins can have substantial eye appeal even if they're worn smooth from use, as long as the smoothness is uniform and the coins are free from defects. On the other hand, even a coin graded Very Fine—a relatively high level of preservation in the circulated range—can be very unattractive if it has a large gash which obliterates several letters in one of the mottos. That same coin would be desirable and eye-appealing if it were worn smoothly on both sides and had no visible problems.

Determining eye appeal can be quite subjective. Yet, there are certain constants. A Mint State coin with peripheral tonation rings is viewed by almost everyone as beautiful, for example, if the colors are attractive and the toning is natural. Few would dispute the eye appeal of a coin with an ocean-green periphery which fades into rings of sky blue, then into a very delicate rose-gold or sunset-tan center. Conversely, few would dispute the ugliness of a coin that looked as if a subway train had run over it, or a coin with black spots penetrating the surface.

Here's a basic rule of thumb: If a coin looks ugly to you, it probably is. In this case, beauty is very definitely in the eye of the beholder—and *you* are the beholder.

No matter how many coin dealers or certification services tell you that a coin merits a certain grade, follow your own intuition: If you don't like the way the coin looks, don't buy it. If, on the other hand, you think a certain coin is incredibly beautiful, chances are a lot of other people will agree with you. So always trust your instincts.

PROOF COINS

The term "proof" does not signify a grade or a level of preservation. Rather, it refers to the manner in which certain coins were manufactured. Proof coins are meant to be showpieces, so the Mint strikes them two or more times to give them greater detail than the coins it manufactures for circulation. Coins made for circulation are called "business-strike" coins.

Proof coins are sold by the Mint during their year of issue at a price that includes a premium over and above their face value. Through 1998, the U.S. Mint charged $12.50 for a current-year proof set of the five regularly issued U.S. coins (the cent, nickel, dime, quarter, and half dollar). Since the face value of these coins totals only 91 cents, the proof set's price included an added premium of $11.59. In 1999, the Mint included five statehood quarters in the proof set and raised the price to $19.95. (For information on ordering current proof sets directly from the Mint, write to: The United States Mint, P.O. Box 13576, Philadelphia, PA 19162-0011.)

Proof coins are graded on the same 1 to 70 scale as coins manufactured for circulation. Normally, proof coins do not enter circulation, and in such cases they are graded from 60 to 70, just like Mint State "business-strike" coins. However, some do circulate. Thus, it is possible for a proof coin—despite its shiny, chromium-like brilliance—to have a grade below the Mint State range, between the numbers 1 and 59.

Proof coins are graded according to the number of "hairlines," or tiny pin scratches, visible on their surfaces. In order to grade a proof coin with any degree of accuracy, you will need a magnifying glass; a 5- or 7-power glass would be very helpful. A bright light would also assist you. Halogen lamps are especially useful in grading proof coins.

To grade a coin, proof or otherwise, you should hold the coin tightly between your thumb and forefinger and tilt and rotate that coin under a halogen lamp. Caution: When using a magnifying glass, be careful not to move the magnifying glass; move only the coin. When viewing a coin, you should tilt and rotate the coin, but always keep the magnifying glass in a stationary position under your eye.

A proof coin with many heavy hairlines is usually not very valuable. Such a coin often will be assigned a grade between 60 and 64. Proof coins relatively free from these tiny hairline scratches often will be graded 65 and above. Other differentials affecting proof coins will be discussed in the next section.

COIN GRADING STANDARDS

The Professional Coin Grading Service (PCGS) is perhaps the largest business of its kind in the world. Since its founding in 1986, PCGS has authenticated and graded millions of rare coins worth hundreds of millions of dollars and encapsulated them in hard plastic holders. It is no exaggeration to say that PCGS—and other companies that followed it—revolutionized the business of buying and selling rare coins by facilitating their sale on a sight-unseen basis.

In 1997, PCGS shared its grading secrets with the public through the publication of a major new book, *The Official Guide to Coin Grading and Counterfeit Detection.* I served as editor of the book, which was published by House of Collectibles, an imprint of Random House.

The following is an excerpt from that book, incorporating the basic PCGS coin-grading standards.

Mint State Standards
MS-70: Perfect Uncirculated

Marks: An MS-70 coin has no defects of any kind visible with a 5X (5-power) glass. **Note: Minor die polish, light die breaks, and so on are *not* considered defects on business-strike coins.**

Strike: The strike is razor-sharp and will show 99+ percent of the detail intended.

Luster: The luster is vibrant and undisturbed in any way. Any toning will be attractive. Only the slightest mellowing of color is acceptable for red copper.

Eye Appeal: The eye appeal is spectacular—the ultimate grade!

MS-69: Superb Gem Uncirculated

Marks: A virtually perfect coin. It usually takes an intense study of the surfaces to ascertain why the coin will not grade MS-70. Only the slightest contact marks, nearly invisible hairlines, the tiniest planchet flaws, and so on are allowable for this grade. **Note: Slight die polish, medium die breaks, or slight incomplete striking are *not* defects.**

Strike: The strike is extremely sharp and will show 99+ percent of the detail intended.

Luster: The luster will be full and unbroken. Any toning must be attractive. Only the slightest mellowing of color is acceptable for red copper, and only the slightest unevenness of color for red-brown and brown copper.

Eye Appeal: Superb!

MS-68: Superb Gem Uncirculated

Marks: A nearly perfect coin, with only slight imperfections visible to the unaided eye. The imperfections (tiny contact marks, minuscule hairlines, a small lint mark, etc.) will almost always be out of the range of the coin's focal points.

Strike: The strike will be exceptionally sharp.

Luster: The luster will be full (or virtually so) and "glowing." Any luster breaks will be extremely minor and usually restricted to the high points. Slight unevenness in toning is acceptable, as long as it is still attractive. Red copper may show some mellowing, and there may be some unevenness of color for red-brown and brown copper.

Eye Appeal: Exceptional, with no major detractions.

MS-67: Superb Gem Uncirculated

Marks: Any abrasions on the coin are extremely light and/or well hidden in the design and do not detract from the coin's beauty in any way. As with MS-68 coins, the fields on smaller coins are usually nearly flawless, especially on the obverse. On large silver coins with smooth devices (Morgan dollars, for instance), the flaws will usually be found in the fields; on large gold coins (such as Liberty Head $20s), the fields will usually be superb in this grade, with only minor flaws in the devices.

Strike: The strike will be very sharp and almost always full.

Luster: The luster will be outstanding. Any toning (even if slightly uneven) must be attractive and not impede the luster in any way. Red copper can have mellowing of color, and there can be unevenness of color for red-brown and brown copper. Minute spotting, if present, should be virtually unnoticeable.

Eye Appeal: In almost all cases, the eye appeal will be superb. Any negativity will be compensated for by another area that is spectacular.

MS-66: Gem Uncirculated

Marks: There may be several noticeable, but very minor, defects. If marks or hairlines are in an important focal area, they must be minimal and compensated for by the rest of the coin's superbness.

Strike: The coin will be well-struck.

Luster: The luster will be above average (usually far above average), and any toning should be attractive and should only minimally impede the luster. Red copper can have mellowing of color, and there can be unevenness of color for red-brown and brown copper. Very minor spotting may be present, although it should be noticed only upon close examination. A dipped coin must be "fresh" in appearance and never give the impression of having been cleaned.

Eye Appeal: The eye appeal will almost always be above average for a gem-quality coin, and many MS-66 coins will be superb in this category. Any negative factors must be compensated for in another area.

MS-65: Gem Uncirculated

Marks: There may be some scattered marks, hairlines, or other minor defects. If the flaws are in a main focal area, they must be minor and few. Hidden marks and hairlines can be larger. On dime-type and smaller, they almost always must be in the devices or must be very minor if they are in the fields. On larger coins, there can be marks/hairlines in the fields and in the devices, but no major ones.

Strike: The coin will be well-struck.

Luster: The luster will be at least average (almost always above average), and any toning can only slightly impede the luster. Copper coins can have mellowing of color for red and unevenness of color for red-brown or brown coins. **Note: There can be a little minor spotting for copper coins.**

Eye Appeal: The eye appeal will be average or above. This is a very nice coin. However, there are many ways a coin can grade MS-65. This grade (or MS/Proof-64) may have the largest range of eye appeal. A coin may grade MS-65 with scattered light marks, but with great luster and strike—or a coin with virtually no marks but a slightly impeded luster also could be MS-65. The overall eye appeal still must be positive or the coin does not merit MS-65.

MS-64: Choice Uncirculated

Marks: There may be numerous minor marks/hairlines, several significant marks/hairlines, or other defects. There may be a few minor or one or two significant marks/hairlines in the main focal areas. On minor coinage (dime coinage and lesser), there may be several marks/hairlines in the fields or main focal areas, but none should be too severe. On larger coins, these marks/hairlines may be more severe in the fields or main focal areas. However, a severe mark/hairline would have to be of a size that would preclude grading the coin MS-65, though not so severe as to reduce the coin to MS-63. If there are several fairly heavy marks/hairlines in obvious areas, the coin would grade MS-63.

Strike: The strike will range from average to full.

Luster: The luster can be slightly below average to full, and toning can impede the luster. On brilliant coins, there may be breaks in the luster caused by marks or hairlines. Red copper can be considerably mellowed. There may be noticeable spotting for this grade, although heavy or large spotting would reduce the grade to MS-63 or below.

Eye Appeal: The eye appeal can range from slightly negative to very positive. This is a nice coin, so anything too negative would preclude the MS-64 grade. Balance is a key. A coin with marks/hairlines in obvious focal areas would have to have great luster or some other positive factor to attain MS-64. A coin with less severe marks/hairlines hidden in devices could have impaired luster or some other problem and still be graded MS-64. Coins with deficiencies and no redeeming characteristics are graded MS-63 or lower.

MS-63: Choice Uncirculated

Marks: There may be numerous marks/hairlines, including several major marks/hairlines in main focal areas. If there are distracting marks/hairlines on the major devices, the fields should be relatively clean. If there are distracting marks/hairlines in the fields, the devices should have less disturbance.

Strike: The strike will range from slightly below average to full.

Luster: The luster can be below average to full. The toning can seriously impede the luster. On brilliant coins, there can be significant breaks in the luster. Red copper can be considerably mellowed. There can be noticeable spotting, including several large spots or a group of small ones. **Note: If the luster is poor, then the coin would *not* be graded MS-63, even if the strike were full and the marks/hairline were acceptable for the grade.**

Eye Appeal: The eye appeal can be slightly negative to very positive. The "average" MS-63 will have neutral eye appeal (noticeable marks/hairlines, average to above-average strike, and average luster). However, quite a few coins are graded MS-63 because of their negative appearance. If either the luster, strike, or marks/hairlines are below the standards set forth here, then one of the other criteria must be exceptional for the coin to attain MS-63.

MS-62: Uncirculated

Marks: The marks/hairlines may cover most of the coin. If the marks/hairlines are light, they may be scattered across the entire coin. If there are several severe marks/hairlines, the rest of the coin should be relatively clean.

Strike: The strike can range from very weak (some New Orleans Mint Morgan dollars, for example) to full.

Luster: The luster can range from poor to vibrant.

Eye Appeal: The eye appeal will be negative to slightly positive. The negativity in this grade usually involves excessive marks/hairlines and/or the strike and/or lack of luster and/or unattractive toning. There can be one to three of the major criteria that contribute to negative eye appeal. Even coins with overall positive eye appeal usually have one or two areas that are negative. Thus, a coin with numerous marks/hairlines but with average strike and luster may grade MS-62, while a coin with just a few marks (probably in the wrong places) and weak strike and luster also may grade MS-62.

MS-61: Uncirculated

Marks: There may be marks/hairlines across the entire coin. There may be several severe contact marks/hairlines. If there are numerous large marks/hairlines in the main focal areas, the fields should be cleaner, although they still could have some contact marks/hairlines. On larger coins (half dollars and larger), there may be areas with almost no marks/hairlines.

Strike: The strike can range from very weak to full.

Luster: The luster may be poor, average, or full.

Eye Appeal: The eye appeal will be very negative to very slightly positive.

MS-60: Uncirculated

Marks: Numerous. The marks/hairlines will probably cover all of the coin's surface. On larger coins (half dollars and higher), there may be some areas that have few or no marks/hairlines. The marks/hairlines can be large and in prime focal areas. **Note: Sometimes the mark is *not* from "normal" contact with other coins or from circulation, thus would be considered damage and the coin might not be graded.**

Strike: The strike can range from very weak to full.

Luster: The luster may be poor, average, or full.

Eye Appeal: The eye appeal can be very negative to neutral.

Circulated Standards
AU-58: Choice About Uncirculated

Wear: There will be slight wear on the highest points of the coin. In some cases, 5X magnification is needed to notice this wear, and sometimes it can be noticed by slowly tilting the coin in the light source. This method often may show the slight friction as discoloration. Very often, the obverse will have slight friction and the reverse will be full Mint State (often MS-63 or higher).

Marks: There are usually very few marks for this grade. Instead of marks, the principal detractions on the typical AU-58 coin are rub or hairlines. The few marks should not be major or in prime focal areas. A coin that would grade AU-58 from a wear standpoint, but has numerous marks, would be graded AU-55 or lower.

Strike: The strike can range from below average to full. **Note: A very weak strike would be downgraded to AU-55 or lower.**

Luster: The luster can range from poor to full. There will be noticeable breaks in the luster on the high points. These areas will be visible to the unaided eye, but should be less than 10 percent of the surface area.

Eye Appeal: The eye appeal is usually very good. Since marks are usually very minor, the eye appeal will be determined mainly by strike, luster, and originality. Many AU-58 coins are lightly cleaned or dipped uncirculated coins that are no longer considered uncirculated because of the light cleaning or rubbing that is now present. These coins can be just as attractive as coins that are graded AU-58 because of slight circulation—and sometimes even more so. Often these coins will have fewer marks than low-grade uncirculated coins.

AU-55: Choice About Uncirculated

Wear: There will be slight wear on the high points and some friction in the fields. The reverse will now usually show wear similar to that on the obverse. In a few instances (coins stored face up that have acquired friction), the reverse will still be uncirculated.

Marks: There usually will be several minor marks/hairlines and a couple of major ones. These should be scattered between the devices and fields, with nothing too severe on the prime focal areas.

Strike: The strike will range from slightly weak to full.

Luster: The luster can range from poor to full, although the areas of wear will not show full luster. There will be breaks in the luster covering 10 to 25 percent of the surface.

Eye Appeal: The eye appeal is usually good. The main criteria will be surface preservation, lack of and placement of marks/hairlines, the luster remaining, and originality.

Proof Standards
Proof-70: Perfect Proof

Marks: There can be no defects visible with a 5X glass. A Proof-70 coin is 100 percent free of hairlines, planchet flaws, lint marks, and any other mint-caused or post-striking defects.

Strike: The strike is full, showing all of the intended detail.

Luster: The surfaces are fully reflective (if applicable) and undisturbed in any way. Any toning must be attractive. Red copper must have no breaks in the color, and only the slightest mellowing is acceptable.

Eye Appeal: Nothing short of spectacular.

Proof-69: Superb Gem Proof

Marks: This coin will appear perfect to the unaided eye. Upon magnification, one or two minute imperfections (extremely minor hairlines, a previously hidden lint mark, a flake from the planchet, etc.) will be evident. **Note: Slight die polish, very minor die breaks, or incomplete striking will *not* preclude a coin from attaining this grade.**

Strike: The strike will be full, showing all of the detail intended.

Luster: The surfaces must be fully reflective (if applicable) and not negatively affected by toning or patina. Any toning must be attractive. Slight mellowing of color is allowed for red copper and only the slightest unevenness of color for red-brown and brown copper.

Eye Appeal: Superb! **Note: Darkly toned proof coins will *not* grade Proof-69.**

Proof-68: Superb Gem Proof

Marks: A Proof-68 coin will have minor defects barely visible to the unaided eye—defects that usually go unnoticed at first look. These will usually include one of the following: virtually undetectable hairlines, a small planchet flaw, or an unobtrusive lint mark. Such defects, no matter how minor, should not be in a conspicuous place such as Liberty's cheek or the obverse field.

Strike: The strike will be full, showing virtually all of the detail intended.

Luster: The coin must be fully reflective (if applicable) or virtually so. Any toning must be attractive, but slight unevenness is allowable. Some mellowing of color is allowed for red copper and some unevenness of color for red-brown and brown copper.

Eye Appeal: The eye appeal will be exceptional. Any hint of negativity will be compensated for in another area.

Proof-67: Superb Gem Proof

Marks: Any defects visible to the unaided eye will be minor. These could include unobtrusive hairlines, one or more very minor contact marks, a stray lint mark or two, a well-hidden planchet flaw, and so on. If the eye is immediately drawn to a defect, that will almost always preclude the coin from grading Proof-67.

Strike: The strike will be full or exceptionally sharp.

Luster: The reflectivity must be nearly full (if applicable). Toning may be dark or uneven, but not both. Red copper can have mellowing of color, and there can be unevenness of color for red-brown and brown copper. Minute spotting, if present, should be virtually unnoticeable.

Eye Appeal: Superb, or nearly so. Any negativity must be compensated for in another area. Darkly toned coins are almost always penalized at least one grade point at this level—for example, a Proof-67 coin that is dark would grade at least Proof-68 if the toning were attractive or nonexistent.

Proof-66: Gem Proof

Marks: A Proof-66 coin can have a few light contact lines/hairlines, but nothing detracting or concentrated in one area. It may have small lint marks or planchet flaws, but any defects must be minor. If the eye is drawn to a flaw, the rest of the coin must be superb to compensate for it.

Strike: The strike must be sharp and will almost always be exceptionally sharp.

Luster: The reflectivity will usually be excellent (if applicable). Any toning must be positive, and reflectivity must be good (if applicable). A Proof-66 coin may have some extremely positive attributes that offset slightly too much negativity in another area. For instance, Coin X has two or three too many hairlines to qualify as Proof-66, but the toning is fantastic, the devices are heavily frosted, and the eye appeal is outstanding, so the coin is graded Proof-66 anyway. Red copper can have mellowing of color, and there can be unevenness of color for red-brown and brown copper. Very minor spotting may be present.

Eye Appeal: Overall eye appeal for this grade is great, since this coin just misses Proof-67. Any deficiency in toning (too dark for Proof-67 because of impeded reflectivity, "splotchy" almost to the point of being negative, etc.) will be slight. If the coin is brilliant, the deficiency usually will be minuscule—contact/hairline/slide marks that preclude a higher grade.

Proof-65: Gem Proof

Marks: There may be several minor problems. These may include light contact, hairlines, lint marks, planchet flaws, or other minor defects. Since there may be several minor problems, there are many ways to attain the grade of Proof-65. For example, a coin with virtually no hairlines may have slight contact/slide marks on the high points and still grade Proof-65. In another case, a coin with no contact/slide marks might still grade no higher than Proof-65 because of minor but noticeable hairlines. Any other minor defects, such as lint marks or planchet flaws, should be unobtrusive.

Strike: The coin will be well-struck and, in most cases, very sharp.

Luster: The reflectivity will be average or above. Any toning present can impede the reflectivity only slightly. On untoned coins, the reflectivity can be moderately subdued, but coins with "washed-out" surfaces cannot be graded Proof-65. Red copper can have mellowing of color; copper coins can have minor spotting.

Eye Appeal: The eye appeal will be average or above. This is a coin almost everyone finds attractive. The comments for eye appeal under MS-65 are just as relevant for Proof-65. There is a wide range in the appearance of Proof-65 coins. Any slightly negative factors must be compensated for in another area.

Proof-64: Choice Proof

Marks: There may be numerous minor problems. These may include contact marks, many small hairlines, or several large hairlines. Other defects—such as lint marks or planchet flaws in focal areas—may be allowed.

Strike: There can be some weakness in strike. **Note: This is the highest Proof grade where some distracting weakness of strike in the major devices is allowable. Weakness in stars and other minor devices is not usually enough to reduce the grade.**

Luster: The reflectivity can be impeded. If the coin is toned, the reflectivity can be noticeably subdued. On untoned coins, there can be dullness or a "washed-out" appearance, but these coins should have fewer contact lines/hairlines than a coin with more of the mirror surface intact. Red copper can be considerably mellowed. There may be noticeable spotting for this grade, although large or numerous spots would reduce the grade to Proof-63 or lower.

Eye Appeal: The eye appeal can range from slightly negative to very positive. This is an attractive coin. However, there can be some negativity in toning (too dark, hazy, splotchy, etc.)—or, with untoned coins, there can be dullness in the mirrored surface. The amount of hairlines acceptable for this grade is directly proportional to the eye appeal. If a coin has great contrast (frosted devices), the hairlines or other defects can be quite noticeable. On a coin that has less contrast and is either darkly toned or dull brilliant, the hairlines must be minor.

Proof-63: Choice Proof

Marks: There may be immediately noticeable defects. There may be quite a few contact marks/hairlines or a group of concentrated hairlines, lint marks in prime focal areas, medium-to-large planchet flaws, or a combination of these or other defects. Obvious "slide marks," which usually result from an album's plastic sliding across the devices, will almost always result in a grade of no higher than Proof-63.

Strike: The strike can range from average to full. This is the highest Proof grade where considerable weakness of strike is allowed. If the coin is poorly struck, a grade of Proof-62 or below would be appropriate.

Luster: The reflectivity can be below average to full. On untoned coins, the surfaces are often dull—and on toned coins, there can be dark or uneven toning that will seriously impede the amount of reflectivity. Red copper can be considerably mellowed. There can be noticeable spotting, with several large spots or numerous small ones. **Note: If the mirrored surface is almost totally obscured, the grade of Proof-63 will *not* be attained and a grade of Proof-62 or lower is warranted.**

Eye Appeal: The eye appeal can be slightly negative to very positive. The "average" Proof-63 coin will have neutral eye appeal (noticeable hairlines, well-struck, slightly dulled surfaces). Some coins can still grade Proof-63, even if one or more of the major criteria are negative, but that must be compensated for by strength in another area.

Proof-62: Proof

Marks: There may be some light contact marks, numerous light hairlines, medium-to-heavy hairlines, or a combination of the above covering most of the coin's surface. There also may be concentrated patches of hairlines, with some areas remaining relatively free of contact marks/hairlines.

Strike: The strike can range from extremely weak to full.

Luster: The reflectivity can range from below average to nearly full. On toned coins, there may be very little of the mirrored surface left, and with brilliant coins the reflectivity may be almost completely impaired by hairlines.

Eye Appeal: The eye appeal will be negative to slightly positive.

Proof-61: Proof

Marks: The surfaces may have some contact marks and numerous light-to-heavy hairlines. There may be several small marks hidden in the devices. The entire surface may be covered with contact marks/hairlines, or there may be several areas with concentrated hairlines and some others relatively free of them.

Strike: The strike can range from very weak to full.

Luster: The reflectivity will range from poor to slightly impaired.

Eye Appeal: The eye appeal will be very negative to very slightly positive.

Proof-60: Proof

Marks: The surface may have quite a few contact lines or myriad medium-to-heavy hairlines and may have several marks. There should be no large marks for this grade. If there are large marks, the grade would be Proof-58 or lower.

Strike: The strike can range from very weak to full.

Luster: The reflectivity may range from poor to slightly impaired.

Eye Appeal: The eye appeal can be very negative to neutral.

Proof-58: Circulated Proof

Wear: There usually is very little wear on the high points. With Proof coins, wear usually takes the form of slight friction in the fields. Since the mirrored surfaces of Proof coins are so delicate, any minor circulation or mishandling will cause marks and hairlines to become immediately apparent. In some cases, the reverse may have no impairment and will grade Proof-60 or higher. **Note: It is much easier to discern wear on a Proof than on a business strike. Proofs and prooflike business strikes reveal marks/hairlines much more easily because of the mirrored surface.**

Marks: There could be a few major marks. There can be scattered contact marks, with a few allowed on the devices and in the fields. If there are more than a few marks, a Proof coin would be graded Proof-55 or lower.

Strike: The strike can range from average to full. **Note: A weak strike would be downgraded to Proof-55 or lower.**

Luster: The reflectivity will be somewhat impaired. This is not always true with Proof-58 coins, since many coins in this grade will have full reflectivity, which is disturbed only by hairlines, marks, or minor wear.

Eye Appeal: The eye appeal is usually very good. There usually is nothing other than slight contact marks/friction on Proof-58 coins. Appearance is usually *not* the problem with this coin.

Proof-55: Circulated Proof

Wear: There will be slight wear on the high points and up to half of the fields will have friction. The reverse will now be impaired in most cases.

Marks: There may be several marks and quite a few contact marks/hairlines. These should be scattered about and should not be concentrated on prime focal areas.

Strike: The strike will range from slightly weak to full.

Luster: The reflectivity may be severely impaired. Up to 50 percent of the mirrored surface is now slightly to fairly severely impaired. There can be a few areas that have lost complete reflectivity.

Eye Appeal: The eye appeal is usually good. The main criteria will be surface preservation, lack of and placement of marks/hairlines, reflectivity remaining, and originality.

Proof-53: Circulated Proof

Wear: There will be obvious wear to the high points. Friction will cover 50 to 75 percent of the fields.

Marks: There may be several minor and major marks/hairlines. There can be scattered marks/hairlines in all areas of the coin, including prime focal areas, but a severe disturbance in those prime areas will result in a lower grade. Some small areas may have heavy concentrations of hairlines.

Strike: The strike will range from below average to full.

Luster: The reflectivity may be severely impaired. The amount of "mirror" still visible will depend on the original depth of the mirrored surface.

Eye Appeal: The eye appeal now is a function of surface preservation, lack of and placement of marks/hairlines, reflectivity remaining, and originality.

Proof-50: Circulated Proof

Wear: Wear is evident. There can be friction in the fields ranging from half to all of the unprotected areas. The high points will have wear that is very obvious to the unaided eye.

Marks: There may be many marks/hairlines. Many times, hairlines and small marks will now start to "blend" into the surfaces. These will appear as discolored areas.

Strike: The strike will range from below average to full.

Luster: The reflectivity may be completely impaired. There may be parts of the surface with no mirror at all. The Proof surface may be visible only around protected devices.

Eye Appeal: The eye appeal is now a function of surface preservation, lack of and placement of marks/hairlines, reflectivity remaining, and originality.

NOTE: COINS THAT GRADE PR-45 AND BELOW ARE GRADED ESSENTIALLY THE SAME AS REGULAR STRIKES. SINCE THE CRITERIA FOR DETERMINING THE OVERALL GRADE WILL MOSTLY BE THE SAME FOR BOTH MINT STATE AND PROOF COINS, THESE GRADES ARE LISTED ONLY UNDER THE MINT STATE STANDARDS MENTIONED EARLIER, WITH ANY EXCEP-TIONS NOTED.

CHAPTER 8

TRADING COINS
LIKE STOCKS

Buying and selling many rare coins today is sometimes like buying and selling shares of common stock.

When you buy five shares of a popular stock such as Xerox or Federal Express, those shares are said to be "fungible." That means they duplicate each other—they're alike and they're traded in like-kind units. You can buy five shares of Federal Express and sell five shares of Federal Express and on each end you'll have a relatively clean paper transaction, facilitated by computer technology and the magnetic media to which we're so accustomed in this modern electronic age.

Rare coins can now be traded in very similar fashion. Let's suppose, for instance, that you buy five 1881-S Morgan dollars (silver dollars made in 1881 at the San Francisco Mint, with an "S" below the eagle on the reverse). And let's say these coins are graded Mint State-65 and cost you $100 apiece. Six months later, if 1881-S Morgan dollars graded Mint State-65 have increased in value to $150 apiece, you'll be able to sell any or all of your five coins for $150 each just as if they were shares of your favorite stock.

Rare coins didn't always enjoy this high degree of liquidity. What gives it to them today is a process known as "coin certification." In recent years, we have witnessed the development of highly skilled "certification services"—companies which, for a fee, will render an opinion as to a coin's grade, or level of preservation, on the 1 through 70 scale.

After assigning a grade to a coin, these services encapsulate that coin in a tamper-resistant, sonically sealed, hard plastic holder, along with a small paper insert which indicates the level of preservation. Coins encased in such holders are said to have been "certified." The grade assigned to a coin by a certification service gives buyers and sellers a reasonable ballpark idea as to its level of preservation, and some dealers might even make a sight-unseen offer for such a coin, based upon its certified grade.

Remember what I said earlier:

As of this writing, the four leading certification services—the ones that can be relied upon most for the consistency and accuracy of their grading standards—are the Professional Coin Grading Service (PCGS) of Newport Beach, California; the Numismatic Guaranty Corporation of America (NGC), of Sarasota, Florida; ANACS of Columbus, Ohio; and the Independent Coin Grading Company (ICG) of Englewood, Colorado.

The founder of PCGS, coin dealer David Hall, is the man who devised the system of encapsulating coins and trading them sight-unseen. This system is now accepted and used throughout the rare coin industry. NGC soon followed suit under the direction of John Albanese, a professional numismatist widely respected for his knowledge and integrity.

Right from the inception of NGC, Albanese took a strong consumer protection stance. To reassure consumers that no conflict of interest exists in NGC's grading practices, he initially prohibited the company's principals from buying or selling coins. Although Albanese sold his interest in NGC, the company is still a leader in coin certification.

PCGS is owned by coin dealers and they remain active in the market. However, PCGS's published anti–self-interest policy prohibits anyone who actively trades coins from grading for it. In fact, the company has achieved tremendous acceptance, and its grading judgments are highly respected.

ANACS came into being as an arm of the American Numismatic Association, the world's largest coin club. In 1990, the ANA sold its grading service to Amos Press of Sidney, Ohio, publisher of *Coin World* and other hobby periodicals.

ICG, founded in 1998, is the youngest of the major grading services. However, it already ranks among the leading firms in terms of the volume of coins that it certifies and encapsulates, apparently because it handles large quantities of high-grade modern U.S. coins.

Grading coins is subjective, but PCGS, NGC, ANACS, and ICG bring relative consistency to the process—and a high degree of accuracy—by using a consensus approach. Coins submitted for evaluation are examined by several different graders, and if the majority agree upon a grade, that's the one assigned.

All four services accept coins from the public for certification. Each service, however, has specific submission requirements. To obtain information about the services, including a free list of submission centers, write to them as follows:

Numismatic Guaranty Corporation of America, Inc.
P.O. Box 4776
Sarasota, FL, 34230

Professional Coin Grading Service
P.O. Box 9458
Newport Beach, CA 92658

ANACS
P.O. Box 182141
Columbus, OH 43218-2141

Independent Coin Grading Company
7901 East Belleview Ave., Suite 50
Englewood, CO 80111

COMPUTER GRADING

Although consensus grading by expert human graders has been extremely successful, the major certification services have spent considerable time, effort, and money exploring the possible use of computers to make their results even more consistent and accurate. In May 1990, PCGS began using a computer—dubbed *The Expert*—to help grade Morgan silver dollars.

The Expert simulated human thought processes and, from early indications, was able to grade coins consistently in accordance with the standards established for Morgan dollars by PCGS.

This noble experiment has been suspended, but it provided considerable food for thought.

The Expert graded coins on a step-by-step basis, very much the way human graders do. Indeed, it was programmed with information gleaned from the experts on the PCGS staff. Much can be learned from reviewing these steps, for knowing what's involved in determining a grade can help us become better graders ourselves—and smarter buyers. You should familiarize yourself with the computer's "thought process" so that you can use the same approach yourself.

According to information provided by PCGS, *The Expert* graded each coin on the basis of the following steps:

1. **Image capture.**

   Multiple images of the coin, obtained under various lighting conditions, are captured in digital form, using a special camera. Looking at this in human terms, it's equivalent to tilting and rotating the coin under a halogen lamp to search for imperfections.

2. **Image enhancement.**

   All of the captured images—or the most significant ones—are computer-enhanced to bring out important features of the coin. In human terms, this is the equivalent of using a magnifying glass to examine the coin carefully.

3. **Low-frequency marks analysis.**

   The key areas of the coin are examined in great detail to identify, classify, measure, and score all flaws. This is similar to using the magnifying glass to scrutinize the most important areas of the coin for scratches and other imperfections.

4. **High-frequency marks analysis.**

   Secondary portions of the coin are examined to identify flaws that exist in busy background areas such as the hair, letters, and rim. These flaws are then classified, measured, and scored by the computer, and it takes them into consideration when assigning a grade. This is what you do yourself when you check the areas which aren't of prime importance on the coin when you're grading it or looking for imperfections.

5. **Mirror and luster.**

   A light-flow and reflectance analysis is used to precisely measure the "mirror," or reflective quality, of the coin, as well as its inherent luster. This is of particular importance on special silver dollars which are said to be *proof-like*.

   Proof-like silver dollars (and their counterparts in other coin series) look like proof coins—coins produced by a special slow process with multiple strikings and brilliant, mirror-like surfaces. In reality, however, they're unusually bright and attractive "business-strike" coins, the kind intended for use in circulation.

   Proof-like Morgan dollars enjoy an especially wide following among collectors. These coins have reflective backgrounds (fields) and frosted raised parts (devices). Frequently, the contrast between the fields (the background areas of a coin) and the raised parts—such as the portrait, the stars, the date, and the lettering—creates a lovely cameo look.

   To the untrained eye, a proof-like coin looks very much like a proof, just as its name suggests. Its brilliant, mirror-like surface lends particular credence to this notion. But the PCGS computer is capable of distinguishing a proof-like Morgan dollar from a proof.

6. **Strike.**

Key areas of the coin are examined to measure the strength of the strike. One of these areas is Miss Liberty's hair, especially the portion above her ear.

7. **Eye appeal.**

Dozens of aspects of the coin are examined to define such qualities as satin smoothness, light flow, "flash," color, and toning—aspects that serve to establish the mood or eye appeal of the coin. (See the previous chapter for a detailed discussion of eye appeal.)

8. **Synthesis.**

The computer draws upon thousands of parameters—constant values for various grades—which have been stored in its memory, and synthesizes these with the key components of the coin. Among the factors evaluated during this process are front and back nicks or other flaws, strike, luster, eye appeal, mirror surface, toning, key-area metrics, and exceptional conditions.

9. **Final grade.**

The results of synthesis are then combined, using a complex set of master rules to establish the final grade for the coin.

COIN GRADING SCAMS

Leading coin grading services have broadened rare coins' acceptance and credibility throughout the investment community with their strict, consistent grading and their incorruptible judgments. However, there have been many copycats, and some of these are far less reliable, far less consistent, and not nearly as honest.

Some of the other coin-grading organizations *are* honest and consistent but, by their own admission, they grade according to standards which aren't nearly as strict as those set forth by PCGS, NGC, ANACS, and ICG. One such service which deserves particular mention is the Numismatic Certification Institute (NCI).

NCI was owned by a very large coin company, the Heritage Capital Corporation of Dallas, Texas. Heritage admitted that NCI's grading standards are about one point more liberal than those of NGC and PCGS. But this doesn't mean that NCI was bad. In fact, there were many people who collected NCI-graded coins exclusively. NCI was a highly respected service and is not to be confused with scam operators. But you should beware of con men who try to sell you NCI coins and use a pricing structure intended for coins from PCGS and NGC. Because the grading of NCI coins is more liberal, their prices are lower than those of comparably graded coins from the two leading services. NCI is no longer operating but coins graded by that service sometimes appear in the marketplace.

The following chart will give you an idea of the comparable values of coins that have been graded by various certification services. In each case, the price shown is the fair market value, as of October 1995, for an 1881-S Morgan dollar graded Mint State-65. Keep in mind that while the *grade* is the same in each case, the actual condition—or level of preservation—of the coin you would receive may vary considerably from one service to another, since some use much stricter standards. The stricter and more consistent the standards, the higher the price will normally be.

This list should provide you with guidance as to which services have strict grading standards and which have standards that simply don't make the grade.

Grading Service	October 1995 Fair Market Retail Value for 1881-S Morgan Dollar in MS-65
Numismatic Guaranty Corporation of America	80
Professional Coin Grading Service	80
ANACS/Amos Press, Inc.	78
Numismatic Certification Institute	50
International Numismatic Society Authentication Bureau, Washington, DC	40
Grading Service "X" (many—beware!)	20

RESUBMISSIONS

Dealers sometimes remove certified coins from their plastic holders and resubmit the coins to the same grading service or a different service in hopes that they will receive higher grades. In the great majority of cases, these resubmitted coins come back the second time with the same grade. Occasionally, though, "borderline" coins—those at the high end of one grade—will be upgraded to the next higher level.

There is strong incentive to resubmit certain coins, since the difference in value between one grade and the next—between Mint State-64 and Mint State-65, for example—can be many hundreds of dollars. There is nothing unethical about this practice, but buyers and sellers should be aware of it. In time, as computer grading is perfected, we will see far fewer resubmissions and they will be far less successful.

TRADING COINS LIKE STOCKS

All certified coins can be—and are—traded in much the same way as stocks. In practice, however, those most commonly traded sight-unseen are the coins which are most fungible—those which exist in relatively large quantities in Mint State-65 and Mint State-64 condition, the two grades most favored by the broad spectrum of investors. These include common-date Morgan silver dollars, Saint-Gaudens double eagles, and Walking Liberty half dollars.

Extremely rare coins—those costing, say, $25,000 or more—can certainly be traded sight-unseen, and on many occasions they are. However, these coins are more likely to be scrutinized, and bought on a "sight-seen" basis, by a prospective purchaser.

The coins most likely to be traded like shares of stock are popular issues with many "like-kind units"—coins which exist in relatively large numbers in high, investment-quality grades.

Independent certification of rare coins, while recommended, does not guarantee protection against the normal risks associated with volatile markets. The degree of liquidity for certified coins will vary according to general market conditions and the particular coin involved. For some coins, there may be *no active market at all* at certain points in time.

WALL STREET'S FLIRTATION WITH THE COIN MARKET

The rare coin market built up tremendous momentum during the 1980s. Annual surveys by Salomon Brothers, a respected New York City brokerage firm, consistently found rare coins to be among the most rewarding investment vehicles, regularly outperforming more conventional forms such as stocks and bonds. Thousands of investors with little or no knowledge about coins began to include them in their portfolios—and this, in turn, led seasoned Wall Street professionals to take a closer look at the phenomenon. Apparently, they liked what they saw, for as the decade neared a close, several major brokerages were actively involved with coin-related investment funds or poised to take the plunge.

A *Business Week* article reported at the time that investors were "flipping over the coin market." And it wasn't hard to understand why. Over a short period in 1989, rare coins were acknowledged to have increased in value a remarkable 40 percent. The rocket ride was propelled, to a great extent, by coin certification and sight-unseen trading. A number of high-powered brokers came to view certified coins as being much like stocks in their liquidity. Once a major grading service vouched for the grade of a coin and sealed that coin in an airtight plastic holder, would-be buyers all around the country stood ready and willing to buy it—without even having seen and examined it first—at a price level established by the marketplace.

Merrill Lynch was the first big Wall Street firm to put its prestige and resources behind a coin investment fund. In 1986, it established the Athena Fund, a limited-partnership fund which used investors' shares to purchase $7 million worth of ancient coins and antiquities. Encouraged by the initial success of this venture, it launched a second one—Athena Fund II—in 1988, this time with $25 million. In both instances, investors bought shares, and managers appointed by Merrill Lynch used the pooled resources to acquire rare coins and antiquities. The idea was to sell these in five to seven years and divvy up the profits among the investor partners.

In 1989, Kidder, Peabody announced plans for a $40 million limited-partnership fund featuring U.S. coins, and that drove already-rising coin prices to even greater heights. Then, as now, U.S. coins occupied center stage in the rare-coin marketplace, and the prospect of having tens of millions of dollars spent in this pivotal area triggered a buying spree even more dramatic than Merrill Lynch's ancient coin purchases had done. Traders rushed to accumulate desirable coins, anticipating massive new activity and price gains.

Unfortunately for them, May 1989 turned out to be not the starting point of a big new surge, but rather the very zenith of an upward market cycle that was running out of steam. Almost at once, prices began to soften and slip, and analysts quickly recognized that the boom of the 1980s had gone too far, too fast. Wall Street's flirtation with coins had created unrealistic expectations and driven prices unreasonably high for many coins that weren't especially rare. Common-date silver dollars in very high levels of preservation—while certainly aesthetically appealing—often were available by the thousands, for example, so it didn't make sense for them to carry huge premiums.

While some firms and individuals in the traditional financial community had dallied with rare coins during the late 1980s, others had viewed this relationship with suspicion. These skeptics felt relief—and a sense of vindication—when coin prices started to falter. The skid accelerated when the overall U.S. economy entered a deep recession in the early 1990s. And the downturn worsened when firms such as Merrill Lynch and Kidder, Peabody turned their backs on rare coins, breaking off their courtship when the going began to get rough. This dealt a severe psychological blow to the coin market, and had the ironic side effect of sharply reducing the value of the coins in those companies' limited-partnership funds.

Wall Street brought undeniable excitement to the coin market, along with the potential for spectacular price gains. The excitement lasted only briefly, and the price potential was never fully realized. But they have given way to stability and a greater sense of proportion. Today's expectations may be more modest, but they're also more realistic. The coin market may not have stars in its eyes anymore, but it has its feet on the ground—and with or without Wall Street, there's ample cause to be bullish about its future.

MARKET CYCLES

Fungible, generic coins such as common-date Morgan silver dollars and Saint-Gaudens double eagles ($20 gold pieces) tend to follow definite market cycles. They move up and down in value within fairly regular ranges of price and time.

By tracking these cycles and timing your buy-and-sell activity to coincide with the market's valleys and peaks, you can reap some handsome profits. You might, for example, purchase an 1881-S silver dollar graded Mint State-65 for $85 at the market low, then sell it within a matter of months for twice that amount when the cycle turns upward.

The following chart will give you a good idea of how coins can rise in value dramatically during a short period. The prices listed here show how twenty-seven of the most popularly traded Morgan dollars rose in value between March 24, 1989, and May 19, 1989. The valuations have been taken from the *Certified Coin Dealer Newsletter*, which used the American Numismatic Exchange as its source. These coins declined in value dramatically after their meteoric rise.

COIN (DATE AND MINT MARK)	GRADE	POPULATION: PCGS/NGC	3/24/89 VALUE	5/19/89 VALUE	CHANGE
Morgan Dollars					
1878-S	MS-64	2,991/558	$ 125	$160	+28%
	MS-65	858/222	685	830	+21%
1879-S	MS-64	10,678/2,305	97	160	+65%
	MS-65	7,109/1,496	310	535	+73%
1880-CC	MS-64	1,012/138	307	405	+32%
	MS-65	336/34	1,850	2,350	+27%

COIN (DATE AND MINT MARK)	GRADE	POPULATION: PCGS/NGC	3/24/89 VALUE	5/19/89 VALUE	CHANGE
1880-S	MS-64	15,584/3,013	97	155	+60%
	MS-65	10,730/1,958	310	535	+73%
1881-CC	MS-64	1,861/241	360	400	+11%
	MS-65	903/93	970	1,240	+28%
1881-S	MS-64	28,046/4,757	100	155	+55%
	MS-65	17,236/2,989	310	535	+73%
1882	MS-64	1,116/276	220	245	+11%
	MS-65	235/39	1,385	1,775	+28%
1882-CC	MS-64	2,658/227	185	225	+22%
	MS-65	920/88	845	1,000	+18%
1882-S	MS-64	9,132/1,806	99	160	+62%
	MS-65	5,519/1,245	310	535	+73%
1883	MS-64	2,740/349	102	160	+57%
	MS-65	1,297/149	530	820	+55%
1883-CC	MS-64	3,925/422	180	215	+19%
	MS-65	1,656/173	675	900	+33%
1883-O	MS-64	6,871/1,055	105	155	+48%
	MS-65	1,666/304	405	680	+68%
1884	MS-64	1,532/243	120	160	+33%
	MS-65	543/72	710	1,110	+56%
1884-CC	MS-64	3,963/388	175	230	+31%
	MS-65	1,423/121	690	900	+30%
1884-O	MS-64	11,178/1,675	98	155	+58%
	MS-65	2,895/411	315	535	+70%
1885	MS-64	5,212/846	99	160	+62%
	MS-65	2,165/438	322	555	+72%
1885-CC	MS-64	1,649/227	390	410	+ 5%
	MS-65	720/80	1,340	1,760	+31%
1885-O	MS-64	13,354/2,078	99	155	+57%
	MS-65	4,504/943	315	535	+70%
1886	MS-64	9,422/1,557	100	160	+60%
	MS-65	4,125/747	315	535	+70%
1887	MS-64	11,745/2,082	100	160	+60%
	MS-65	3,756/901	310	535	+73%
1888	MS-64	3,000/513	120	160	+33%
	MS-65	804/179	665	895	+35%
1888-O	MS-64	1,265/236	180	235	+30%
	MS-65	257/45	1,720	2,025	+18%

COIN (DATE AND MINT MARK)	GRADE	POPULATION: PCGS/NGC	3/24/89 VALUE	5/19/89 VALUE	CHANGE
1889	MS-64	1,633/494	155	210	+35%
	MS-65	233/50	1,800	1,900	+ 5%
1890-S	MS-64	576/113	325	365	+12%
	MS-65	145/25	1,510	2,000	+32%
1896	MS-64	2,828/599	104	160	+54%
	MS-65	774/176	685	995	+45%
1897	MS-64	1,361/241	150	160	+ 7%
	MS-65	315/41	1,140	1,500	+32%
1897-S	MS-64	736/204	225	285	+27%
	MS-65	230/74	980	1,350	+38%

THE SCOTT TRAVERS EIGHT-STEP MARKET-CYCLE BUY-SELL PLAN, OR HOW TO MAKE A FORTUNE IN COINS IN EIGHT EASY STEPS

Earlier, I showed you how to use three simple steps to gauge the current psychology, or "temperature," of the coin market. Following is a list of eight easy guidelines to help you take advantage of this knowledge—and predictable market cycles—to maximize your profits from rare coins.

1. **Follow market cycles.**
     Determine the low and high points for any particular coin in which you may be interested. In an active market, many coins trade within definite ranges. For example, in the late 1980s, a number of common-date Morgan silver dollars graded Mint State-65 tended to move up and down within a trading range from $100 to $500.

     You can get a good feel for how the market performs by studying past issues of the *Coin Dealer Newsletter*, a weekly publication—widely referred to as the "Greysheet"—that lists the current values of all commonly traded U.S. coins. Examine a number of Greysheets covering a period of several months and you'll start to see a pricing pattern emerge. You can obtain a book with many past issues for $24.95 postpaid by writing to the *Coin Dealer Newsletter*, P.O. Box 11099, Torrance, CA 90510.

2. **Locate and identify large coin promoters.**
     A number of very large coin companies run regular promotions featuring certain types of coins. Two such companies are Blanchard & Co., Inc. of Louisiana, and Investment Rarities, Inc. of Minnesota.

Whenever these companies promote a particular coin or series of coins, the surge of activity will cause their prices to rise in the market at large. Let's say, for example, that Blanchard is promoting Liberty Head eagles ($10 gold pieces) graded Mint State-65. In conducting its promotion, the company will distribute advertisements to many thousands of prospective purchasers urging them to buy these coins. That, in turn, will generate demand which will put upward pressure on the prices of *all* Mint State-65 Liberty Head eagles.

Your key to making a profit is to *sell* the kinds of coins that are being promoted. Keep in mind that the market for these coins is probably at its peak during the time the promotions are being run. Once the advertisements stop, demand will decrease and prices will fall.

What you must do is *anticipate* which coins will be coming up for promotion and buy some before the campaign begins. To do so, you should get on the mailing lists of large coin companies that run these types of promotions. Then, pick out a popular coin that these dealers are likely to promote but which they are *not* promoting at the moment. Check to see whether that coin is at the low or high end of its market cycle, following the approach outlined in Step 1. If it's at the low end, the time is probably right to buy some, since this coin has two big pluses: Its market cycle is due to head back up and it's due to be promoted.

3. **Actually buy the coin.**

When the time comes to actually make a purchase, ask your dealer to check the current buy and sell prices on the Certified Coin Exchange (CCE). This is a sophisticated electronic trading mechanism which enables buyers and sellers worldwide—dealers, collectors, and investors alike—to determine what the ballpark value of any particular certified coin is at a given time. Dealers trade coins among themselves on this system. Be careful. If a dealer on CCE is offering a certain coin for sale at $1,000, but the three highest offers to buy that kind of coin are only $100, you need to find out why. Are the buy offers too low, or is the sale price too high?

Another excellent way to keep track of sight-unseen prices for certified coins is to purchase the *Certified Coin Dealer Newsletter*. This weekly publication, popularly known as the "Bluesheet," is available by subscription at a rate of six months for $65. The address is P.O. Box 11099, Torrance, CA 90510.

Coins in the very highest grades have performed the best, and coins grading 65 are the most popular. Keep in mind, however, that while popularly traded generic coins—common-date Morgan silver dollars graded Mint State-65, for example—can make you a lot of money, some of the rarer coins might make you a lot *more* money.

4. Don't get scared.

The coin market can be extraordinarily volatile. This will make it harder to anticipate the direction of the market, and heighten the odds that you'll guess wrong now and then, even though you've done all your homework perfectly. You may find that instead of going *up* in price, a coin you have identified as a good bet for promotion or cyclical gain actually goes *down*.

This doesn't mean you should immediately sell that coin and lose money. Often, such coins will bounce right back in a matter of just a few days. In fact, this may be a prime opportunity to acquire more specimens.

Psychologically, the low point of the market is one of the most difficult times for people to buy. But, in fact, that's when the market is really the strongest—and the high point is when it's the weakest. Only after a market cycle has run its course do most people look back and see what was really happening. Often, the time when people have the greatest resistance to buying is when market values are at the bottom and things look bleak—yet that's when they should really be buying the most.

5. Continue to accumulate.

The Professional Coin Grading Service, the Numismatic Guaranty Corporation, and ANACS all issue periodic reports listing the number of coins of each type, date, and mint mark that they have certified in the various grade levels. Check these reports to see which coins have low "populations" (as PCGS calls them) or "censuses" (the equivalent term used by NGC). This will help guide you in determining which coins you should buy, for coins of which fewer examples have been certified are likely to appreciate in value more rapidly.

Your accumulation period should be a time of extreme caution, and you should limit your purchases to coins which have been independently certified by PCGS, NGC, ANACS, or ICG.

6. Take your profit.

By the time you reach this point, some of the coins you accumulated in Step 5 may have risen in value appreciably. For that matter, some of the coins you bought in Step 3 (and possibly saw decline in value in Step 4) may also be showing handsome gains. Perhaps certain coins you purchased for $250 each are now selling for $500. Now is the time to cash in some of these chips.

Use your intuition. But, if you see a tidy profit, don't hesitate. Sell. *If you see that you've achieved an impressive profit, go to the cash window and celebrate.*

If something rises in value dramatically in a very short period, that increase may be the result of an artificial run-up or some other temporary phenomenon. When you see an immediate run-up, that—more than ever—is the time to consider selling right away.

The coin market operates in a series of condensed, contracted boom-and-bust cycles which take anywhere from two months to two years to run their course. At times, a coin will go up from $150 to $500, then down to $150 again, within a matter of just a few months. Other times, it may take a couple of years for this process to be completed.

7. Cash out nonperformers.

If you're not prepared to hold out for the long term, don't let your ego blind you to reality. Take your loss and go on to something else that will be a better performer in the current marketplace.

A coin can be considered a nonperformer if it hasn't increased in value over an extended period and in fact has a long-term trend of *decreasing* in value.

8. Use your common sense.

Whether you're buying or selling, trust your judgment. Don't let a dealer sway you by building up a coin or knocking it down. If the coin looks ugly to you, don't buy it. And if a coin you're selling looks extremely attractive to you, don't let the dealer convince you it has problems, and don't accept less than you think it's worth. The dealer may be trying to take advantage of you. Shop around and look for a higher offer; don't be afraid to go to a second dealer and ask what *he* would pay. Use your common sense—and your own sensibility.

There you have it: the Scott Travers eight-step buy–sell plan. Continue to perform these eight simple steps and you have an excellent chance to make a lot of money over an extended period.

Obviously, you'll need more expertise to take full advantage of marketplace situations and opportunities. For a more detailed discussion of how to buy and sell coins, I urge you to read my book, *How to Make Money in Coins Right Now* (House of Collectibles/Random House (2001). This will take you behind the scenes in the rare coin market and equip you with the knowledge you need to be successful in complex marketplace situations.

COINS, THE COMPUTER REVOLUTION,
AND THE INTERNET

The automobile revolutionized daily life in America at the turn of the 20th century. The computer is doing the same at the turn of the 21st and the dawn of the new millennium. And its impact is apparent in the coin collecting hobby, just as everywhere else.

The Computer Revolution is rapidly transforming virtually every aspect of American life, and coin collecting is very much caught up in the excitement and the change. Indeed, the applications of computer technology seem certain to have an increasingly profound impact on the hobby—and the business of buying and selling coins.

Personal computers are no longer status symbols; they're standard equipment today in millions of American homes. They're linking the occupants of those homes with each other and with a vast network known as the Internet, and fundamentally changing the way people get information and communicate. In the process, they're making the world a smaller place.

Scott Travers Home Page on the World Wide Web. *Set your Internet browser to: http://www.pocketchangelottery.com for your starting point in numismatics. (Photo courtesy the author)*

The Computer Revolution has had a profound effect already on the coin hobby, and I expect to see even more dramatic changes in years to come. Some of these may not be for the better; until this new frontier is fully tamed, for instance, unscrupulous individuals may twist this new technology into a tool for exploiting the unwary. The real and potential advantages, however, far outweigh any drawbacks.

Recent History   The marriage of coins and computers first manifested itself during the 1980s with the establishment of computerized coin trading networks which facilitated the trading of coins on a sight-unseen basis. Sight-unseen trading diminished significantly during the first part of the 1990s, when lingering malaise in the rare-coin marketplace led to the departure of many big-money investors, who had been the principal buyers of such material. And this, in turn, greatly reduced the need for computer trading networks.

By the mid-1990s, however, the Computer Revolution was influencing rare coins, and the people who collect them, in even more personal and fundamental ways. By then, many millions of Americans had linked up with each other through on-line computer services, and this was giving coin collectors—and hobby organizations—a powerful new method to communicate among themselves and reach out to potential new recruits. It also loomed large as a marketing tool for dealers and a vehicle to expedite trading among collectors.

Coin Collecting On-Line   The Internet is sometimes described as the "information superhighway." In reality, it's more like a grid of interlocking highways through which you can travel to just about anywhere in the universe of humanity's collective knowledge.

This ultimate information superhighway is a loosely connected universe of computer networks and bulletin boards that brings together data on just about every conceivable aspect of human experience. The Internet encompasses more than 6,000 separate "newsgroups," or series of public messages and responses about related topics. The hottest place in cyberspace, however, is the Internet's World Wide Web, where a click of the mouse on hyperlinked text lets you visit any area of interest.

Originally developed as a means of communication between the U.S. military establishment and scientific researchers at institutions of higher learning, the Internet now serves a fast-growing segment of the general public. According to some estimates, nearly 40 million persons from the United States and Canada are surfing the Internet. Software and dial-up connections are available from various Internet service providers, and the only cost beyond the initial outlay is usually a flat monthly fee—typically about $25. On-line services such as America Online (AOL)—while offering a "gateway" to the Internet—want to be perceived as a "community." AOL attempts to retain the attention of "members" by offering unique or unusual proprietary content.

If you collect coins, your first destination should be a place called **rec. collecting.coins**—a kind of town square where hobbyists gather from all around the world to exchange information, ideas, and opinions related to their hobby. Technically speaking, this is a *newsgroup*—one of many specialized rest stops on the Internet where people of like interests congregate.

There are two principal ways to reach this newsgroup:

• A direct link to the Internet through an Internet service provider (ISP) such as AT&T Worldnet or EarthLink.

• A connection to the Internet through an on-line service such as America Online (AOL).

If you are linking to the Internet, you'll travel from place to place on the World Wide Web with software known as a *browser*. You'll need to configure your browser to give you quick access to **rec.collecting.coins** and its many postings.

If you're using America Online, you can get to **rec.collecting.coins**—as well as AOL's other coin-related resources—by following a few simple steps:

• Select "Keyword" or press the control and K keys at the same time.

• Next type the word "newsgroups," and press return.

• This will call up a list of various options. You can "search all newsgroups," and enter the word "coins." The option to add or read **rec.collecting.coins** will appear.

Keep in mind that in this newsgroup—or, for that matter, wherever you may pause to browse or chat on the Internet—not everything you see on your screen will be factual information. A great deal may be merely gossip or hearsay. So keep an open mind, but don't suspend your common sense or check your skepticism at the door.

One of the most valuable Internet services offered by PCGS.com is a daily price guide known as CU 3000. This chart, compiled by PCGS, tracks the market performance of 732 different coin types in up to nine different grade levels, showing not only their current retail value but also their high and low prices for the previous twelve months and their highest-ever value since 1970. These listings are accompanied by easy-to-follow graphs. David Hall and John Dannreuther, two of the founders of PCGS, deserve high praise for their pioneering work in developing this service. The PCGS site also contains an excellent bulletin board.

American Numismatic Association on the Internet   In June 1993, the ANA went on-line with CompuServe and Prodigy, giving it a forum in a vibrant new marketplace with several million "shoppers." In 1994, it staked out a position on the Internet as well, increasing its exposure exponentially.

To convey its message as efficiently as possible, the ANA has established what it calls the Numismatic Information Network—NIN, for short. The association's former executive director, Robert J. Leuver, was instrumental in developing this program, having recognized at a very early stage the enormous potential of computer networking. ANA's Internet sites and posts are efficiently and intelligently executed by Susie Nulty, the association's computer architect and MIS manager.

Through NIN, the ANA posts regularly updated information at its locations on the Internet. Among other things, it furnishes transcripts of its *Money Talks* radio program, as well as press releases and membership information. It also is

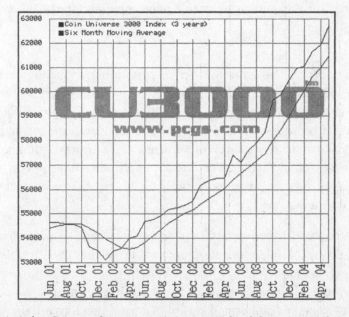

CU3000 coin index. Price performance statistics in graphical format are only a mouse click away. (Courtesy PCGS.com)

geared to receive correspondence from its 25,000-plus members, or from the general public. E-mail enables it to expedite requests for library materials, for example—and provides a handy means for prospective new members to seek information and application forms. The ANA's address on the Internet's World Wide Web is: www.money.org.

Photography Using Computers   *E-mail* (short for *electronic mail*) is a form of correspondence in which one computer user sends a message directly to another user's electronic mailbox. The recipient finds the message when he or she goes on-line and checks the log of mail that has arrived.

Taking e-mail one step further, some collectors have purchased inexpensive *scanners*—devices that convert regular photographs into digital form—and used these to create digitized images of their favorite coins, which they then save as electronic files and transmit via computer to other coin enthusiasts. A standard desktop scanner, complete with software, might cost $100 to $150. Brand-name scanners cost a little more—perhaps $250 to $300. The quality of scanned digital images is excellent from a technical standpoint—and if the original photograph is sharp and clear, the digitized version will be likewise. This is a great new way for collectors to show off their coins and possibly set up trades.

Even inexpensive scanners are capable of scanning superb digitized images of coins directly from the coins themselves. Just place the coin or slab on the glass scanner surface, and—similar to a photocopy machine—you have an exceptional photograph.

On-Line Auctions   There are a number of coin firms conducting auctions online, and some of these are real-time: You can see the bids increase before your eyes, or even submit a bid of your own. With the explosive growth of personal computers and on-line services during the last few years, the marketplace has witnessed rapid expansion as well in the size and frequency of on-line auctions of collectibles, including coins. This trend is likely to continue in years to come, if only because so many more potential coin buyers will be computer-literate and able to participate on-line.

Computers are also performing a valuable function as a means to compile, store, and access useful information about coin auction results of the past. I strongly suspect that before too long, databases will be available showing the prices realized of all coins ever sold at major auctions. Some auction companies have already compiled and posted lists of their own previous sales results. This type of information would be of great interest and value to a researcher cataloging an auction, or to a collector or dealer seeking information about a particular coin. Many coin companies already are computerizing their inventories for ready reference. These include two of the nation's leading coin auction firms—Auctions by Bowers and Merena of Wolfeboro, New Hampshire, and Heritage Numismatic Auctions of Dallas, Texas.

Risks in Buying Coins On-Line   In many respects, the Internet is a new frontier—a vast, largely uncharted territory with seemingly limitless potential. But like the Western frontier of the late nineteenth century, its potential is accompanied by very real dangers and serious risks. Before taking part in on-line coin auctions, you should learn as much as possible about this relatively new market medium and arm yourself with the knowledge you will need to deal with the dangers lurking there.

Computerized coin auctions offer convenience and excitement, but to date they have been subject to far less regulation than more traditional auctions, and that has created a climate in which abuses can—and do—occur. Part of the problem stems from the fact that on-line auction companies often serve merely as conduits, providing the Internet "auction rooms" where individual dealers conduct the actual sales. Bidders gain a sense of false confidence, reasoning that the large on-line auction firms will safeguard their interests and protect them from fraud and misrepresentation—when, in fact, they may be at the mercy of the individual dealers. The volume of complaints arising from on-line auctions suggests very strongly that these are not always tender mercies. And rather than cracking down on such abuses, some of the on-line auction firms have disavowed responsibility, leaving victimized bidders to fend for themselves.

All too many coin dealers holding on-line auctions use this forum to dump their inferior material—items that would be more difficult to sell in traditional auctions or face-to-face transactions. They then add insult to injury by placing high reserves on the coins—bloated prices below which the coins cannot change hands. Typically, they do this with "raw" or uncertified coins, since market values are better defined for coins that have been graded and encapsulated by a major third-party certification service. If the bidding level reaches the inflated reserve placed on a coin by a dealer, he or she gets a maximum return on a coin with minimal value. If the reserve isn't met, the dealer simply puts the same coin up for sale—with the same excessive reserve—in the next on-line auction, and the next one after that, until at length some unwary and unlucky bidder does claim this dubious "prize."

For anyone bidding in on-line auctions, I have three major recommendations:

Make sure you're doing business with a reputable dealer. If you don't know and trust an on-line auction dealer from personal experience, do some digging. Check to see whether he or she is a member of the Professional Numismatists Guild (PNG), an industry organization that polices its members' ethics and offers arbitration to settle disputes. Also, scan on-line message boards dealing with coin collecting to see whether the dealer is the subject of any complaints, or post a message yourself seeking information about the firm.

Don't buy uncertified coins on-line. Dealers foisting off inferior material have far more margin for error—error by buyers, that is—when they sell uncertified coins, since the grade levels haven't been established by independent experts. Grading becomes a matter of the auction dealer's judgment, and you can be sure the dealer won't err on the low side.

Even with certified coins, familiarize yourself with market values. In buying certified coins, you can be confident that the grading is correct—or at least not far from the mark. But knowing the grade is only half the battle; you also need to know the coin's market value in that grade. The *Certified Coin Dealer Newsletter*, or "Bluesheet," provides this information for coins that have been graded by the leading services. Keep in mind that with few exceptions, coins in on-line auctions are *not* premium-quality (or "PQ") pieces. On the contrary, they are likely to be coins that barely qualify for the grade they have been awarded by a certification service. Adjust your bidding accordingly, and do *your* erring on the low side.

Buying coins in on-line auctions can be fun. It can be exciting, too; without a doubt, there's a rush of adrenaline and instant gratification when you realize that you're the winning bidder. This is one case, however, where "winning" can make you a loser—perhaps a *big* loser, at that. So be sure you bring a road map when you travel into territory you're not familiar with. Bid cautiously, not carelessly. And don't get caught up unduly in the excitement of the moment. If you do, you may get caught in some unscrupulous dealer's trap—and find yourself stuck with an ill-advised purchase for years to come.

The Future   As this is written in 2004, computers and the Internet already are creating tremendous new excitement in the coin collecting hobby. But as Al Jolson said at the dawn of talking pictures in 1927, "You ain't seen nothing yet!" The future figures to be even more dramatic—and possibly downright startling— in terms of the way the Computer Revolution will change the face of the hobby.

With the advent of technology such as video-teleconferencing over the Internet, we'll soon be able to hold a coin up to a camera, tilt and rotate that coin under a pinpoint light source, and actually enable the people in the conference to view that coin so closely at their remote locations that they can evaluate it fully and determine its grade precisely, just as if they were in the very same room and holding the coin themselves.

This has enormous implications for the way rare coins are bought and sold. It's impossible to achieve the same degree of accuracy in evaluating and grading a coin simply by looking at a photograph. You need to tilt and rotate the coin under the proper lighting—and that will soon be possible once the new technology is perfected. It will certainly give all of us a major new perspective on the way that we collect and invest in coins.

Carlisle Development Corporation, a developer and marketer of collectibles software, has given us a preview of what might be in store for the future. My book, *The Coin Collector's Survival Manual—Revised Third Edition,* was reintroduced as an interactive CD-ROM by Carlisle. The multi-media computer version, maximized for Microsoft Windows 3.1 and Windows 95, features every single word and photograph from the printed book.

The CD-ROM edition includes more than two dozen PhotoProof color images to assist in illustrating the nuances of grading. The software program allows the user to zoom in on images for close inspection of grade-sensitive areas. The Carlisle staff worked long and hard to make this book come to life, and they should be commended for doing an exceptional job while keeping the product's price point to a reasonable $29.95.

We may see significant changes in coin conventions, too, for many of the functions performed by conventions today are available more conveniently online. And future coin auctions undoubtedly will reflect the role of the computer more and more.

Other Destinations On-Line   The more you explore the Internet, the more coin-related destinations you will find. I've mentioned some already, and others will beckon to you as you spend more time and effort learning the electronic ropes. One of the most noteworthy is the official Web site of the American Numismatic Association, the national coin club.

Many coin dealerships now have Internet sites—and while some of these are essentially nothing more than electronic ads with listings of coins for sale, some of them also have worthwhile educational features.

I've drawn up a list of some of the Internet destinations you may find beneficial as a hobbyist. These include commercial locations as well as the Web sites of non-profit and educational organizations. Note: I do not endorse any of the vendors included on this list except myself, and I do not monitor the text or the images found at these sites. I provide this information solely as a convenience to you as a Web user.

A word of caution: Many Web site addresses change on a frequent basis because the Internet is in a state of flux and nothing stays the same for very long. You'll need to conduct a search to see whether a particular dealer or organization has set up a new site. The good news is that for every coin-related Internet site that is no longer available or has moved, there are several brand new ones relating to that area of the hobby, because the Internet is such a fast-growing medium.

If you haven't embarked already, by all means plan a trip on the Internet sometime soon. You'll find it's a journey well worth taking and one that will revolutionize your life as a collector.

Important Numismatic Web Sites

Auctions
eBay
www.ebay.com

Teletrade
www.teletrade.com

Grading Services
ANACS
www.anacs.com

Independent Coin Grading Company
www.icgcoin.com

Numismatic Guaranty Corporation of America, Inc.
www.ngccoin.com

Professional Coin Grading Service
www.pcgs.com

Information Resources

Certified Coin Exchange
www.certifiedcoinexchange.com

Scott Travers Rare Coin Consumer Protection Homepage
www.pocketchangelottery.com

U.S. Coin On-line Encyclopedia
www.coinfacts.com

U.S. National Numismatic Collection/Smithsonian Institution
americanhistory.si.edu/csr/cadnnc.htm

Worldwide Coin Show Directory
coinshows.com

Organizations

American Israel Numismatic Association
www.amerisrael.com

American Numismatic Association
www.money.org

American Numismatic Society
www.amnumsoc.org

British Art Medal Society
www.bams.org.uk

Canadian Numismatic Association
www.nunetcan.net/cna.htm

Canadian Numismatic Research Society
www.nunetcan.net/cnrs.htm

CoinMasters On-line Coin Club
www.coinmasters.org

Combined Organizations of Numismatic Error Collectors of America
conecaonline.org

Early America Coppers
eacs.org

International Bank Note Society
www.public.coe.edu/~sfeller/IBNSJ

John Reich Collectors Society
www.logan.com/jrcs

Numismatic Bibliomania Society
www.coinbooks.org

Professional Numismatists Guild
www.pngdealers.com

Society of U.S. Pattern Collectors
www.uspatterns.com

Token & Medal Society
www.money.org/clubs/tams

Periodicals
Canadian Coin News
www.canadiancoinnews.com

The Celator
www.celator.com

The Coin Dealer Newsletter
www.greysheet.com

Coins Magazine
www.krause.com/static/coins.htm

Coin World
www.coinworld.com

Numismatic News
www.krause.com/static/coins.htm

World Coin News
www.krause.com/static/coins.htm

Book Merchants
American Numismatic Rarities, LLC
www.anrcoins.com

Brooklyn Gallery Coins & Stamps
www.brooklyngallery.com

Charles Davis Numismatic Literature
www.abebooks.com/home/numismat

George Frederick Kolbe Fine Numismatic Books
www.numislit.com

Scott Travers Information Services
www.pocketchangelottery.com/travers3.htm

Stanton Printing & Publishing
www.numis.net/jtstantom.com

Federal Reserve Banks
Atlanta
www.frbatlanta.org/

Chicago
www.frbchi.org/

Minneapolis
http://woodrow.mpls.frb.fed.us/

New York
www.ny.frb.org/

Philadelphia
www.libertynet.org/~fedresrv/fedpage.html

St. Louis
www.stls.frb.org/

U.S. Department of the Treasury/Mint/B.E.P.

www.bep.treas.gov/
www.treas.gov/mint/
www.usmint.gov/

E-Mail Addresses for Editors of Publications

Beth Deisher
Editor, *Coin World*
bdeisher@coinworld.com

Barbara Gregory
Editor, *Numismatist*
anaedi@money.org

David C. Harper
Editor, *Numismatic News*
harperd@krause.com

Ed Reiter
Senior Editor, *COINage* magazine
EdEditor@aol.com

Robert R. VanRyzin
Editor, *Coins* magazine
vanryzinr@krause.com

CHAPTER 9

HOW YOU CAN MAKE BIG PROFITS FROM SMALL COINS

Many coins rise in value, but often there's great disparity in how much—and how fast—they go up.

You can reap big profits by acquiring the coins with the greatest potential, and in this chapter I show you how to spot these coins quickly and easily. I've put together the ultimate list of secret insider tips—tips available nowhere else in the world—revealing how coin dealers operate and what happens behind the scenes in the marketplace.

Before we go behind the scenes on the sellers' end, let's first take a look at the principal *buyers* of coins and get a better idea how people in general play this money game—how they go about parlaying their small change into big net gains.

For the purposes of our discussion, there are four major groups of people who seek to acquire coins and then put them together—to a greater or lesser extent—systematically: (1) accumulators, (2) collectors, (3) collector/investors, and (4) investors.

Accumulators get their coins out of circulation—from pocket change, at the bank, or possibly in their travels to other countries. The unifying thread is that accumulators don't buy coins; they obtain them for face value.

Collectors, too, look for interesting coins in pocket change. But unlike accumulators, they also *buy* coins—and however they obtain them, they derive great pride and pleasure from assembling their acquisitions into sets. Some collectors purchase coins with million-dollar price tags; others buy coins costing only 50 cents. Whatever the outlay in money or time, true collectors savor the thrill of the hunt. They get much of their satisfaction from *finding* a worthwhile coin—whether that coin is an 1804 silver dollar costing a million dollars or a 1968 Lincoln cent worth only 5 or 10 cents, and whether they find it in pocket change or in a dealer's showcase.

The final two groups of coin buyers we'll consider are collector/investors and investors. These people's interest centers on coins of the highest grade (or level of preservation) and greatest rarity, and in almost every case they acquire them through purchase, rather than discovery. The coin investor looks upon his holdings not so much as a collection, but rather as a portfolio. Nonetheless, the prudent investor acquires and assembles coins systematically. And to maximize his return, he diversifies his holdings, just as he would do with stocks or bonds.

The greatest share of profits has gone to knowledgeable buyers who are either collectors or collector/investors who have studied coins first and who have bought coins based upon their own judgment. A lot of people think that if they send money to an investment advisor in the rare coin field they will make money, but historically this has not been the case.

ACCUMULATORS

Although the accumulator tends to be involved with lower-grade and lower-valued coins than either the collector or the investor, there are still many ways that this type of person can—and does—put together coins in an organized manner.

It's possible, for example, to assemble a complete set of Lincoln Memorial cents by date—or even date and mint mark—from coins found routinely in pocket change. The earlier Lincoln cents with the "wheat-ears" design on the reverse have largely disappeared from circulation, but a good cross-section of Lincoln Memorial cents can still be found, going all the way back to 1959, the year they were introduced. Not being as deeply committed to the hobby as the collector, the typical accumulator probably would be satisfied to acquire just one Lincoln Memorial cent of every date, from 1959 to the present, without going on to consider mint marks, as well.

Jefferson nickels would be another good series for the accumulator. These coins have been issued continuously since 1938 without a significant change in design, and many early dates turn up quite routinely in pocket change. Again, the accumulator would probably be content to save just one coin from every year, rather than seeking one coin from every date and mint. That would greatly improve the odds of being able to find a complete set in circulation. The toughest pieces to locate would probably be the "war nickels" minted from 1942 to 1945. Nickel was urgently needed for war-related purposes during those years, so five-cent pieces were made from a substitute alloy—and silver was used in that alloy. Most of these coins have been pulled out of circulation because their silver content gives them premium value. However, they do show up from time to time.

Yet another goal for the accumulator would be to assemble sets of "clad" Roosevelt dimes and Washington quarters—those produced since 1965, without any silver content. As with war nickels, the earlier dimes and quarters have been saved because their silver makes them worth more as metal than as money. No similar reason exists for saving the later coins, so with a little searching these can be found for every date. It might take time; it might be necessary to go to the bank, obtain some rolls and look through them. But all these coins can be found, at least by date.

Frequently, people accumulate the coins of other nations when they take international trips. They bring these coins home, put them in little envelopes or perhaps a special album, and treat them as mementos of their travels.

Sometimes coin accumulations end up being very much like collections. An accumulator would verge on becoming a collector, for example, if she started saving coins with similar themes—coins depicting animals, for example, or coins portraying ships, or possibly coins that were issued by a number of different countries for Olympic Games.

People who collect very expensive coins believe that the value of individual coins is enhanced by assembling them into sets—that the whole, so to speak, is worth more than the sum of its parts. The truth of this has been demonstrated on numerous occasions when exceptional collections have been offered for sale: Their completeness has resulted in substantially higher premiums. There's no reason why this shouldn't apply, as well, to casual accumulations. And whatever the dollars-and-cents value of such an accumulation, there's no doubt at all that the more time and effort someone invests in coins, the more emotional reward he will gain.

COLLECTORS

Collectors place heavy emphasis on completeness—much more so than accumulators do. While accumulators might be satisfied with a date set of Lincoln Memorial cents, for example, collectors would be more inclined to put together a set with not only every date but also every mint-mark variety. And they might very well extend the set back to the start of the whole Lincoln series in 1909. Such a set would require more time and effort, not to mention more expense, but true collectors have this dedication.

Often, collectors assemble sets of coins according to die varieties. Dies are pieces of steel that impart the design to a coin. You might think of them as cookie cutters. Or picture a rubber stamp and a piece of paper: The stamp corresponds to the die and the piece of paper represents the planchet—the metal blank struck by the die. Different sets of dies may vary somewhat in certain details; perhaps the date is slanted on some or the mint mark is slightly larger. The coins that result can then be differentiated, and collected, according to these varieties. Many collectors put together sets by date, mint mark, *and* die variety.

One of the great attractions of coin collecting is the diversity it provides. Coin collectors can—and do—pursue their hobby in almost innumerable ways. Some collect coins by metal, seeking to acquire a representative example of each coin struck in a specific type of metal, such as silver or gold. Others specialize in particular denominations (silver dollars, for instance) or series (Lincoln cents, perhaps) or time period (such as the twentieth century). And, as noted earlier, collecting coins by themes is another very popular approach—and this offers limitless possibilities. The theme can be broad and general, such as animals, ships, or monarchs. Or it can be quite narrow: I know of several collectors who specialize in coins that depict men or women wearing glasses.

More and more collectors have turned in recent years from date-and-mint collecting to a broader kind of approach in which they collect by *type*. In fact, this may be the single most popular method of collecting coins today. A person who collects by type seeks to obtain a single representative example of each different type of coin—one Lincoln cent, for instance, to represent the whole Lincoln series.

To a great extent, the growing popularity of type collecting reflects the fact that coins have risen in value so spectacularly. Purchasing one example for every date and mint can be prohibitively expensive at current market levels, especially in very high grades, so many collectors content themselves with just one coin from each of the different series.

Since they are acquiring only one coin to represent an entire series, most type collectors want that coin to be a particularly nice one. Thus, they seek the highest-grade piece they can find and can afford. Typically, this will be a common-date coin—since such a coin, of course, would be far more affordable than one of the scarcer and more expensive "keys" in the same high level of preservation. A "key" is a low-mintage, high-value coin. Obtaining one of these is a key to completing the series to which it belongs—hence the name.

Collectors with a great deal of patience and perseverance attempt to assemble "matched" sets of coins. These are sets in which all the coins are exactly the same—or very nearly so—not only in grade but also in appearance. If one coin is toned a certain way, all are toned that way. If one is brilliant and lustrous, so are all the others. It takes time, effort, money, and sometimes a little luck to put together a perfectly matched set, but the final result can be a breathtaking achievement—one that will be a source of enormous satisfaction and potentially significant profit.

COLLECTOR/INVESTORS AND INVESTORS

Collector/investors and investors both are impelled by the profit motive: Making money from coins is important to both these groups. But while the investor looks upon coins as commodities, the collector/investor values them as well for their beauty and historical significance.

The coins with the best track records as money-makers are those with the lowest mintages and those in the highest levels of preservation—in other words, those with the greatest rarity and quality. If profit potential is paramount in *your* scheme of things, you ought to be seeking coins that exist in the fewest numbers or that have the fewest flaws—those which haven't passed from hand to hand and betray few nicks and scratches. If you enjoy a challenge and have a well-padded wallet, you might go after coins with *both* these attributes—those which are both rare *and* well preserved.

Investors tend to favor high-grade examples of common-date coins. These coins are said to be "generic," because even though their dates and mint marks may be different, they resemble each other closely in appearance and value. Generic coins exist in significant numbers, even in high grades such as Mint State-65.

To a far greater extent than the investor, the collector/investor is interested in completeness. She shares the collector's impulse to start and finish a set. The collector/investor is a healthy, vibrant breed—one that we're seeing more and more today as the coin business grows into a thriving, bustling multibillion-dollar marketplace.

A lot of coin investors, and even collector/investors, have made mistakes in the past by failing to diversify their holdings. Simply stated, they've put all their eggs in one basket, and all too often the basket has had a hole in it. Perhaps they've heard of a friend or neighbor who made a real killing—a 50-percent profit—on 1881-S Morgan silver dollars, so they've taken all their money and bought up a quantity of 1881-S Morgan dollars graded Mint State-65. But it may have been their misfortune to buy at the top of the cycle, and instead of *making* money, the coins may have decreased in value.

My advice to collector/investors and investors is very simple: Acquire coins by type. For someone with only limited knowledge of coins, this is an excellent way to gain familiarity with the different kinds of coins that are available. It also has the advantage of building in protection against a market decline that hits one kind of coin especially hard. Take the case I just cited, where Morgan dollars suffered a cyclical decline. Chances are that rare-date gold pieces, early type coins, and a number of other coins may not have experienced the same kind of setback, and may have even held their own or gone up. A portfolio containing *all* these different coins would be much more likely to weather any storm and stay on an even keel.

When you collect or invest in coins by type, you're basically getting one representative example of each major kind of U.S. coin that was struck for people to spend. This can be extremely educational—and never underestimate the importance of education in helping you manage an investment. It also can deepen your aesthetic appreciation for U.S. coinage and stimulate your interest in pursuing one or more areas in greater depth—including certain areas you may not have thought about before, if you were aware of them at all.

SECRET TIPS TO HELP YOU MAKE MONEY

Whether you're a collector, an investor, an accumulator, or a combination of some of these, you can profit greatly from inside knowledge. With this in mind, I'm going to share some tips with you—some secret tips—and offer some valuable insights on how coin dealers operate. I've gleaned this information from years as a market insider and, to the best of my knowledge, it isn't available anywhere else except in this book.

The following information doesn't apply to every single dealer, but it does apply to *some*—even *many*. It's up to you to determine which dealers it applies to and which it doesn't apply to—and that's really a matter of using your common sense.

Dealers have an uneven knowledge of coins. Many dealers are specialists in certain areas, and their in-depth knowledge is limited to the one or two certain areas in which they specialize. If they deal in silver dollars and you bring them some Buffalo nickels for an appraisal, they're really not going to know the Buffalo nickel series that well. They might have a working knowledge, but not an intimate one. As a result, these dealers often have a tendency to overprice material in areas outside their specialties—areas about which they don't have special knowledge. They're afraid a more knowledgeable buyer may take advantage of them.

This should make you wary of buying coins from these dealers outside their specialties. At the same time, however, it also can present some exceptional opportunities. If you look closely at *all* the coins in these dealers' stock, you frequently can find a scarce die variety—or even one of the valuable varieties described in Chapter Two of this book. Invariably, you will find it among the coins outside the dealer's specialty. And when you do, you can "rip" it—get it at a price considerably cheaper than what you might have to pay a specialist. In fact, you might be able to turn right around and sell it to a specialist at a profit. This is what's known in the trade as "cherry-picking" a dealer's inventory.

A good way to learn about coins, and develop the ability to cherry-pick, is to go to pubic auctions, where many rare coins of all different kinds are sold in a single place in a concentrated period of time. Make notes before each auction as to which coins you feel are valuable and which you believe to be special varieties. Then see what kind of prices these coins bring at the auction, when knowledgeable professionals are bidding on them. If your selections attract unusually spirited bidding and strong prices, you've probably picked some real cherries.

Dealers can't always grade coins consistently. Many dealers are not all that astute at grading coins. They're excellent businesspeople and fine entrepreneurs; they're honest, well-meaning, hard-working people. But many smaller dealers just aren't all that proficient at grading coins.

Don't take it for granted that a dealer *is* proficient at grading unless he happens to be a market insider—a dealer who is employed by one of the leading grading services, for example, or possibly even a dealer who *owns* a grading service.

Again, this creates tremendous opportunities for *you*, assuming that you're willing to take the time and effort to gain and sharpen that edge. You can acquire a good basic knowledge of grading within six months by reading up on the subject, then attending public auctions and examining as many coins as possible. At that point, you might very well be able to spot instances where dealers have graded coins too conservatively. That would enable you to pick up some real bargains. A note of caution: This is sophisticated stuff, and I would recom-

mend that you not risk any sizable sum of money unless and until you're absolutely sure of your ability. And, above all, don't pretend to be an expert unless
you really are.

Dealers don't heed their own advice during market cycles. Although they
may know better, many dealers tend to get caught up in the ebb and flow of current market activity. Dealers may know in principle that if certain kinds of
coins—let's say Morgan dollars—are increasing in value at a frenzied pace,
they're probably at or near the top of their market cycle. If they went by the
book, they would stand back and say to themselves: "Wait a minute, these coins
have increased 100 percent in three weeks. This increase is just too great; it's a
speculative frenzy; I don't think it's going to last. What's going to happen when
all these people decide to sell their coins and take some profits?"

But dealers are only human, and that makes them prone to common human
frailties such as greed. Consequently, some will get greedy and continue to buy
these coins for their inventory, even though their better judgment tells them the
market cycle is already at the top. And this can be very profitable for *you*. Even
at the top of a cycle, many dealers will still let you realize your profit and sell
your coins back to them because they think the market's going to go even
higher. Conversely, at the bottom of a cycle, you'll have the opportunity in
many cases—not all the time, but many times—to buy coins at bargain-base-
ment levels. At the bottom, many dealers fall prey to yet another basic human
emotion: despair. They become pessimistic and fail to see the light at the end
of the tunnel. The herd mentality infects dealers just as it does any other group,
so often they'll give you a chance to buy coins inexpensively at the bottom of a
cycle.

Thus, in a surprising number of cases, you can sell at the top, because a number of dealers will continue to buy at the top. And you also can buy at the bottom, because so many dealers don't follow their own advice and buy coins
when everyone else is selling.

**Dealers borrow money for their coin activities and are caught short if the
market falls quickly and without notice.** It isn't unusual for the coin market to
fall very quickly and without any notice. In fact, that's the way it usually *does* fall.
When it does, dealers are often caught short financially. What we notice is that after the market retreats, dealers are temporarily unable to buy any more coins. But
this doesn't mean that your coins are now worthless, or worth a great deal less
than they were before. It's just an indication of temporary market illiquidity.

Let's say a dealer is willing to pay you $100 for a certain coin on a Friday afternoon—then, on Monday morning, he doesn't want to buy it at *any* price, or offers you only $5. This kind of drop is simply too dramatic, and you should flatly refuse to sell the coin. Use your common sense: Hold out until the cashflow position of that particular dealer—or perhaps of dealers in general—turns around. My experience has been that if you wait a week or so, the cash flow will improve and you'll be able to sell your coin for a much better price. It may be substantially less than the $100 you were offered on Friday afternoon, but it certainly will be substantially more than the $5 Monday morning offer.

Dealers are your No. 1 source of inside information. One good way to anticipate what may be due to increase in value is to check the price guides and see which coins *haven't* gone up in value for a while. Chances are, some of these coins have been at the bottom of their cycle and now may be ready to move up. And an excellent way to confirm your hunch would be to call a number of different dealers and ask them if they have these coins in stock and whether you can purchase them at the going price. If they *don't* have the coins, or won't let them go at the current market price, you can be pretty sure the supplies are thin—and that would reinforce the likelihood of higher prices soon.

Don't tip your hand, or start speculation, by calling a hundred dealers and asking for one or two particular coins. A better approach would be to ask about a number of different coins—ten or twenty, perhaps—and somewhere in that list include the one or two coins in which you're really interested. If you call a hundred dealers and few of them can provide the coins you want at the going price, that's a sure sign that the coins are ripe for a price increase.

Another tipoff would be if you learned that a certain major dealer has been buying specific coins in significant quantities. Let's say you discover that a mail-order dealer with substantial resources has become an aggressive buyer of high-grade Buffalo nickels. You could logically conclude that this dealer was preparing for a big promotional push on Buffalo nickels. That, of course, would stimulate interest—and heightened interest translates into higher prices. By acting quickly and purchasing high-grade Buffalo nickels yourself *before* the dealer's advertising started to appear, you could put yourself in a position to capitalize on the flurry of new activity. In a sense, you could ride the dealer's coattails.

Prices tend to move quickly during a promotional blitz, rising sharply while the push is on and then falling just as sharply once the campaign is over. Thus, you should view this as a short-term situation. Strike while the iron is hot, then take your profits and celebrate.

Dealers don't use magnifying glasses. Everyone should use a magnifying glass in examining coins—but, quite surprisingly, many dealers don't use a glass all the time. As a result, they sometimes overlook imperfections. This is to your advantage when selling coins to these dealers, but may be to your detriment when you buy. I recommend that you use a 5- or 10-power glass when you look at a coin. And be sure that the magnification and lighting conditions are consistent every time. If possible, coins should be viewed under a pinpoint light source such as a tensor lamp or a halogen lamp. Halogen lamps are becoming increasingly popular in examining proof coins. They enable the viewer to spot small hairline scratches quite readily on these coins.

Dealers are small entrepreneurs with families to support and a need for regular income. A dealer is entitled to a reasonable profit on the coins you buy from him; after all, he's in business to make money. However, I don't recommend that you buy into monthly programs where you give a dealer a set amount of money—say, $100 or $200—every single month to buy you coins. In certain months, there just won't be any great buys available.

Monthly programs are especially inadvisable as a method of acquiring pricier coins. If you're talking about investing 25 or 50 thousand dollars a month, you're far better off to establish a relationship with a dealer and have him call you if a suitable coin becomes available. Otherwise, you're putting too much pressure on the dealer, forcing him to get you something extraordinary when it just might not be available in the marketplace.

Dealers would be happy to take your money each month, in every kind of market, because they have families to support and they need a steady income. But that wouldn't always be best from *your* standpoint.

Dealers have a vested interest in buying coins. If you go to some dealers with a coin worth $1,000 and ask "Hey, what's this worth?" you might be told: "I'll give you $50." Needless to say, these dealers would be all too happy to buy such a coin for $50 and then turn around and sell it at a huge profit. That's why I recommend that you get your coins independently certified—a process I discussed at length in Chapter Eight.

Dealers sometimes handle coins improperly, even leaving fingerprints on the coins. When showing your dealer valuable coins—or *any* coins, for that matter, you should pay close attention and ask him politely not to touch the coins on the obverse or reverse. All too often, some dealers handle coins carelessly, sometimes even dropping them. Don't take for granted that just because someone buys and sells coins for a living, he'll treat your coins with care and pick them up only by the edges. He may *know* the right way to handle coins, but he may not always practice it, especially with regard to someone else's coins.

With certified coins, this really isn't a problem. These coins have been encapsulated in sonically sealed, tamper-resistant holders that protect them from such mishandling. What's more, the grading services will not encapsulate a coin if it has any visible residue on its surface which might cause it to deteriorate at a later date. If a certified coin does deteriorate after being encapsulated, the grading service that certified that coin will buy it back.

Dealers who buy coins in quantity often withdraw their public offers to buy these coins just before major conventions. A number of dealers post "bids" to buy coins that they haven't even seen. They place these bids on computer trading networks that are known as "sight-unseen" systems. If you're selling coins through a sight-unseen system, always check to see if any major coin conventions are taking place or are imminent. You can do this by looking in *Coin World* or *Numismatic News*, the two leading weekly coin newspapers; both publish detailed coin show schedules. Dealers often withdraw or lower their bids before a major convention, since they don't want to be locked in at a high level—with an obligation to buy at that level—if the market suddenly plunges at the convention.

The coin market is a thin marketplace; at any given time, there may be no more than half a dozen dealers with bids posted on the sight-unseen trading network for certain rare coin types. If all of them withdraw or lower their bids for those coins at the same time—and this does happen—the sight-unseen bids will be substantially lower.

As a rule, dealers attend conventions from Thursday through Saturday. With that in mind, don't sell your coins on a Friday afternoon if you know there's a major convention taking place. You might get much better prices by waiting till Monday morning, when the dealers return from the show and reinstate their normal sight-unseen bids.

Dealers sell rejects, or "off" coins, to other dealers at prices below the wholesale level. I recommend that you establish a working relationship with one or more dealers and ask them about the deals they may have available. Most dealers have certain coins they're willing to sell at discounted prices, but often they prefer to sell these coins to other dealers. By making your interest known, you can sometimes gain access to such deals.

For instance, a dealer may have a certain coin that's been in his stock for six months, and he may just be tired of seeing it. He may say to himself: "You know, it's not that great a coin. I paid $500 for it, but I'd be willing to sell it to another dealer for $300 just to get rid of it. It's not the nicest coin I've ever seen, so I don't want to sell it to a retail client." If you were able to buy this coin for $300, you might be able to turn around and sell it to somebody else for $350 or $400, so it might be a very good deal for you. You might even find it attractive and decide to keep it yourself. Beauty, after all, is often in the eye of the beholder.

By establishing a good relationship with a dealer, you can put yourself in a position to purchase cut-rate coins even before they're offered to other dealers. Remember, you *pay* for the special coins; you pay top dollar for exceptional coins that the dealer *wants* his retail clients to have. So why not cut yourself in on bargain coins when those become available?

Dealers absolutely obey the law and file IRS reports on you if you buy coins for cash. The law requires coin and bullion dealers to file a report with the Internal Revenue Service any time you—or your agent or representative—pay more than $10,000 in cash for coin purchases during a given calendar year. And whether they tell you about them or not, the dealers absolutely do file these reports. Never buy coins for cash; always pay by check. Further details on this subject can be found in Chapter Thirteen.

LEGAL ADVICE

When I need legal advice about a numismatic matter, I often turn to Armen R. Vartian, an attorney in Manhattan Beach, California, who specializes in art and collectibles issues. Vartian is Legal Counsel to the Professional Numismatists Guild (PNG), former General Counsel to the American Numismatic Association (ANA), and represents many leading coin dealers and auction houses in the country, as well as individual collectors and investors.

Based on my discussions with Vartian, here are a few suggestions on what to consider when doing business with a coin dealer.

- How did you learn about the dealer? Some dealers advertise in numismatic publications, where they know that potential customers already know some-

beautiful that even if some of your coins fail to appreciate monetarily, you still come out ahead because you get *aesthetic* appreciation.

Of course, you would prefer to gain *both* types of appreciation, and that's where *One-Minute Coin Expert* comes in. By following the guidelines and using the secret tips I've given you in this chapter, you'll have a big head start in picking coins with the potential to realize tremendous gains.

CHAPTER 10

HOW TO CASH IN
THOSE BIG PROFITS

Congratulations! You've looked in the cookie jar, searched the attic, checked your pocket change—and now you're ready to go to the cash window and celebrate. You've found some coins that are valuable, other coins that are extremely valuable, and still other coins that may even be super-rarities.

Maybe you've discovered a circulated 1932 double eagle ($20 gold piece) worth $5,000. Or possibly you've come up with a circulated 1797 Draped Bust half dollar with 15 stars on the front, which is worth a tidy $18,500. These coins are easy enough to sell; dealers all over the nation want to buy them. I'll provide you with details later in this chapter on how to sell them.

But suppose you've really struck it rich. Suppose, for instance, you've found a circulated 1870-S three-dollar gold piece worth half a million dollars. It's easy enough to sell this coin, too. But it's not quite so simple to obtain the full value for a coin in this rarefied price range. You may have dealers across the country beating a path to your door and wanting to buy it for $300,000. You may even find a couple of dealers willing to buy it for $400,000. But if you want to sell it for its full value, you may have to wait a little while—or even longer—in order to maximize what you can sell it for.

Generally, the higher the price you ask for your 1870-S three-dollar gold piece, or any other extremely valuable coin, the longer you'll have to wait for a buyer. But this is not unique to rare coins. It's much like what you would encounter, for example, if you tried to sell your house.

A friend of mine owned a house in New Jersey, where the real estate market was depressed at the time. He decided to move with his family to a different part of the state, and he foolishly bought a house there without first making sure to sell his first house. He was confident he could sell it with no problem at all if he simply lowered the price somewhat.

Surprise! Many months elapsed without a single offer on the old house, leaving my friend in a major cash-flow bind since he needed the proceeds from that house to help finance the new one.

Big-ticket coins are sometimes very much like real estate. If you own a coin for which you paid $100,000, selling it may not be as quick and easy a deal as you might think. You can't simply take it to any of a thousand willing dealers, all of whom have $100,000 in cash on hand and are pleading with you to let them buy that coin.

Selling your extremely valuable coins is similar to selling your house. You might be able to sell that coin, or that piece of real estate, almost instantaneously; maybe you'll simply get lucky. In most cases, though, especially in instances where the coin is worth a whole lot of money, the process of selling is a much longer one and one which requires some planning and some good, quick-witted common sense on your part.

A few years ago, a rare and beautiful U.S. gold coin was sold for more than $1.5 million. The coin is an "ultra-high-relief" 1907 double eagle, or $20 gold piece, designed by renowned sculptor Augustus Saint-Gaudens. This coin was graded Mint State-68 on the 1 through 70 scale by the Numismatic Guaranty Corporation.

This probably was not an instantaneous sale; this was not a spur-of-the-moment transaction where a coin dealer had the coin in his hip pocket and said to himself, "You know, I think I might want to sell this coin because I need the money." This wasn't a situation where he just went out and walked up to someone who said, "I'll give you a million-and-a-half for it," and then the coin dealer said "okay" and the buyer took $1.5 million out of his back pocket and put the money on the table.

Transactions such as this involve detailed negotiations—frequently extended ones. They're planned far ahead of time and the people selling these coins give careful consideration to psychological factors in the marketplace.

Financial service professionals regard stocks as being "continuously liquid." At any given time, you can take a share of stock and sell it for the price that's published in the newspaper or the current trading price of that stock—and for every share you sell, you'll receive a uniform price. At any given time, that stock is salable.

To a certain extent, some coins which are not great rarities enjoy this same advantage. We often see $1,000 coins and $500 coins and $100 coins which, for all practical purposes, are continuously liquid. But when we start talking about large groups of these coins, or coins which have fancy price tags, these coins lack continuity of liquidity. These coins are not always readily salable at any given time.

Let's say a dealer has three boxes of coins and he takes them to a show, figuring he can sell them under current market conditions for $2 million. But when he gets to the show, where many other dealers have a chance to examine the coins, the best offer he gets is only $1 million. Chances are that dealer wouldn't sell those coins. He would wait until the next show, figuring he would get a better offer. He might have to wait a month to find the right buyer, the person willing to pay $2 million—or close to $2 million—for those coins, but the difference in price would make the wait worthwhile.

In this case and other cases like it, the "right buyer" is the person who:

- *Needs the coin*—a dealer who needs it to sell to a collector; a collector who needs it to complete a collection; a collector-investor who needs it for a type set.

- *Appreciates the coin*—someone who appreciates its cultural, artistic, or historical significance; someone who appreciates its rarity; someone who appreciates its high grade; someone who likes the design of this kind of coin; someone who finds the toning unusually attractive.

- *Has the money to pay for the coin*—someone who can pay for it within a reasonable time.

If someone is buying a coin for a million dollars, he can't be expected to pay for it tomorrow. And if he is able to pay for it tomorrow, he, in turn, will expect the seller to extend advantageous terms. If he can pay for it within a month or two, that's fine. When I speak of someone who can pay for the coin, I don't necessarily mean a dealer with the money in his hip pocket. It could instead be a dealer who knows a private collector who wants that particular coin, or a dealer who can secure the proper financing. This ability, coupled with his own financial resources, would enable him to give you the best possible price for the coin you're selling.

Unless all three of these factors are involved, there won't be any sale.

This is really no different from what you would encounter in trying to sell a house. Unless you were lucky enough to find the right buyer—someone who needed your house, appreciated your house, and had the money to buy it—you wouldn't be able to swap your "For Sale" sign for one reading "Sold."

THE MONEY SUPPLY

The coin market's money supply is governed by four basic factors: cash flow, debt payments, bank collateral, and market fluctuations.

Cash flow is the two-way pattern of payments: money received by a dealer and money spent. If a dealer sells a coin for $1,000 but doesn't get paid by his client for thirty days—even though the dealer had to pay for the coin right away—that dealer may very well have a cash-flow problem. This type of negative cash flow, multiplied by a number of different deals, could have a significant impact on that coin dealer's ability to pay a strong price for your coins at any given time.

Just about everyone has *debt payments*, and coin dealers are certainly no exception. Dealers who maintain coin shops often have heavy debts, including mortgage payments and installment-loan payments on expensive computer equipment. These debts can sometimes limit their ability to wheel and deal freely in buying and selling coins.

Many dealers also are repaying loans for which they have used coins as *bank collateral*. When the market goes down, many dealers in a sense "hock" some of their coins in order to obtain needed cash. In the late 1980s a dealer might have taken $500,000 worth of coins to the SafraBank of California, or some other institution offering such a service, and been able to obtain a loan for 50 percent—or sometimes as much as 70 percent—of the coins' value, based on the current sight-unseen prices on the computerized trading network. Some banks still offer such loans.

Dealers have to make payments on such loans—and if coin prices go down further, they have to come up with more coins (or other assets) to keep the value of their collateral at 50 or 70 percent of their loan balance. Otherwise, they have to repay the money. Thus, a declining market can place a particular strain on dealers using coins as collateral—and, in the process, magnify the weakness of the money supply in the marketplace as a whole.

Market fluctuations can never be predicted with pinpoint accuracy, but they certainly play a role in determining how much—or how little—money will be available. Dealers' profits are maximized in a rising market, and that in turn gives them more money to spend on buying coins.

SALES OPTIONS

There are three primary methods by which you can sell your coins: direct sale, electronic trading networks, and public auctions.

Direct sale is a highly personalized, specialized area which won't be covered in great detail in this book because it involves such subjectivity—such interpersonal chemistry between the seller and buyer. I don't recommend the direct sale approach because in many cases, the person buying the coins has a vested interest in the outcome of the transaction.

The buyer might say your coins are worth nothing when, in fact, they're really worth thousands—or even millions—of dollars. That's why third-party certification is so important. If you have coins and you don't know what they're worth, you should get them independently certified before you attempt to sell them.

Electronic Trading The principal network through which you can sell your coins electronically is the Certified Coin Exchange (CCE). You'll have to get your coins certified beforehand by one of the two leading coin-grading services.

The Certified Coin Exchange accepts coins certified by either the Professional Coin Grading Service (PCGS) or the Numismatic Guaranty Corporation of America (NGC).

To use this trading option, you'll need to have a dealer submit your coins to NGC or PCGS. Both firms will be happy to provide you with a free list of member dealers. You'll find these dealers extremely helpful. Once your coins are certified, the dealer you select will help you again in determining the current sight-unseen bids. Just ask him to show you the computer screen or a printout of the current high bids. Chances are, the dealer will charge a commission of 10 or 15 percent to handle the sale for you. And that is certainly fair and reasonable.

The electronic exchanges will be of greatest use to you in selling coins that are fungible—high-grade examples of common-date coins that resemble each other in appearance and value and thus are interchangeable. These coins are said to be commoditized, and they lend themselves readily to sight-unseen trading, especially when they trade for less than $250 apiece.

As I explained earlier, these coins are continuously liquid for all practical purposes—unless you have several million dollars' worth that you want to dump at one time. The coin market has a number of small entrepreneurs, and if you try to sell several million dollars' worth of anything, it's not going to be as easy as selling a smaller quantity with a lower market value. You could certainly do it; a transaction in the millions could certainly be consummated. But it probably would take a lot more time and effort.

Auction Sales Auction sales offer some highly significant advantages to you as a seller, and I happen to like this particular option very much. These sales bring many prospective buyers together in one place, and that can produce competitive bidding that will drive up the prices you receive.

In a conventional auction, your coins are showcased in a beautiful catalog, where they are described very attractively—and possibly pictured, as well. This helps produce a sort of mystique, a sense that the auction coins are special. And that, in turn, enhances the prices they realize.

Conventional auctions do have a downside, however. First and foremost is the fact that substantial time will pass between when you consign the coins and when you receive your money. Typically, it takes about two to three months for coins to come under the gavel after they're submitted to an auction company for sale in the conventional manner. Then, after the auction, another thirty to forty-five days will pass before you receive your money.

Clearly, the time lag involves a serious risk. Let's say you consign some coins to an auction house in January and they don't come up for sale until March. If the coin market experienced a cyclical decline and your coins went down in value 10 or 20 percent from January to March, you would receive a lower return. And this kind of cyclical decline isn't uncommon. There are ways to protect your coins from selling at auction for unacceptably low prices, and I'll discuss these shortly. However, there's no way to force bidders to pay January prices in March when the March prices are lower, and you should keep this in mind when deciding whether to sell your coins at auction.

The growing volatility in the marketplace has increased the possibility that coins could go down in value after being consigned for public auction. This has given rise to a quick and easy new method of selling coins at auction. One company calls this method the "express auction." Another calls it the "bullet auction." Whatever the name, it's a method that greatly reduces the delay of the conventional auction route.

Suppose you have a coin whose value has risen 200 percent since you acquired it and you want to cash out and take your profit. At the same time, however, you want to be sure of getting the highest price, and you feel the best way to do that is to sell the coin at auction. By consigning the coin to a company that conducts express—or bullet—auctions, you can benefit from the competitive bidding atmosphere of a public auction without enduring the worrisome lag time often inherent in old-style auction sales. There's a good chance your coin can be sold at one of the new, quicker auctions within a few weeks. And the payment will be quicker, too. Companies conducting express auctions require faster payment from successful bidders, and they in turn then pay their consignors almost at once.

This type of auction is becoming an extremely viable alternative. And besides saving you time, it can also save you money. That's because express or bullet auctions tend to be "no-frills" sales, creating substantial savings which then can be passed along. The catalogs for these auctions can't be as elaborate, for example, because of the limited time; they can't make lavish use of full-color illustrations as conventional auction catalogs often do. Because of such economies, the commission you'll have to pay is likely to be significantly lower than at a traditional auction house.

Market secret: If you decide to sell your coins by means of an express or bullet auction, consign them only to a company that also conducts the more elaborate, more traditional kind. These full-service companies have built up large mailing lists and enjoy the patronage of many thousands of clients to whom they can send catalogs for their sales, including the quicker auctions. If a "fly-by-night" firm were to set up one of these quickie auctions, you wouldn't get good results in many cases.

HOW TO PROTECT YOURSELF WHEN YOU SELL A COIN AT AUCTION

There are three potential risks in buying and selling coins.

Probably first and foremost is the *buy risk*—the risk that what you get will be less than what you paid for. As long as you limit your purchases to coins that have been certified, the buy risk will be greatly minimized or even eliminated.

Then there is the *market risk*—the risk that if you buy a coin, instead of going up by 300 percent it might go down a couple of percentage points.

Finally, you have the *sell risk*—the risk that when you dispose of your coins, the payment you receive will be less than what they're worth. To use an extreme example, you might have coins worth $100,000 and some unscrupulous dealer might offer you only $50. If you were naive enough to sell them for $50, the dealer would then go out and sell those coins for their true value and reap the enormous dividend that rightfully should have been yours.

Selling your less expensive coins at auction isn't like selling real estate by the same sales route. Houses and other pieces of real estate often change hands at auction for substantially less than their normal market value—what they would bring if their owners had time to sit tight and wait for the right buyer, the buyer with the combination of ingredients I outlined earlier in this chapter. Desirable coins tend to bring strong prices when sold at auction; there's great competition for these coins.

Sometimes, an auction company will agree to take raw coins—coins that have not been certified—and describe them optimistically in its catalog. This would make these coins appear to be in a higher grade than they actually are. In a sense, this is not unlike what a used car dealer does when he takes a car that's a lemon, represents it to be a cream puff, and sells it on someone's behalf to an unsuspecting consumer. An auction company might be willing to do this on your behalf—so before consigning your coins for sale in the company's auction, you should first ask what grade it intends to assign to each coin.

If the auction company doesn't want to grade your coins in accordance with your wishes, I recommend that you have them independently certified before consigning them. This would establish their actual grade beyond any reasonable doubt. They might not then be graded optimistically in the catalog, but they also wouldn't be given too low a grade. Be sure to have your coins certified only by leading grading services.

Any time you sell your coins, you should seek to take advantage of market trends; in other words, you should try to anticipate upward movements and time your auction consignments so the coins' sale coincides closely with a cycle's high. This, of course, is easier said than done, and even the experts guess wrong now and then.

To protect yourself against the possibility that you may be guessing wrong, and that the market may actually decline before your coins come up for sale, you should work out an arrangement with the auction house beforehand to assign a "reserve" value to each of your coins. If the bidding fails to reach this level, you will then get to keep the coins. You may have to pay a commission on the reserve price, but at least your coins won't be sold for less than they're worth.

The traditional, or three-month, auction route is best suited to coins that are real rarities. These coins need the exposure they receive in fancy catalogs and extensive promotional buildups. Elaborate trappings aren't really "frills" when it comes to great rarities, since it takes this kind of approach to attract the right kind of buyer for such coins.

If you have commodity-type coins such as common-date Morgan dollars graded Mint State-65, you can place these in bullet sales or sell them through the electronic exchanges.

If you have coins that fall somewhere in between, such as beautiful Mint State-65 or Proof-65 Liberty Seated quarters that are worth perhaps $2,000 each, you certainly could consign them to a bullet sale. But these coins should not be sold over the electronic exchanges. Each of these coins has an idiosyncratic quality of toning, of appearance, and the electronic exchanges tend to minimize, rather than maximize, special qualities. These exchanges emphasize the *similarities* that certain coins possess, not their *differences*—and beautiful toning can be a very positive difference that makes a coin more valuable than the norm.

Competition is healthy for sellers; when selling your coins, you want as many buyers as possible competing to purchase them. At an auction, the competition is already built in: The gallery will be filled with people who are vying for your coins. But if for some reason you don't want to sell a coin at auction, you still can stimulate strong competition for that coin—and get the highest price possible—by showing it to twelve or fifteen different dealers and having each one give you a sealed bid. This isn't nearly as effective as the public auction route, but it's better than going to just one dealer and being at his mercy.

Selling your coins can be a pleasurable and profitable experience. Just remember that some coins can be sold more readily than others, and all coins can be sold more readily at certain times than at other times. You can sell a million-dollar coin instantaneously, but you may get only $800,000 for that coin.

With super-rarities, if you want to maximize the amount of money you get, you may have to wait a little while. With coins valued at $10,000—and even $20,000 or $30,000—you can get full value almost immediately.

CHAPTER 11

SCOTT TRAVERS'
SECRET TOP TWELVE

Coins that have great potential to rise in value sharply, but aren't yet performing at close to their potential, are said to be *sleepers*.

Sleepers can be found among certified coins—coins that have been examined, graded, and encapsulated by one of the leading grading services. They also can be found among "raw" coins—coins that haven't yet been certified and encased (or "slabbed") in sonically sealed, hard plastic holders.

Some sleepers have greater potential than others. In this chapter, I reveal a secret list of twelve coins, or types of coins, which are among the biggest sleepers of all—the very best buys—in the current marketplace.

If you have money to spend on rare coins, these are potential purchases that merit your serious consideration, since all are excellent values.

You may not have to buy some of these coins; it's certainly possible to find any or all of them in an old collection or accumulation that may be sitting right now in a drawer or cigar box in your home.

Recently, I performed an appraisal for people who had come into possession of just such a group of rare coins. The people who owned these coins thought they had little or no value—but when I examined them, I found they included a number of rare and valuable pieces, among them low-mintage proofs. At my suggestion, the owners got some of them certified; the coins came back from the grading service with grades as high as Proof-65, making them worth premiums ranging as high as tens of thousands of dollars per coin.

If you do find some of the coins on my secret list—in the cookie jar, in the attic, or in an old collection you received as an inheritance—hold on to them. Because of their great potential, all these coins could rise in value dramatically in the long run, or even in a much shorter term. Think twice before selling them; they could bring you much more substantial returns later on.

If you don't find any of these twelve sleepers but are thinking of investing in coins, these would be excellent items to buy. I've chosen a cross-section of coins with current retail prices ranging from modest amounts to six-figure sums, so you'll find something here for just about every budget.

In buying them, as in selling them, certification is highly advisable. "Slabbed" coins—those that have been certified—enjoy broad popularity and great liquidity in today's coin market, and by limiting your transactions to certified coins you will greatly enhance the security of your investment.

You can buy or sell a number of certified coins sight-unseen through any of the hundreds of coin dealers nationwide who are members of the Certified Coin Exchange (CCE). And while prices fluctuate, you can get a good idea of your coins' current value by referring to the values in the *Certified Coin Dealer Newsletter* (or *Bluesheet*), an authoritative weekly price guide of the sight-unseen market. This publication is also an excellent indicator of which grading services are in favor at any given time, since it lists market prices only for the services whose coins are most widely traded.

Here, then, is my special twelve-coin list:

1.   The certified business strike United States "generic" gold coin.
    As I have said many times in my public pronouncements, when precious metals increase, so do rare coins—and as go the metals, so goes the rare coin market.

We are seeing feverish interest in the metals as this book is being revised in August 2004. Gold is over $400 an ounce. And the interest in gold coins that goes with this is exceptional.

Saint-Gaudens double eagles ($20 gold pieces) graded Mint State-65 cost several thousand dollars apiece in 1988 and sell today for about $1,500. With the possibility of gold reaching for the moon, it's not inconceivable that they could jump to $3,000 or $3,500. In August 2004, you could buy nice Saint-Gaudens double eagles graded MS-65 by the Professional Coin Grading Service (PCGS) or the Numismatic Guaranty Corporation of America (NGC) for $1,500 or so, with hand-selected premium-quality coins trading for just a little bit more. There is a supply of these coins, but not an oversupply. They're available, but strong new demand could push their price substantially higher. They're beautiful coins, and each contains nearly an ounce of gold. With these, as with all my recommendations, I strongly urge you to buy only coins that have been certified.

Gold coins are in demand because of what newsletter editor Maurice Rosen calls the economic justification for owning it—and those with bigger budgets might do well to consider buying some of that gold in the form of high-grade $3 gold pieces. A PCGS MS-65 specimen will run about $8,000, and an NGC MS-65 is about $7,500. These are delightful coins, and if gold goes up $100 an ounce, this type of coin has the potential to enjoy a 40-percent increase in value.

With the kind of activity we're seeing now in gold and the possibility that the yellow metal may rise to $500 or more an ounce, $10 Libs (with-motto Liberty eagles or $10 gold pieces) graded MS-64 appear to be very attractive coins. I like the ones from 1866 to 1907, with the motto IN GOD WE TRUST above the eagle. In MS-64, a with-motto $10 Lib is an $1,100 coin today—and the NGC price is a little bit higher than the PCGS price. You should check the *Certified Coin Dealer Newsletter* to see if there's a difference in price between the two services; sometimes NGC is higher, sometimes PCGS. The $10 Lib is a relatively large coin and is fairly scarce in this condition, both of which heighten its appeal. It was much higher-priced some years ago, and the current price more than doubles from MS-64 to MS-65. I can see this $1,100 coin becoming an $1,800 coin if demand increases as a result of a higher gold price.

Indian $10s graded MS-63 are fabulous coins too, and people really love them. They're large gold coins with an exquisite design by Augustus Saint-Gaudens whose beauty rivals that of his magnificent double eagle. As this is written, MS-63 Indian $10s are priced at $750. I wouldn't be surprised if that price doubled to $1,500. Certainly $1,000 is a realistic expectation at some future time. There's a wide variance of quality with these coins. You might find an MS-63 with lots of minor nicks and scratches on the obverse, and under a glass it might look like an MS-62 or even an MS-61—but at a glance, to the unaided eye, it might appear to be an MS-64 or even marginally an MS-65. Exercise great care in selecting these coins, and be aware of the variance in quality, especially regarding scratches on the obverse.

Warning: Values of these gold coins can be extremely volatile. Learn the idiosyncratic qualities of the generic gold coin market, and consult a competent coin dealer and financial professional before jumping in. These prices are current as of August 2004, but can change dramatically and without notice. Economic conditions could actually push the price of gold downward, and that would make the performance of these coins less than golden.

2. Proof war nickels.

Production of U.S. proof coins was halted by the Mint during World War II. Prior to the suspension, though, the Mint did produce a proof version of one "war nickel": the five-cent emergency issue made at the main Mint in Philadelphia in 1942. This coin has a large "P" above Monticello's dome. (*Note:* Prior to removing nickel from the coin, the Mint also made proof 1942 Jefferson five-cent pieces of the standard copper-nickel composition. To be sure your coin is a war nickel proof, check for the "P" above the dome.)

In Proof-66, a 1942-P war nickel certified by an independent grading service would cost you only about $200 sight-unseen. An extra-nice specimen actually seen before purchase would cost perhaps $225. These are sensational values.

These coins contain silver. They're quite scarce, with a mintage of only 27,600, and a lot of them have deteriorated, making the survivors even scarcer. They're novel—the only proof examples of the war nickel type. Noncollectors appreciate them because of their uniqueness. And, best of all, they're reasonably priced.

Besides being great values, they're also marvelous conversation pieces—something you can keep around the house and impress your friends with. People are fascinated when they see a "nickel" coin made of silver. And because of their unparalleled quality, proof coins showcase this difference best of all.

3. 1955 doubled-die Lincoln cents graded Mint State-63.

In 1955, popular music wasn't the only area of American life that was undergoing major change. Coin collecting, too, was beginning to rock and roll as millions of people with newfound leisure time on their hands began to immerse themselves in hobbies. Coin collecting was one of the principal beneficiaries of this cultural change—and in 1955, the U.S. Mint inadvertently gave this process a major boost by creating a new one-cent piece with a weird and very obvious error.

This coin is known to specialists as the "doubled-die" Lincoln cent. It's instantly recognizable even to novices, though, by the dramatic double images of the date and other features on the "heads" side (the reverse was not affected). This mint mistake came about because of misalignment in a process known as "hubbing" of dies at the Philadelphia Mint. A coin is produced by striking a *planchet*, or blank piece of metal, with two dies—one bearing the design for the head's side, or obverse, the other having the elements for the reverse. On each die, the design is in mirror image. A die, in turn, is produced by striking a piece of tempered steel with a hub—a harder piece of steel on which the design is positive, or exactly the way it will look on the finished coin. To sharpen the impression, workmen give each master die multiple blows with the hub. In rare instances, the hub and die become misaligned between blows—and when that happens, the die emerges with doubling of the images. That's what occurred in 1955.

The problem was discovered, but not before small but significant quantities of the misstruck cents—about 30,000, it's believed—had been mixed with normal coins. Inspectors decided to let the misstrikes go, rather than destroy the whole batch. Soon, the coins began turning up along the East Coast, especially in New England, and sharp-eyed collectors began to set them aside. Most were pulled from pocket change at a fairly early stage, but almost all did circulate at least to a modest extent. As a result, mint-state specimens are extremely elusive. At this writing, a red and brown piece graded Mint State-63 might cost you $2,500. But this is a rare and coveted coin in a series that enjoys tremendous popularity with collectors. A few years from now, $2,500 may look, in retrospect, like a bargain.

4. Trade dollars graded Proof-63 or Proof-64.

After the Civil War, the U.S. government turned its attention abroad and sought to expand its trade with foreign nations. As part of this effort, Congress created a new silver coin called the Trade dollar. This coin was similar in size and appearance to the regular silver dollar, but contained a bit more silver. It was meant for use in the Orient, where merchants preferred to be paid with precious-metal coins.

The Trade dollar was a short-lived and essentially unsuccessful innovation: It remained in production for little more than a decade, from 1873 to 1885, and during the last seven years it was minted only in proof form, for sale at a premium to the public. However, it's a high-priced and highly prized collectible.

Trade dollars graded Proof-63 and Proof-64 are sleepers. Once again, there's a gap between the market prices in Proof-64 and Proof-65. As this is written, a Proof-64 example has a fair market retail value of $ 2,500, while a Proof-65 is worth $6,000. And the difference in appearance between these two coins is very slight.

I especially like Proof-63 Trade dollars. These are priced right now at only about $1,700 each—and like their Proof-64 counterparts, many appear quite similar to Proof-65 pieces when viewed with the unaided eye. You can get a coin that's virtually identical to a Proof-65 except for a couple of hair-lines. And buyers have a tendency to overlook those minuscule hairlines when viewing a coin with great aesthetic appeal. You're getting a coin with almost the same eye appeal for only about one-fifth the price.

Look for a Proof-63 Trade dollar with dramatic contrast between its snow-white devices (the raised portions of the design) and its chromium-like fields (the flat background areas). You might have to pay a somewhat higher price than you would for an ordinary Proof-63, but the extra cost would be money well spent. That type of stunning cameo contrast would make such a coin tremendously appealing to most people who saw it, and they'd probably disregard the hairlines that reduced its technical grade.

Be on the lookout for Trade dollars which have been certified as Proof-63 by one of the leading independent grading services. Many of these coins can be taken out of their holders and sold at a later time for a higher price. I've seen many dealers do just that: They'll buy a certified Proof-63 Trade dollar at a convention for the going price—let's say $1,700—and then take it out of its "slab" and sell it immediately at the same convention for $3,000 to $4,000 to another dealer who thinks that he can get it certified as Proof-65.

Caution: Be careful in purchasing "raw" (or uncertified) proof Trade dol-lars. Many of these coins have been certified and encapsulated and then re-moved from their plastic holders because their owners felt the assigned grades were too low. You may be misled into grading such a coin optimisti-cally and thus paying too much for it.

5. **Proof-64 Variety 3 Liberty Head double eagles (1877–1907).**
    The double eagle, or $20 gold piece, is the largest gold coin the U.S. Mint ever made for use in commerce. Each of these coins contains nearly one full ounce of gold, giving it a value of several hundred dollars just as metal. But many double eagles are much more than merely pieces of metal: They're beautiful, desirable collectibles that often command premiums of tens, or even hundreds, of thousands of dollars.

The double eagle made its first appearance in 1849, so it is, quite literally, a "Forty-Niner." It was, in fact, the California Gold Rush that gave rise to the issuance of this coin. It remained an important part of U.S. coinage for more than eighty years before being discontinued in 1933, at a time when Americans were mired in the Great Depression.

The first double eagle produced by the Mint is known as the Coronet or Liberty Head type because its design depicts a crowned figure of Liberty.

This type, in turn, is divided into three different varieties because of small but important differences in the inscriptions. Double eagles minted from 1877 to 1907 are denoted as Variety 3 because they bear the inscription *IN GOD WE TRUST* and have the words *TWENTY DOLLARS* spelled out at the base of the reverse.

Very few proof double eagles were produced: In most years, the total proof mintage was less than one hundred. Proof-64 examples of the Variety 3 Liberty Head double eagle are almost unknown—yet they can be acquired for about $30,000 each. This sounds like a lot of money, and it is. But it's really quite a bargain—in fact, it's an absolutely phenomenal value—because these coins are so rare and so desirable. In Proof-66, the same coin would probably cost upwards of $85,000, and there's really little difference in the way the two coins look.

In buying proof double eagles, acquire only coins with cameo contrast—that is, a strong contrast between the devices (the raised portions of the design) and the fields (the flat background areas). Ideally, the devices should be frosted and the fields should have a lovely mirror-like sheen.

You can expect cameo proofs to cost a little more than regular ones; they generally sell for 10 to 15 percent, or even 20 percent, above the cost of their counterparts without the cameo contrast. But the difference in price is negligible compared with the increased value this eye-catching feature will impart to your spectacular coin.

Double eagles are very large coins with exceptional appeal to noncollectors. Never underestimate the importance of size as a selling point with such buyers. Investors are smitten with large, bold-looking coins—especially when they're made from gold or silver. That's why silver dollars are so popular with investors, and double eagles enjoy the same kind of popularity.

As the coin market expands and more and more noncollectors enter the field, interest in coins such as proof double eagles will almost surely grow by leaps and bounds. Many of these newcomers will have large sums of money to spend, and many will be drawn to big, beautiful coins made of gold and silver.

The Proof-64 Variety 3 Liberty double eagle is rare. Its aesthetic appeal is awesome. And it has a rock-solid collector base. Add up all these elements and what you have is a coin with almost unlimited potential. We may very well see this coin command a six-figure price tag in the not-too-distant future if the coin market expands as I expect it to.

6. Mint State-65 and Proof-65 copper coins.

Copper coins in general, just about across the board, are really exceptional sleepers. These coins didn't participate to any great extent in the market's spectacular boom of the late 1970s and early 1980s, and while major copper rarities have certainly risen in value over the years, their growth has been far more limited than that of similar coins in gold and silver.

The reasons for this are partly physical and partly psychological. Copper coins are susceptible to unsightly—and irreversible—discoloration, and this can cause permanent impairment of their surfaces and substantial reduction in their value. Damage of this type can be averted with proper precautions, but instead of being familiarized with the precautions, investors have been systematically discouraged over the years from even considering copper coins. This has created a deep-seated bias against these coins in many buyers' minds.

Concern is certainly warranted, but blind rejection of all copper coins is an overreaction. Besides closing their minds, investors who harbor this prejudice are also closing the door to profits that are potentially very sizable.

Matte-proof Lincoln cents were made by the U.S. Mint from 1909 to 1916. Their surfaces have a dull, almost sandblasted type of look, very unlike the mirror-like appearance of most other U.S. proof coins. Identifying these proofs can be tricky for the uninitiated, so I advise you to buy only coins that have been certified. In grading these coins, and copper coins in general, independent grading services distinguish between those that are fully original in color (certified as "RD" for "Red"), those that have some original color but also some toning (certified as "RB" for "Red and Brown") and those that are fully toned (certified as "BN" for "Brown"). Fully red Proof and Mint State coins are considered the most desirable, but many buyers favor copper coins with toning, since these are less susceptible to possible surface damage.

I particularly like matte-proof Lincoln cents that have been certified by one of the leading independent grading services as Proof-65 RB (Red and Brown). As this is written, these coins can be obtained for just $150, and that's an incredible value. They're extremely underrated and very, very difficult to obtain. At $1,400, matte-proof Lincolns certified as Proof-65 RD (Red) are also excellent buys. Often, a coin certified as Proof-65 Red and Brown can be resubmitted to a grading service and then will be assigned a new grade of Proof-65 Red, effectively almost quadrupling its market value.

Matte-proof Lincolns graded Proof-64 RD (Red) are also very good values. As of this writing, these coins are priced at $500 each, and I consider that a phenomenal bargain. But don't buy a Proof-64 with the idea of resubmitting the coin to an independent grading service in quest of an upgrade to Proof-65. With these particular coins, there's a big difference between 64 and 65 and I don't think you'll be able to buy a Proof-64 RD for $500, resubmit the coin, and get back a Proof-65 RD worth $1,400. It really doesn't happen in this area. But the Proof-64 still represents a terrific value.

7. **Proof-66 nickel three-cent pieces, Shield nickels, and Liberty Head nickels.**

Nickel coins never have enjoyed the same kind of respect as their gold and silver cousins, but often they're rarer—and should be more valuable— in very high grades and with very sharp strikes. Being a harder metal, nickel doesn't yield crisp design details as readily as gold and silver when struck. And nickel coins are more prone to environmental damage over long periods of time, so fewer survive in pristine levels of preservation.

Surviving populations of nineteenth-century nickel coins are quite small in Proof-66, and at the height of the coin market's boom in 1989 some of these coins were bringing many thousands of dollars. Today, those same coins change hands for a great deal less. A coin that sold at auction for $8,000 in 1989 might well be available now for less than $1,000. And it's still every bit as rare.

Caution: Even though they may have been certified by one of the leading grading services, Proof-66 three-cent nickels, Shield nickels, and Liberty Head nickels should be free of carbon spots—that is, intense toning areas which appear to be black. If a coin has any of these spots, you should reject it, no matter how high the grade at which it has been certified.

8. **Capped Bust half dimes.**

The term "half dime" sounds strange to us today, since we're so accustomed to calling our five-cent piece the "nickel." In reality, however, the nickel as we know it is a relatively recent innovation. The five-cent piece wasn't introduced in its present size and composition until 1866. Up to then, and even after that for a few additional years, Americans used a small silver coin called the half dime.

Half dimes were among the earliest U.S. coins, making their first appearance in 1792. One of the earliest types was a coin known as the Capped Bust half dime, which showed Miss Liberty wearing an old-style cap. Half dimes of this type are very, very popular and also quite rare in top condition.

In Proof-66, Capped Bust half dimes are an exceptional value. They're far from inexpensive: At present, the sight-unseen price is about $28,000. But that's not much more than the comparable price for a Proof-65 example, which currently is worth $23,000.

These coins demonstrate that something can be a really terrific value even if it carries a hefty price tag.

9. **Franklin half dollars graded Proof-66 or Mint State-66 or higher.**
    For several years, knowledgeable coin market insiders, including some of the nation's leading dealers, have been quietly acquiring superbly toned Franklin half dollars in very high grades—Proof-66 or Mint State-66 and above.

You would think that if you went to a coin show and walked from table to table trying to find nice Franklin halves, they'd be plentiful. These are, after all, modern coins—coins produced as recently as 1963. And their mintage levels certainly weren't small by comparison with previous U.S. half dollars. Judging from their modest values in some of the price guides, you'd probably figure you ought to be able to find hundreds of these coins— maybe even buy them by the bag. You might expect to go up to Harry J. Forman, a highly regarded Philadelphia dealer who specializes in late-date U.S. coins, ask him for a roll of 1950 Franklin halves in Mint State-66, and have him produce not only a roll of 20 coins but a bag of 100 rolls.

This is one case, however, where even Harry Forman wouldn't be able to help you—for despite their seemingly plentiful mintage figures and despite what any price guides may say, high-grade Franklin halves are surprisingly scarce. And they're just not available in quantity.

It's true that the prices are modest. At this writing, a 1950 Franklin half dollar graded Mint State-66 by an independent grading service is priced at only about $375 sight-unseen. The problem is, hardly any 1950 halves are available in Mint State-66—at this price or even a higher price.

While insider dealers are aware of this situation and are seeking to benefit from it, collectors and investors as a whole haven't yet caught on. Thus, while the supply is low, the demand so far has also been relatively low. That has served to hold down the prices, at least on paper. Once additional people start looking for these coins and trying to obtain them, I look for the prices to rise dramatically. And since the present levels are so affordable, making these coins potentially attractive to such a broad spectrum of buyers, the price increase could be amazingly sharp.

I wouldn't be surprised to see high-grade Franklin halves that currently sell for $300 apiece soar in value to $1,000 each within a relatively short time. I wouldn't be at all surprised to see those 1950 halves in Mint State-66, now worth $300, skyrocket to the $1,000 range within the next ten years.

I don't expect this type of huge price increase to happen in the short term—within the next two years; I see it coming a little bit farther down the road. Therefore, if quick profit is your goal, you're probably better off buying something else. But if you can wait ten years, or even fifteen or twenty years, this is a great growth area.

10. Draped Bust dollars.

Silver dollars hold powerful appeal for investors. They're big, attractive coins with precious-metal content—assets that are quintessentially tangible. Early silver dollars, those produced in the nation's formative years, provide the added bonus of great rarity. Many of these coins had very low mintages, and the number of surviving examples is exceedingly small, especially in very high grades. Some are all but unknown even in the lowest Mint State levels.

Most of the very earliest U.S. silver dollars belong to a group known as the Draped Bust type. These coins bear a right-facing bust portrait of Miss Liberty with a garment draped over her shoulder, hence the name. The most famous of all U.S. silver dollars, the 1804, belongs to this group. Only fifteen specimens of this highly publicized rarity are known to exist, and all are accounted for as of this writing. One of them was sold at public auction in 1999 for $4,140,000, the highest price ever paid at auction up to that time for a single coin.

Unless you're a person of very substantial wealth, you probably can't expect to ever become the owner of an 1804 silver dollar. But the other Draped Bust dollars, from 1795 to 1803, are also highly desirable—and those can be obtained for significantly less than their world-renowned 1804 cousin.

None of these coins is cheap; all carry six-figure price tags in Mint State grades. But all have great potential to move up in value—perhaps to the seven-figure range—within the coming years as more and more institutional money enters the coin market. This is the type of coin that holds the greatest appeal for affluent members of the baby-boom generation, and the type that institutional investors will be seeking and acquiring with the greatest dedication.

Draped Bust dollars come with two different designs on the reverse. On the earliest examples, from 1795 to 1798, the reverse depicts a small eagle. In Mint State-67, one of these coins would cost more than $300,000 at the present time. From 1798 to the end of the series in 1804, the reverse portrayed a heraldic eagle.

The heraldic-eagle dollars from 1798 to 1803 strike me as particularly good investments at this time. The sight-unseen price is just $225,000 for a piece certified as Mint State-67 by one of the leading independent grading services, and you could probably get a super premium-quality specimen for not much more than $300,000. These are coins that may very well be trading for close to a million dollars a few years from now. Again, let me stress that you should buy only coins that are certified in these grades by one of the leading independent grading services.

These are very definitely not pocket-change rarities; they're about as far removed from that as anything in all of U.S. coinage. But they're coins that every collector dreams about owning someday—and coins that are dreams-come-true for a fortunate few.

Draped Bust dollars are exceedingly scarce even in the higher circulated grades. But specimens in Extremely Fine and Very Fine condition are findable treasures; Bust dollars in these grades are much more likely to turn up in your attic or cookie jar than a pristine Mint State example. You probably won't discover a Mint State piece unless it was purchased by someone in your family over the years.

If you do come across a Draped Bust dollar, don't sell it. These are coins with enormous investment potential and you should keep them.

11. Seated Liberty dollars graded AU-50 to AU-55.

Seated Liberty coins have always been special favorites of mine. They held sway in Americans' pocket change for more than half a century, from the late 1830s through the early 1890s, and they seem to me especially evocative of that period in U.S. history—one that saw a battle to the death between the North and South, a westward migration toward the nation's "manifest destiny," and the country's first tentative steps as a prime-time player on the international stage. These coins are distinctly nineteenth-century in appearance, and yet they embody a level of competence—in terms of both design and quality of production—not fully achieved on the nation's earliest coinage. Best of all, from a coin collector's standpoint, they include many issues that are scarce or even rare.

The Seated Liberty portrait appeared on five different U.S. coins, from the half cent through the silver dollar, but the dollar had by far the lowest mintages, typically below 100,000 and occasionally even below 10,000. The coin was produced on a regular annual basis from 1840 until it was discontinued in 1873, but it saw little use in circulation except in the West, where hard money enjoyed a special status.

In mint condition, Seated dollars can be very pricey. Their price tags are more reasonable, though, in grades just slightly lower. Circulated specimens certified in grades such as About Uncirculated-50 or AU-55 are available for just a few hundred dollars, and some of these possess even greater eye appeal than pieces that, while technically uncirculated, don't have much pizzazz. They're just as historic, with mintages just as low, and they're very attractive additions to any collection.

12. Common-date Barber silver coins in Mint State-64 or 65, or Proof-64 or 65.

The Barber silver coins, which replaced the Seated Liberty half dollar, quarter, and dime in 1892, brought continued uniformity to Americans' spending money. All three had the same design on the "head's" side, and the half dollar and quarter were virtually identical on the reverse as well. These are also known as Liberty Head coins, but many collectors today refer to them by the name of their designer, Mint chief sculptor-engraver Charles E. Barber.

The Barber coins had something else in common with their Seated Liberty predecessors: They wore well in circulation, remaining serviceable for decades. As evidence of this, they still could be found occasionally in circulation as late as the 1950s—some forty years after the Mint discontinued their production. People *did* use them for years and years, and the great majority ended up in well-worn condition. As a corollary of this, relatively few were preserved in mint condition, or even in the highest circulated grades. Unlike Morgan dollars, which saw only limited use, the Barber coins served the nation long and well in commerce, but collectors are paying the price for this today. You can expect to pay thousands of dollars for Barber coins in upper-level mint-state grades—MS-66 or higher—and in corresponding Proof grades. They're more reasonable, however, in the mid-level grades of

MS-64 and 65 and Proof-64 and 65. You'll pay hundreds of dollars even for common-date examples, but they're worth it. These coins are genuinely scarce, and growing numbers of hobbyists are pursuing them. Remember, too, that proof Barber coins seldom were made in quantities exceeding 1,000.

Warning: The rare coin marketplace can be volatile. As this is written, all twelve coin types described in this chapter are excellent values. However, rapid changes in the marketplace could alter that situation; any or all of these coins may very well have experienced dramatic price increases (or decreases) by the time you read this. For that reason, you should check their prices carefully before making a purchase, and compare them to the prices listed here. In fact, you should do this before buying coins of any kind.

If any of these coins are selling for prices substantially higher than those listed here, use caution in considering their purchase. They may have already enjoyed the appreciation anticipated in this chapter, and thus may no longer be "sleepers." In that case, they will be removed from this special list in future editions of this book.

CHAPTER 12

COINS AND
PRECIOUS METALS

Tangible assets.

Those two words express an entire world of financial commitment by investors.

In the late 1970s and early 1980s, the United States was wracked by a devastating combination of rampant inflation and high interest rates. Understandably nervous about the nation's economy, a great many Americans shifted large portions of their financial resources from conventional investments such as stocks, bonds, and real estate into tangible assets—things they could see, hold, and touch.

Rare coins became the focus of unprecedented public demand. People who had never collected coins poured millions and millions of dollars into the rare coin marketplace. They did this not because they wanted rare coins *per se*, but because in a sense coins were an offshoot of the single most coveted tangible asset of all: gold. Silver was also in great demand during that period, but gold was really the centerpiece of this massive investment move to tangible assets. People were buying gold almost by the truckload, driving the price of the timeless yellow metal to an all-time high of $887.50 an ounce on Jan. 21, 1980 (intra-day London high).

Gold is a universally recognized store of value. It's rare, aesthetically appealing, and remarkably resistant to corrosion. For all these reasons, it has long been used as a medium of exchange in many countries. In fact, the monetary system of the United States was originally based upon gold.

It has often been said that the value of gold doesn't change; what changes is how much everything else is worth in relation to gold. Thus, when gold rises in price from $350 to $400, what's really changing is the value of the dollar, not the value of the gold.

Gold is a mirror of the economic and political environment. When economics and politics are stable, the price of gold is relatively stable; in such a climate, in fact, the price of gold might even decline somewhat. But in times of economic and political instability, when the money supply is inflating, gold tends to increase in price—sometimes remarkably so.

During the turbulent period of the late 1970s and early 1980s, many analysts issued dramatic proclamations boldly predicting that gold would rise in price to levels never attained and hardly imagined before. Some foresaw a time when the price would soar as high as thousands of dollars per ounce.

These predictions haven't come true—at least so far. As this book is written, the price of gold is hovering at less than $300 an ounce. But even now, many financial advisors are flashing the buy signal for gold, arguing with conviction that its price will reach one thousand dollars an ounce in the not-too-distant future.

THE HARD-MONEY MOVEMENT

For many years, a dedicated group of financial advisors has been urging people to divert substantial portions of their money from bank accounts and other traditional savings repositories into tangible assets such as gold, silver, and numismatic (that is, collectible) coins. Well-known authors such as Howard Ruff, James Dines, and John P. Dessauer have been quoted widely as advocating the acquisition of "core holdings" containing these "hard" assets.

Sure, these experts say, you might want to invest in the stock market. Sure, you might want to put some of your money into bank accounts and into other traditional investment vehicles. But the possibility exists—and it's more than just a remote one—that this nation and indeed the entire world could face turbulent economic and political times in the months and years ahead, and at least a percentage of your holdings should be invested, as an insurance policy, in gold or silver or both.

Leaders of the hard-money, tangible-asset movement really do make a persuasive case. It certainly is possible that we could see instability in the world. Despite the easing of tensions and apparent dawn of democracy in Eastern Europe, trouble spots remain in a number of other locations. This became apparent in August 1990 when Iraq invaded Kuwait, precipitating a crude-oil crisis and heightening concern around the globe.

A protracted oil crisis could push up the price of gold significantly. An economic debacle such as the savings-and-loan crisis of the 1980s could prompt the United States government to print a lot more money, and that could cause massive inflation—yet another scenario that probably would cause gold and silver to soar in value. There is, by the way, a widespread misconception that inflation means nothing more than higher prices. Actually, inflation means expansion of the money supply; in an inflated economy, there's more paper money around but each individual note is worth less.

Those who preach the gospel of acquiring tangible assets were scornful when government officials minimized the problems of the S&Ls and their impact on Americans' pocketbooks. They're similarly contemptuous when economic optimists tell us inflation is licked and won't be resurfacing soon. These "hard-money people" are sometimes accused of being doomsayers. Clearly, though, some of their critics are looking at events through rose-colored crystal balls.

Don't get the wrong impression about hard-money advocates. These people are very much like you and me. They invest part of their money, much of the time at least, in standard investment vehicles. More so than most of us, though, they believe in "hazard insurance" for their portfolios. They're acutely aware of the very real risks that exist in the world, and they're firmly convinced of the need to prepare financially for the worst. Gold, silver, and other tangible assets provide this kind of insurance, they believe.

People who purchase hard assets tend to cherish their privacy; they don't want the government knowing what they're buying and what they're keeping. In the early 1980s, these people were dismayed when the U.S. government put into place strong regulations governing transactions involving gold bullion. Under these regulations, buyers and sellers of gold bullion items must have their dealings reported to the Internal Revenue Service.

At that point, many of these people turned to rare coins, since these were not—and are not currently—subject to the same IRS reporting requirements. Rare coins are a relatively private investment.

Although the regulations dampened some buyers' enthusiasm for gold bullion, they haven't discouraged the leaders of the hard-money movement. These true believers remain as convinced as ever that the yellow metal's future is as bright as gold itself.

GOLD'S TWO PERSONALITIES

Gold and silver and other precious metals—but particularly gold—have what might be called two personalities. One of these is their long-term historical value; the other is their short-term price performance.

Gold has been aptly described as "financial insurance." John P. Dessauer, a noted financial advisor, has commented that gold is "better financial insurance than the FDIC will ever be." It has held its value for investors since the dawn of history, dating all the way back to the days of the pharaohs.

In the short term, however, gold can—and does—rise and fall in price quite unpredictably, and often very substantially. This is where some investors encounter difficulties: They focus too strongly on the short-term personality and lose sight of the metal's long-term aspect. They start out by purchasing gold as long-term insurance, but then get preoccupied with the profit motivation and try to make a killing on the metal. It's very important to keep the two goals separate.

Everybody should own at least a certain amount of gold as protection against the unexpected. Silver serves that function, too, and so does platinum. But gold has always enjoyed a primacy among the precious metals. Owning gold has been the way to preserve at least a minimum standard of living during times of political calamity. It has also been the best way—and sometimes the only way—to obtain safe passage out of a troubled land to a place where you can live in greater comfort and security. Gold was the ticket to freedom, for example, for thousands of Vietnamese refugees following the fall of Saigon in 1975.

How much gold should you own? That's like asking how much life insurance you should own. And the answer is much the same: You should own all the gold you can comfortably afford.

BULLION COINS

Bullion coins provide a convenient way to own precious metals—including not only gold but also silver and platinum. Although it is made in the form of a coin and carries a statement of value, a bullion coin is meant to be saved, rather than spent. It's intended to serve as a pocket-size investment, not a unit of commerce.

You can spend a bullion coin, but you'd lose a lot of money if you did, since the face value of such coins—the denomination placed on them by the government—is usually far lower than the value of the metal itself. The one-ounce gold American Eagle, for example, carries a face value of only $50, but the coin could be worth $300 or more as a piece of gold, and would cost that much to purchase.

Numismatic coins—rare coins—rise and fall in price in accordance with collector demand. Their value is determined by how scarce or common they are, and truly rare collector coins often sell for tens, hundreds, or even thousands of times their intrinsic worth. Bullion coins, by contrast, rise and fall directly in proportion to the value of the metal they contain. A one-ounce gold bullion coin, for example, would typically be priced just a little higher than the current market price of an ounce of gold. This small premium—generally less than 10 percent—covers such costs as production, distribution, and promotion.

As this is written, investors have their choice of a number of different gold, silver, and platinum bullion coins. In gold, they can choose from among such popular items as the American Eagle, the Canadian Maple Leaf, and the British Britannia. The American Eagle and Maple Leaf both have silver counterparts. And the Maple Leaf is made in platinum, too.

Bullion coins offer several attractive features. They're affordable, highly portable, easy to store, and readily salable. And the fact that they are coins—with legal-tender status in the country where they were issued—greatly enhances their liquidity.

Numismatic coins—precious-metal and otherwise—are sensitive not only to changes in demand among collectors but also to changes in global wealth. Their value tends to rise and fall in concert with personal income around the world. They have benefited, for instance, from the great wealth created in Japan. These coins are in demand from people who want them, like them, intend to keep them, and can afford to pay for them. At times when the world is reasonably sound economically and there's healthy economic growth, the likelihood is strong that numismatic coins will continue to appreciate in value.

WHAT'S IN STORE FOR PRECIOUS METALS?

It's safe and easy to say that precious metals—particularly gold—will rise in price substantially in a time frame of fifty or sixty years. Historically, the long-term trends have almost always been higher. It's far more difficult to say with any accuracy where the metals will be fifty days or fifty weeks from now. In the short term, their prices can be skewed enormously by an almost endless number of sometimes unforeseeable world events.

The difficulty of making such predictions was underscored during the 1980s. Some highly astute market analysts came out with forecasts that gold would soar well over $1,000—and even over $2,000—before the decade's end. Instead, the yellow metal languished around $400 as the Eighties drew to a close. And it trended even lower during the 1990s.

If John Dessauer is correct, the coming years will offer some golden opportunities to make big money buying gold and other precious metals. To do so, however, you'll need to adopt and maintain a longer-range perspective. The trick will be to buy when the price is right and then hold the metal—through short-term ups and downs—for several years. The chances are good that in time, prices will be much higher and you'll then be able to sell for a tidy gain.

THE ORIGINAL GOLD BUG

James Dines is regarded as one of the founding fathers of the hard-money-asset movement. More than thirty years ago, as a securities analyst for A. M. Kidder and Company, Dines recommended the purchase of gold mining stocks to the firm's clients. Those recommendations panned out extremely well, and admirers have referred to Dines ever since as the original gold bug. This highly respected expert has published *The Dines Letter* for more than thirty years. His advice is eagerly sought on a personal level, as well—and it doesn't come cheap. Dines charges $10,000 for a speech and $5,000 an hour for private consultations.

One of Dines' most memorable—and spectacular—predictions came about 1970, when gold was valued at $35 an ounce and the Dow-Jones Industrial Average was hovering around 600. *The Dines Letter* predicted that these two numbers would cross one day—an almost unimaginable occurrence which actually did take place in January 1980. *Barron's*, the influential financial newspaper, described this in an editorial as one of the most fantastic investment calls ever made.

A few years ago, Dines made the same prediction again, and it seemed just as daring this time as it did before. On July 19, 1990, with gold at $361 and the Dow-Jones Industrial Average close to 3,000, he predicted that these numbers would cross yet again. Later, he said this would happen during the 1990s.

This time, the prediction didn't come to pass. As the Dow-Jones average soared higher and higher, the price of gold stayed stagnant throughout the 1990s. But Dines and other gold bugs aren't flustered as we enter a new millennium. On the contrary, they remain convinced that sooner or later, gold will take off like a rocket and justify their confident predictions. History, after all, is on their side—for that has been the pattern from time immemorial.

Dines made his startling prediction of a second convergence between the Dow-Jones and gold bullion in a fascinating interview that appeared in *The Rosen Numismatic Advisory*, an award-winning newsletter published by distinguished coin market analyst Maurice Rosen. Although the comments and context are ten years in the past as this is written, they represent an intriguing glimpse into the mind of the gold bug. And who's to say they won't prove to be much more on target during the decade to come.

Following are excerpts from that interview. (Copyright 1990, *The Rosen Numismatic Advisory*, P.O. Box 38, Plainview, NY 11803; subscription price $79 per year.)

We've seemed to accustom ourselves to an inflation rate of 4–5% without worry or harm. What will cause inflation to soar and what level might it reach?

We are in a situation where matters are hopelessly out of control. Take the budget deficits which exist in the form of two "sets of books," one which shows us merely in a terrible fix, the other in a crisis situation. Look at the Saving & Loan crisis which started off as a "cost" in the $10–20 billion area—now up to $500 billion and counting! When you consider that the entire Money Stock (M-1) is about $810 billion you can see how enormous the problem really is. But that's just the first shoe; next are the banks which are in a worse situation because they are so thinly capitalized, with tons of bad loans and overpriced assets.

To bail out the S&Ls and the banks will cause massive amounts of money creation which in turn will cause inflation to skyrocket. Much higher inflation rates are virtually guaranteed, as are soaring prices for the whole inflation hedge sector. So, although your coin market is calm now, it will be performing superbly at some point in the future.

In 1980 the national debt was $1 trillion; now it's $3 trillion. The budget deficits continue apace, the banking situation disintegrates, our trade balance worsens, and on and on, yet the system is holding while gold is struggling. Why worry?

The Inflation Bubble is taking us through stages. The deflation of 1980–87 allowed further growth and expansion. Inflation asset values got too ahead of themselves in the '70s and corrected in the '80s. Since about 1982, gold has been in a broad trading range between 300 and 500. It's still way above 35. This is a huge base building area as we still digest the deflationary influences of the

1980–87 era—the biblical seven-year period of hard times. I see an increasing trend of inflation into the mid-1990s. What the peak rate will be hinges in what the politicians do. If they will continue to be as stupid as they have been we might get frightening high levels. If not, I can see 15–30% inflation.

Referring to the June 25, 1990, Wall Street Journal *article on gold, how did you arrive at your predictions of $2,000 and of $3,000–$5,000 gold prices?*

It's actually a compromise. If you want to bring the buying power of gold to where it was in 1934 before all this started you can come up with even substantially higher objectives. Old-time newsletter editor Vern Myers once told me $50,000 in gold would be needed to put things back into balance. But, I feel $2,000–$5,000 would monetize gold enough so we could get back to a system that worked and we could tie down a lot of the remaining debt. Another way to look at it is by technical analysis using Fibonacci numbers, a method which has proven itself eerily accurate several times in the past. Since the 1980 high was $875, a Fibonacci multiple of 3 equals $2,665 and a multiple of 5 equals $4,375. Allowing for the sure-to-come panic at the end of this bullish gold move, $3,000–$5,000 is entirely possible.

Furthermore, the collapse of communism—something I've been predicting as far back as 1980—will be enormously bullish for gold as pent-up demand by ex-communist masses is unleashed. It all seems to be coming to a head later this decade; that's why I predict gold is at an absolutely bargain price today.

Besides the actual metal, I also recommend gold mining shares. I see them as being the absolutely best performing group over the next few years. Here, geographical diversification is important, which would include North American, Australian, and South African issues. As the price of gold gets closer and closer to the Dow, just imagine the panic scramble that would result as individual stock investors and the big institutions buy into the relatively small gold-mining share industry. I'm sure you'll experience the same mad scramble of money coming into the rare coin market.

What advice do you have for rare coin investors in the years ahead?

I am adamantly against short-term trading. You should only buy for the long term. Like real estate, there's no more to be made and there are more collectors every year. There's huge pent-up demand, from China, Europe, and Russia to India and Africa. All of them will be competing for coins. You'll have more liquidity and greater acceptance from funds and banks. They are portable, beautiful works of art. The grading services have increased confidence and lowered spreads between buyer and seller.

Buyers of certain rare coins should not be overly concerned with price, as the opportunity to buy them does not come around often; buy them and lock them away. This is a good time to grab them as others get discouraged. This is like the early 1960s to me all over again. Of course, high inflation will send rare coin prices to the moon, and current psychology is all in favor of the smart investor buying now.

PRECIOUS METALS AND RARE COINS: SIMILARITIES AND DIFFERENCES

Bullion coins contain a relatively high amount of precious metal. Rare coins often contain little or none. Bullion coins' value comes from the metal itself. These coins are purely an investment in precious metal. Rare coins derive their value from collector demand—and this demand, in turn, stems from such factors as the coins' design and date. Rare coins can be partly a bullion investment, but they're mainly an investment in collector taste.

With bullion coins, the margin is very small between a dealer's bid and ask prices; with rare coins, the margin is much higher. The margin is the spread between what a dealer will pay for a coin and what he'll sell it for. With bullion coins, this spread may be only 3 or 4 percent, and sometimes even less. With rare coins, a spread of 15 or 20 percent is quite routine.

Bullion coins are standardized, and it isn't important to grade them; rare coins aren't standardized, and subtle differences between two similar coins can translate into a major variation in value. With bullion coins, you can buy ten, fifteen, or twenty pieces and they'll all be the same; you won't need a magnifying glass to inspect them. That's not true with rare coins. Even if a rare coin comes in a holder from a leading grading service, with an insert tab indicating its grade, that doesn't mean the coin is exactly the same as another coin in the same kind of holder with the same grade written on its tab. It also doesn't mean that the coin won't be graded differently if it is submitted again to the same service.

Bullion and bullion coins are subject to government regulation, but at present collector coins are not. Any time a person buys or sells bullion coins, the dealer has to fill out a Form 1099-B naming that person. A person buying or selling collector coins is entering into a relatively private transaction, as this book is written.

Bullion prices move up or down over a longer period; collector coins experience dramatic price changes almost instantaneously. In recent years, bullion has traded within a rather narrow price range, moving up or down only 10 or 15 percent even over a fairly extended period. Rare coins normally trade within a 5- to 15-percent price range, but it isn't uncommon for them to rise or fall as much as 20 to 50 percent in a short period. Volatility has been much more of a factor in the rare coin market than with bullion.

Bullion enjoys a much wider market than rare coins; the rare coin market is composed of thinly capitalized entrepreneurs. The market for gold is global and ranks among the world's most fully developed. It's also the most liquid of all the commodity markets. The rare coin marketplace is dramatically smaller. A few big investment firms tested the waters—Kidder, Peabody and Merrill Lynch, among them. But at this writing, the rare coin industry doesn't yet enjoy the full participation of companies such as this.

COIN AND PRECIOUS METAL PRICES

Does a correlation exist between the prices of precious metals and those of rare coins? There has been considerable discussion and analysis regarding this possibility. After all, both of these assets are in a sense indicators of where wealthy people think the economy and political events are headed.

In a "micro-sense," as economists would refer to it, there isn't really a day-to-day correlation. If a rare coin is valued at $10,000 and gold goes from $300 to $325 an ounce, the value of that coin isn't going to change. However, in a broader sense, or "macro-sense," as economists would call it, a correlation does exist in the long run.

In the early 1970s, gold was extremely strong and so were rare coins. From 1974 to the early part of 1977, gold was in the doldrums and so were rare coins. Then, from 1977 to 1980, rare coins and gold both did extremely well.

Take a look at the accompanying chart entitled "Does Spot Gold Matter?" In it, you'll see the "spot" price of gold—the market price of one troy ounce of the metal—traced from January of 1985 to June of 1990, along with the corresponding prices for common-date Saint-Gaudens double eagles and Liberty Head double eagles ($20 gold pieces).

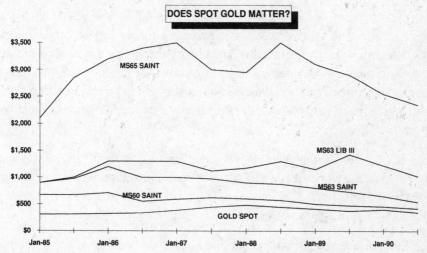

Graph of gold bullion and "semi-numismatic" coin price performance. (Graph courtesy Coin Dealer Newsletter)

In this chart, Saint-Gaudens double eagles graded Mint State-60 and Mint State-63 correlate somewhat with the spot price of gold. So do Mint State-63 Liberty Type 3 double eagles. But Mint State-65 Saint-Gaudens double eagles, which are really collector coins, show very little direct correlation. At one point, these coins were actually decreasing in value at a time when gold was increasing.

We can conclude from this chart that the price of gold is an important psychological factor in the rare coin marketplace, but it doesn't necessarily stimulate gold coins to rise or fall in value. It does affect the value of what we would call "semi-bullion" numismatic coins—coins like Mint State-60 Saint-Gaudens double eagles. But its impact is less direct, and may even be negligible, on higher-grade coins that are pure collectibles.

CONCLUSIONS

Coins with high precious-metal content have substantial intrinsic value, and even if they weren't worth a single penny more as collectibles, they'd still command a premium based upon the bullion they contain. A $20 gold piece has just under an ounce of pure gold, so the least it will be worth at any given time is the current market value of that much gold.

Gold and silver and other precious metals provide a solid floor—a minimum market value—for the coins in which they are used. At the same time, they enhance the appearance and appeal of these coins, and this gives them greater allure as collectibles.

The price of a numismatic coin is a product of supply and demand, and gold and silver content can influence this equation by increasing the level of demand. A rare coin can be worth many thousands of dollars without containing a bit of precious metal; many cents and nickels bring very fancy prices. But, in practical terms, a great many buyers have shown a decided preference for coins that contain gold or silver.

The impact of precious metal is far more direct in "bullion" coins. The value of these coins at any particular moment is directly linked to the price of the precious metal from which they're made. If the price of gold or silver goes up or down even marginally, the prices of bullion coins will do likewise.

Bullion coins essentially are economic hedges—a convenient form of insurance against inflation. Numismatic coins are collectibles, but their long-term price performance has given them the dimension of good investments as well.

HOW TO PROSPER DURING A BULL MARKET IN GOLD

This section was written in 2004 by award-winning newsletter publisher Maurice Rosen. The opinions expressed are his own. Readers are advised to seek competent professional advice before acting on this or any other financial forecast.

by MAURICE H. ROSEN, Numismatic Counseling, Inc., Plainview, NY
A Courageous Forecast—Special to One-Minute Coin Expert, Fifth Edition

The price of gold hit a record high of $887.50 on January 21, 1980, a price it had not seen for almost a quarter of a century. Within the next several years, that high price will be revisited and exceeded, possibly vaulting the $1,000 level. What will cause this and how can you prepare for and prosper from such a tumultuous event?

Gold reached an important bottom of $250 in 1999 and revisited this exact level in 2001. Its price has been climbing since, albeit with occasional corrections along the way. The 2-decades-plus long bear market has ended. We are in a bull market that can last for several more years and carry to levels not seen before. Credit a tremendous, pent-up inflationary experience for what is to come, the result of extremely high government spending, mounting deficits and the declining value of the dollar vis-à-vis other currencies. This should all unfold over the next few years.

At the same time, investments in such areas as quality rare coins, common bullion coins, and the popular $20 gold pieces, will be experiencing rip-roaring bullish markets as high demand soaks up available supplies. Those who recall the 1970s with memories of excitable and climbing tangible asset markets will be well prepared for what is in store. Here is my suggested guide for you to best position yourself for this bull market.

WHY GOLD WILL SOAR IN PRICE

The bear market ended in 2001. The value of the dollar is headed down. Compared to the immense value of paper dollars and paper obligations that have been created over the years, gold is substantially undervalued. The lid has been held down for as long as it can be held down for. Soon it will blow, with the result being a much higher gold price.

ACTIONS TO TAKE

Your actions in this developing bull market depend on whether you are more of a trader or a long-term holder. A trader should be mindful to be buying weakness and selling strength. When gold suffers one of its occasional sell-offs (usually on the order of at least 5% to 10%), you should be adding to your holdings. On the other hand, whenever the gold price seems to be running away on the upside or, perhaps, stalls in its ascent, consider lightening your position.

A long-term holder will hold tight to his or her position until it appears that the primary bull market is ending. Additions to your portfolio are best made during those periods of weakness. The market will be calmer, prices will be more attractive, and better selections will be achieved. The long-term holder should not be overly concerned during these normal corrective periods. He or she should most definitely not be prematurely intimidated out of a carefully built position.

BEST COINS TO BUY

Rare Coins

The market for rare coins should perform strongly over the next few years. Be guided by the counseling elsewhere in this book which emphasizes quality, certification, rarity, and value.

QUALITY: During previous rare coin bull markets, high-quality coins were always in feverish demand. They would often fetch prices greatly in excess of published quotes as anxious buyers vied to acquire coins they expected would continue climbing in price. Therefore, paying premiums (though I would suggest you pay *reasonable* premiums) is a good strategy to own the coins that will be strongly demanded in the future at even greater premiums.

CERTIFICATION: Concentrate your rare coin buying to coins certified by the leading authentication and grading services.

RARITY: You want to acquire coins that possess a high combination of rarity and collector demand. Such coins are in constant demand, have many buyers for each offered coin, and will be highly liquid—these are quick sellers when you want to get out.

VALUE: The price you pay determines how good your investment will be. When you are buying coins as an investor, you should be aware of what the coin is worth in the wholesale marketplace. Pay as reasonably close to that price as possible since it is likely that when you sell you will be realizing a wholesale price at the time. Retail prices are generally for collectors building collections. You want to do better. Get value from the beginning, and you will be on the right path to profits.

Common Gold Coins

The two common types of the American $20 gold piece have served investors well in the past. There's every reason to believe they will serve investors well in the future, too. Your options are several, including:

- $20 Liberties, Type 3, 1877-1907, circulated grades of Very Fine, Extremely Fine or About Uncirculated. The appeal of these coins is their American heritage and their low prices. Each coin contains 0.9675 oz. of gold, and is usually priced to reflect a premium-over-actual gold content of approximately 15% to 25%. There have been times when premiums were higher. There are a lot more gold coin "products" on the shelf now, so competition is high, but the premium is a reasonable one.

- $20 Liberties, Type 3, 1877-1907, Mint State grades of MS-60 to MS-63.

- $20 Saint-Gaudens, MS-61 to MS-63. Though more costly than the circulated versions, these pieces add a numismatic flavor that is great appeal. These Mint State coins should be certified by a leading grading service—a requirement that doesn't always apply to the circulated coins.

CAUTION CAN BE GOLDEN

Gold at higher levels over the next several years will make the coin market shine as brightly as ever. Rare coins of every metal and common gold coins will perform admirably for these investors who use care and prudence to acquire worthy selections. But just as every bull market has a beginning, it also has an end. Be mindful of extreme signs of a topping market; visit the cashier's window, and add up your profits!

CHAPTER 13

COIN DEALERS, DRUG DEALERS, AND THE GOVERNMENT

Because they combine great value with small size and easy portability, rare coins hold special appeal for people who want to keep their wealth concealed and be able to move it around.

Most of the time, these people's motivations are perfectly legitimate; they're reputable investors who wish to maintain low profiles. But the very same attributes that make coins attractive to legitimate investors and collectors have also caught the eye of profit-minded people on the wrong side of the law.

This is not a strictly modern-day phenomenon. Centuries ago, pirates hoarded coins in chests of buried treasure. In recent years, however, space-age criminals have found an updated way to use rare coins—and bullion coins, too—to their advantage.

One of the most intriguing examples of this came to light in 1988, when Heritage Numismatic Auctions, Inc. of Dallas, one of the nation's largest and best-known coin auction companies, held a public sale featuring valuable gold coins that federal agents had confiscated from members of an international drug ring.

The drug dealers had purchased large numbers of coins—rare coins and bullion coins, as well—to help conceal the proceeds from their illicit activities. And I do mean *conceal*: They had transformed some of the coins, quite literally, into modern-day buried treasure by hiding them in underground caches.

To put the story in proper perspective, we have to go back two years earlier, when members of the drug ring were arrested on a variety of drug, racketeering, and tax-evasion charges. Hoping to obtain lighter sentences, they agreed to a plea bargain—and part of that agreement called for them to forfeit their coins.

Finding these coins wasn't a simple matter of going to one of the suspects' safety deposit box. The coins were hidden in three separate locations: buried in plastic bags beneath a Nebraska field, in a briefcase under a rock pile in the Colorado Rockies, and stashed on the Hawaiian island of Maui.

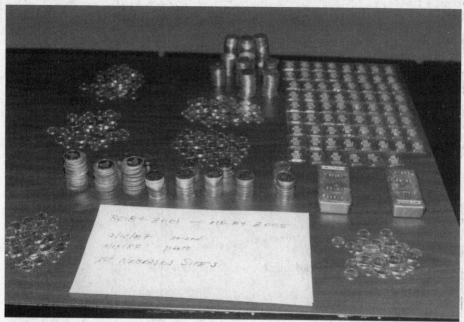

Part of the 982 gold coins valued over $2 million, all buried treasure of drug dealers. It was all sold at public auction at the direction of the U.S. government. (Photo courtesy Heritage Capital Corp.)

"It was very much like treasure hunting," said Thomas J. Dolan, one of the agents who coordinated the investigation for the federal Drug Enforcement Administration. "Part of it was out in the guy's backyard, and we went in with a bulldozer and a map."

One of the conspirators had drawn up a crude map showing the location of one hoard of gold coins buried by the ring in the small town of Crawford, Nebraska—population 1,320. The map said the coins could be found between two pine trees seventeen paces apart, and it showed a "white cliff with a crack" as a point of reference.

The ground was frozen the day DEA agents went to retrieve the treasure, so they brought in a backhoe to help with the excavation. They found the coins just where the map said they would be—sealed inside Tupperware containers.

A second cache of coins was buried elsewhere on the property, but this one proved easier to unearth. A hole had already been dug at this site, then covered with a 2 × 10 board and mounds of earth.

In Colorado, the conspirators apparently ran out of Tupperware. This time, the coins were found in a briefcase that was wedged in a rocky crevasse. The

DEA had no trouble determining the owner: The briefcase was tagged with a United Airlines baggage claim check.

One of the leaders of the drug cartel apparently had some knowledge of the coin market, for the treasure included a number of unusually rare and desirable items. Among the highlights:

- A virtually complete set of Liberty Head double eagles ($20 gold pieces).

- An almost complete set of Saint-Gaudens eagles ($10 gold pieces).

- Dozens of early $10 gold pieces.

- Two high-relief 1907 double eagles.

- An 1879 stella (or $4 gold piece), a rare pattern coin worth tens of thousands of dollars.

The bullion portion of the cache contained nearly $1 million worth of bullion-type gold coins and bars, including 1,132 Canadian Maple Leafs, 399 South African Krugerrands, 303 Russian Chervonets, and two 100-ounce bars. Heritage sold these items privately for the government.

Coins being counted and listed at the burial site. When the spot was discovered, a 2' × 10' board was covering a skillfully dug hole. (Photo courtesy Heritage Capital Corp.)

Heritage sold the numismatic material at two auctions in October and December 1988, where the coins brought approximately $2 million—well above pre-sale expectations. This money was placed in the U.S. Treasury's general fund.

The drug ring involved in this case operated out of Denver, but had "tentacles" in San Diego and South America, according to the DEA.

Tom Dolan, who is group supervisor of the DEA office in Denver, said the drug dealers purchased the coins and bullion "as one of the ploys they used" to hide their ill-gotten gains. They also spent large sums of drug-related money to acquire other items such as real estate and stocks.

The Comprehensive Crime Control Act of 1984 empowers the DEA and other federal agencies to confiscate and sell any items which they believe were purchased with the proceeds of illegal activities, such as drug trafficking and racketeering. Often, the proceeds from such sales are shared on a pro-rata basis with state and local law-enforcement agencies who assist in making the arrests and seizures.

According to the DEA, the Heritage auction represented the largest public sale of confiscated collectibles ever arranged by the agency. Most of the coins were high-grade circulated specimens. However, there were also a number of proof and Mint State pieces. This was not the first time coins seized by the government had been sold on the public's behalf; however, it was easily the biggest such sale ever held.

Among the other collectibles confiscated and sold in recent years were a group of Tiffany lamps and a 1963 Ferrari GTO automobile. The car was sold privately for $1.6 million, according to Steve Boyle, a spokesman for the U.S. Marshal Service, which arranges most such sales.

CASH AND YOUR COIN PURCHASES

The U.S. Treasury Department has promulgated a new regulation which—while apparently aimed in part at identifying drug dealers—could also have implications for coin dealers and their customers.

For years, there has been a federal rule requiring that the Internal Revenue Service must be notified of any cash transaction of $10,000 or more. But the Treasury broadened this on July 24, 1990, to require the reporting of "related" cash transactions over a twelve-month period which, in their aggregate, total $10,000 or more. This rule was made retroactive to Dec. 31, 1989.

For those who are anxious to preserve their financial privacy, this rule poses serious potential problems.

CHAPTER 14

TREASURE BURIED
AT SEA

From time immemorial, shipwrecks have fired man's imagination with visions of treasure buried at sea—tantalizingly near but forever beyond his reach. That lore has grown with time, as man has expanded his sphere of influence around the globe—giving him access to still greater treasures but forcing him to expose them to even greater risks as he transported them.

Only in recent years has recovery of those riches from the bottom of the sea evolved from an impossible dream into a realistic possibility. Advances in technology, especially since the late 1900s, have given explorers tools they never had before to pinpoint the locations of these wrecks, reach them with recovery gear and snatch their precious cargos from watery graves that once seemed inviolable.

A 1986 photograph taken by robot sub nearly 8,000 feet below the surface of the Atlantic Ocean showing the undistributed gold coins and ingots on the seabed where they had been since September 1857. The researchers of the Coumbus America Discovery Group nicknamed the site, "the Garden of Gold." (Photo courtesy California Gold Marketing Group)

With each success, the pace of exploration has picked up added impetus, propelling new quests, triggering new discoveries and lengthening the list of recovered riches. These treasures, in turn, have done much more than merely enrich their finders: They have had a profound impact on many important segments of world commerce—including the market in collectible coins.

Shipwrecks have yielded fabulous caches of gold and silver coins, bars, ingots and artifacts—some of them rare and valuable far beyond their content as precious metal. Rather than depressing the prices of existing examples, these finds have actually strengthened the market by stimulating new interest and broadening the base of potential purchasers. In the process, they have added a patina of drama and romance—for the stories behind these coins transform them from mere objects of value into living pieces of hand-held human history.

The successful recoveries also have provided crucial insights into how burial at sea affects treasure coins. In the late 1970s, for example, a hoard of 1854-S gold coins was retrieved from shallow water off the California coast—and experts found that while the salt water hadn't harmed the coins, they had been damaged by sand. This led some hobbyists to fear that all shipwreck coins would be similarly pitted and difficult or impossible to curate. For a time, in fact, it created a bias against such coins. But gold coins recovered in several subsequent salvage operations, including the one on the *SS Central America*, emerged from the ocean virtually unscathed. Salvors and coin experts now understand that seawater alone has little or no effect on gold coins, especially if the water is relatively deep and still. In fact, it may help preserve them.

There are countless shipwrecks around the globe, spanning the ages from ancient times to the recent past. Some hold little interest for treasure hunters, bearing no cargos deemed worthy of the effort and expense required to salvage them. Others, however, have driven the adventurous to dream and dare—and sometimes even to die—in the pursuit of the fabulous wealth they contain.

In recent years, some of these adventurers, abetted by experts in science and technology, have overcome nature's formidable defenses to reach and reclaim the riches long hidden at the bottom of the sea. Others have taken significant steps toward realizing similar successes. Their triumphs are the stuff of legends and the plot lines of pulsating books and movies.

A review of just a few such sagas will make it crystal clear why shipwrecks exert such a hold on people's minds and play such a pivotal role in stimulating the marketplace in gold and silver coins and related items.

THE ATOCHA

The New World was a source of vast wealth for Spain in the Age of Discovery. It was, in fact, the cornerstone of Spanish power during the period when España, not Britannia, truly ruled the waves. That power was shaken when the British fleet defeated the Spanish Armada in 1588, but it remained formidable—and regular infusions of gold and silver from America kept it so. One such infusion was planned in the late summer of 1622, when a fleet of 28 ships embarked for Spain with a rich cargo of silver from Peru and Mexico, gold and emeralds from Colombia, and pearls from Venezuela.

The Spanish colonies depended upon goods from the mother country and they, in turn, sent back shipments of precious metals and gems. These were transported in convoys of merchant ships accompanied by warships known as galleons. Typically, the treasure was carried on the larger, heavier galleons while the merchant ships held cargos of agricultural goods. It was customary for one warship to sail at the head of the fleet and one at the rear to discourage and repel attacks by enemy vessels.

The Tierra Firma fleet began its journey in Cartagena on July 24, 1622. It arrived in Havana a month later, but delayed its departure from there because a large Dutch fleet was in the area. Finally, on Sept. 4, it set sail for Spain. It had been at sea for only a day when it found itself being overtaken by a hurricane as it entered the Florida straits. By the morning of Sept. 6, eight of the ships had been sent to a watery grave by the fierce storm. *Nuestra Senora de Atocha*, the 112-foot galleon at the rear of the convoy, struggled to withstand the wild winds and 15-foot waves, but she was no match for nature's fury. The savage sea lifted her and hurled her onto a reef, ripping a huge hole in her bow. She quickly disappeared beneath the surface, carrying 260 men to their deaths. There were only five survivors—three crewmen and two slaves who lashed themselves to the stump of the mizzenmast, the only part of the ship still above water, and clung to it until rescuers reached them the next morning.

The rescuers attempted to enter the wreckage, but the hatches were tightly sealed and the water depth of 55 feet made recovery operations impossible. Marking the site, they moved on to other ships where men and treasure could still be saved. On Oct. 5, a second hurricane swept through the area, completing the destruction and burial of the *Atocha*. Spanish salvagers searched for the ship for many years thereafter, but never found a trace. The loss dealt a crippling blow to Spain's economy, forcing her to borrow funds to help finance war with the Dutch and French.

The tale of the *Atocha* continued to kindle dreams as decades turned into centuries—and with good reason. At the time she met her end, the ship contained a cargo of exceptional opulence, including more than 1,000 silver ingots weighing 24 tons in all, 180,000 silver pesos, 125 gold bars and discs and 1,200 pounds of worked silverware. Little wonder, then, that the thought of extracting this treasure from the ocean's jealous grip put a glint in the eyes of so many hopeful adventurers through the years.

By 1969, man had not only landed on the Moon but also made major strides in solving the mysteries of the sea—and it was in that climate of exploration and discovery that one particularly dogged modern treasure hunter, Mel Fisher, set out that year to find and recover the long-lost treasure of the *Atocha*. Fisher had new technology on his side—including some that he devised himself. To help clear sand from potential underwater wreck sites, he used prop-wash deflectors, or "mailboxes," of his own invention. He and his company, Treasure Salvors, also used specially designed magnetometers. The relentless quest continued for 16 years, even after a 1975 tragedy that claimed the lives of Fisher's son and daughter-in-law and a diver when their salvage boat capsized. Periodic discoveries of isolated artifacts, such as silver bars and cannons, reassured the searchers that they were close to the wreck and gave them the incentive to press on.

By 1980, Fisher and his crew had found most of the remains of the *Santa Margarita*, a ship that went down with the *Atocha*, and retrieved a smaller fortune in gold bars, silver coins, and jewelry from that wreckage. But their focus remained fixed on the main prize—and finally, on July 20, 1985, Fisher's son Kane, piloting the salvage vessel *Dauntless*, sent an exuberant message to his father: "Put away the charts; we've found the main pile!" Within days, the salvors were excitedly at work exploring "the shipwreck of the century" near the Marquesas Keys some 20 miles west of Key West, Fla.

Treasure Salvors had to overcome not only the tragic accident, but also financial problems, power cutoffs, and repeated legal challenges. In the end, though, Fisher's persistence paid off: He and his team recovered more than $60 million worth of riches from the *Santa Margarita* and, especially, the *Atocha*. Much of this treasure has been sold in the intervening years. A substantial portion, however, is preserved at the Mel Fisher Maritime Heritage Society Museum in Key West. Among the items on display there are a solid gold belt and necklace set embedded with gems; a gold chain weighing more than seven pounds; an elaborately tooled gold plate; and gold and silver coins and bars meant for Spanish royalty centuries earlier. Some 200,000 visitors pass through the museum every year—and glimpse not only the wealth of a bygone age but also the dazzling rewards that await the fortunate few who hit the ultimate jackpot in this age of re-discovery.

One-Minute Treasure Tip:

Spanish colonial coins and similar treasure from *Atocha*-era shipwrecks are un-questionably romantic and historic, but they lack the marketability of U.S. double eagles and other gold coins from more recent wrecks, such as the *SS Central America*. These later coins can be easily certified by grading services and sold into an active, ready-made marketplace; the earlier coins, by contrast, are more eso-teric and harder to quantify as collectibles. "Buy them as souvenir trinkets, but not as a serious investment," says coin expert John Albanese—and I concur. The need for caution was underscored several years ago when *Atocha* treasure hunter Mel Fisher pleaded no contest to charges of selling counterfeit Spanish shipwreck coins. Fisher said he was deceived about the coins' origin by the supplier.

THE SS CENTRAL AMERICA

The *SS Central America* occupies a special place on the roster of the world's most famous shipwrecks. The sinking of this ship in 1857 was considered to be America's worst peacetime sea disaster, in both human and economic terms, and the recovery of her treasure more than 130 years later produced such fabu-lous riches that the ill-fated vessel came to be known far and wide as the "Ship of Gold."

A contemporary artist's depiction of the S.S. Central America. (Drawing courtesy California Gold Marketing Group)

The *SS Central America* was a sidewheel steamship used to transport U.S. mail, cargo, and passengers on the Panama Route, a combined sea-and-land journey from San Francisco to New York. The passengers would take one steamship down the West Coast to Panama, travel by train across the isthmus (for the Panama Canal didn't yet exist), then board a second sidewheeler for the last leg up the Atlantic Coast to New York.

When the *Central America* left Panama on Sept. 3, 1857, she was carrying 477 passengers, 101 crew members, 38,000 pieces of mail and a cargo that included more than three tons of California gold. The gold consisted of thousands of coins—many freshly made at the San Francisco Mint—and hundreds of bars and ingots. Much of this treasure was bound for Eastern financial institutions as backing for notes they had issued.

On Sept. 9, the ship encountered an unexpected hurricane; three days later, it sank off the Carolina coast, carrying 425 souls and its rich cargo to a tomb at the bottom of the sea. Reports on the tragedy and stories about the survivors filled the front pages of newspapers across the country, and loss of the precious cargo triggered financial panic in New York. But, within months, the *Central America* faded from public consciousness as the nation's focus turned to the Civil War.

Not everyone forgot the wreck, however. One who remembered the tragic tale—and rich cargo—was Tommy Thompson, an ocean engineer then conducting scientific research at the prestigious Battelle Memorial Institute in Columbus, Ohio. In 1981, Thompson began studying contemporary accounts of the ship's demise and gathering other evidence in an effort to pinpoint her final resting place. As his research proceeded, he assembled a group of associates to assist him in the quest. By the mid-1980s, he had formed a partnership known as the Columbus-America Discovery Group and attracted investments of more than $10 million from 161 partners intrigued by the potential rewards the ship might yield. With the money, he was able to finance sophisticated search equipment and a team of 40 scientists, engineers and technicians.

The team conducted a side-scan sonar search in 1986 and site verification studies in 1987. On Sept. 11, 1988, with competitors closing in, Thompson and his team struck paydirt: An underwater sea robot called *Nemo* located the wreckage of the *SS Central America* at a depth of 2,200 meters on the Blake Ridge, approximately 270 kilometers southeast of Cape Fear, North Carolina. The group converted the underwater robot into a research submersible capable of performing complex tasks at great ocean depths and began the delicate process of retrieving artifacts from the site.

Some of the spectacular gold coins and assayers' ingots recovered from the fabled "Ship of Gold," the S.S. Central America. (Photo courtesy California Gold Marketing Group)

During the months that followed, Thompson and his team recovered more than 7,500 gold coins and 485 gold assayers' bars from the wreckage. Many of the coins were 1856-S and 1857-S double eagles, or $20 gold pieces—and their state of preservation was exceptional, for gold is virtually impervious to chemical reaction with seawater. The coins were of great interest to numismatists not only because of their history and romance, but also because they provided a major new supply of pristine pre-Civil War double eagles, which are considered quite scarce. The treasure also included many privately minted "territorial" coins from Gold Rush California.

My firm, Scott Travers Rare Coin Galleries, was involved in the sale of an 1857-S *Central America* double eagle certified as Mint State-67 by the Professional Coin Grading Service (PCGS), and the buyer now values it far in excess of $100,000 because of its rarity in such spectacular condition. The coin, an example of the scarce "bold-S" variety, is one of just three such pieces in the Central America cache, and 11 of any kind from the ship's spectacular cargo, to receive the lofty grade of MS-67 from PCGS. It remains in the original gold-foil-insert holder used by the company to showcase coins from the ship and signify they were subject to no additional restoration after their recovery from the wreck and initial curation—a crucial consideration in assuring their high quality is pristine.

The Columbus-America Discovery Group was stymied for years in its efforts to market the gold because of legal challenges from insurance companies, which maintained they were entitled to a share of the treasure because they (or their predecessor firms) had paid out claims when the *Central America* sank. At

A sampling of shimmering gold coins recovered from the Central America's cargo. (Photo courtesy California Gold Marketing Group)

length, the two sides reached an agreement whereby the insurers received a small percentage of the coins and ingots.

The discovery group's portion of the treasure was acquired by a consortium called the California Gold Marketing Group, LLC, which oversaw sale of the gold—nearly $100 million, in all—through a network of major dealers. Prominent New Jersey coin expert John Albanese and West Coast dealer Dwight N. Manley were co-founders of the group and Manley was managing member. Bob Evans, Columbus-America's chief scientist, assumed responsibility for conserving the treasure. The California Gold Marketing Group created a $20 million traveling exhibit of recovered gold coins, bars and nuggets for display at coin shows and museums throughout the country. It also sponsored a television documentary about the *SS Central America* and published a 1,056-page reference book, *A California Gold Rush History,* featuring the sunken treasure.

Individual coins from the *Central America* were certified by PCGS and encapsulated in special holders identifying them as having been recovered from the ship. Many of the ingots were used to prepare handsome souvenirs of the "Ship of Gold." Especially noteworthy was a restrike of the 1855 Kellogg & Co. $50 gold piece. Original dies were located and used to strike 5,000 examples of this stunning piece, each containing 2_ ounces of *Central America* gold. The combination of Gold Rush dies and shipwreck gold makes this an unusually attractive collectible.

One-Minute Treasure Tip:

In purchasing certified *SS Central America* gold coins, buy *only* coins with gold-foil inserts in their PCGS holders. These prove the coins are still in their original holders. A blue PCGS insert signifies a resubmission and raises legitimate concern about the accuracy of the assigned grade—concern that can translate into a lower price if the coin is subsequently resold to a knowledgeable dealer or collector. As of this writing in February 2004, you can expect to pay about $12,500 for a gold-foil PCGS *Central America* coin certified as MS-65 and $8,000 to $8,500 for an MS-64 example. Also, keep in mind that *Central America* coins were sold in special boxes accompanied by historical books and serially numbered certificates. The absence of these items would reduce their resale value.

The *Central America* coin sales were good news for collectors who coveted pre-Civil War U.S. gold coins—especially Type I double eagles—in gem condition. Previously, such coins were virtually unknown. The restrictive marketing campaign, limited to just a handful of dealers, caused bad feelings, however, among many other dealers who were not permitted to participate. This has led to an uneven aftermarket—but the ill will has now begun to dissipate as more and more dealers handle the coins. One important factor in smoothing the ruffled feathers was the inclusion of the *Central America* coins in *The Top 100 Coins*, a landmark book by Jeff Garrett and Ron Guth that has had a major influence on the marketplace.

THE SS BROTHER JONATHAN

The *SS Brother Jonathan* was a sidewheel steamship that plied West Coast shipping routes between 1850 and 1865—a time of explosive growth for that region as the California Gold Rush transformed it overnight from a series of sleepy outposts into a stretch of boomtowns. Her final voyage started on July 28, 1865, when she left San Francisco bound for Portland and Vancouver. After just a short time at sea, the ship encountered a gale and her captain, Samuel De Wolf, decided to turn back to Crescent City—but she struck a submerged rock on Saint George Reef and quickly sank to the bottom of the Pacific. Only 19 of the 244 passengers and crew members survived—and even today, this ranks as California's worst shipwreck.

The *Brother Jonathan* was loaded—some have said overloaded—with 500 tons of cargo, including a quartz-stamping mill being sent to an Idaho gold mine; more than 300 barrels of whiskey; machinery for a woolen mill in Oregon; and a small fortune in gold coins—many of them newly struck double eagles from the San Francisco Mint. There were hundreds of smaller gold coins as well, including pristine eagles and half eagles.

The wreck lay undisturbed—and undiscovered—for more than a century. Finally, in 1993, a company called Deep Sea Research (DSR) located the wreck site. Even then, recovery operations proceeded slowly. It was not until Aug. 30, 1996 that DSR's Harvey Harrington and David Slater, exploring the wreck in the two-man submersible *Delta*, spotted gold. The first bags of coins were brought to the surface that day; they contained 564 double eagles, some still in mint condition even after their long stay on the ocean bottom. In all, 875 gold coins were recovered in 1996 and 332 more the following year.

DSR's plans to sell the coins hit a roadblock when the State of California took legal steps to halt the sale. The battle went all the way to the U.S. Supreme Court before DSR prevailed. Despite its vindication, the company gave 200 of the coins to the state to forestall any further legal action. The state agreed to keep them off the market for 15 years. DSR's portion was consigned to Auctions by Bowers and Merena, which dispersed the coins at a memorable auction in Los Angeles on

May 29–30, 1999. Prices were extremely strong; one buyer, for example, paid $115,000 for an 1865-S eagle graded Mint State-64 by the Professional Coin Grading Service. Prior to the discovery of these specimens, mint-state gold coins from the San Francisco Mint had been all but unknown for the early 1860s.

One-Minute Treasure Tip:

The *SS Brother Jonathan* treasure filled a major void by providing collectors with high-grade uncirculated examples of Civil War-era U.S. gold coins—something they could only dream about before then. As a consequence, the coins were readily absorbed at very substantial prices. As this is written in February 2004, you can expect to pay $15,000 for an MS-65 *Brother Jonathan* double eagle, $8,250 for an MS-64 and $6.500 for an MS-63. There is significant demand for these coins, and they will undoubtedly follow the market in years to come.

THE SS REPUBLIC

he *SS Republic* is a recent addition to the list of important shipwrecks located by researchers, and it promises to be one of the most important, with a cargo of precious-metal coins that could be worth as much as $180 million. That would make it the most valuable wreck ever to be salvaged in U.S. nautical history—even more valuable than the storied "Ship of Gold," the *SS Central America*. As plans were being made in late 2003 to undertake recovery operations, ABC News featured the story on "World News Tonight," and I was among the coin experts interviewed for the segment.

The *SS Republic* was just a modest steamship, but her brief career took twists and turns worthy of a Hollywood movie. Her brushes with history were so numerous that one observer has called her "the Forrest Gump of the Civil War era."

The two-decked, 210-foot-long ship started life in Baltimore in 1853 as the *SS Tennessee*. She had a single piston more than 6 feet wide that turned side-wheels 28 feet in diameter. But she also had two masts and sails, which were needed for extra power on ocean runs. The *Tennessee* made a successful voyage to England, then, in 1855, became the first North American steamer to open regular service to South America.

In 1856, the ship ferried Gold Rush miners and soldiers of fortune to Nicaragua. The prospectors crossed the country to board another ship to California; the mercenaries stayed to fight a war meant to establish a new pro-slavery government in Nicaragua. When the mercenaries, or "filibusters," were routed, the *Tennessee* took the remnants of the ragtag "army" back to New York.

The ship then began plying a run between New Orleans and Mexico, but the Civil War's outbreak in 1861 brought another change: It was pressed into service as a blockade runner in the Confederate navy. The following year, Union Vice-Admiral David Farragut captured New Orleans and seized the *Tennessee*, turning her into his flagship. The ship was caught in a gale and damaged off the Texas coast in 1864, ending her military career. But a group of New York investors bought her for $25,000 in 1865, patched up the hull, renamed her the *SS Republic* and put her into service on a route from New York to New Orleans just 34 days after the end of the war.

Northern bankers and businessmen viewed New Orleans as a fertile ground for investment, and began sending substantial shipments of gold to the war-ravaged city in an effort to jump-start its economy. When the *Republic* left New York on Oct. 18, 1865, she was carrying $400,000 in precious-metal coins bound for New Orleans, the South's largest city. The trip was calm and uneventful at first—but on the morning of Oct. 23, an east-northeast gale blew in. By night, it had developed into a hurricane. Caught by surprise, the crew fought valiantly to stay on course, but before long the paddlewheels stalled and the pumps failed. By Oct. 25, the ship was adrift and taking on water; soon, it sank. At least 16 of the 59 people on board perished, most of them during four agonizing days on lifeboats and a raft.

Odyssey Marine Exploration Inc. of Tampa, Fla., a private marine salvage company, spent 12 years searching for the wreckage of the *Republic*. Finally, in August 2003, an underwater robot equipped with a video camera captured a ghostly image of the paddlewheel steamship 1,700 feet beneath the surface of the Atlantic, 100 miles off the coast of Georgia. Barely a month later, a team of 40 technicians, robot operators, field archaeologists and curators began the happy task of retrieving the treasure. By the end of May 2004, Odyssey had recovered more than 51,212 coins with a total face value of $54,500—some 47,096 silver and 4,116 gold coins—plus more than 750 other artifacts. The coins represented approximately 22.7 percent of the $400,000 face value of the overall monetary treasure. At press time, the total retail value of the coins recovered is over $75 million, according to John Albanese, numismatic marketing strategist for Odyssey.

The wreckage of the *Republic* lies well beyond the federal government's authority, which extends 24 nautical miles offshore. Nonetheless, Odyssey sought and received federal permission, known as an "arrest," in staking its claim to exclusive salvage rights. To get that permission, the salvors took the first item recovered from the wreckage—a bottle filled with preserved fruit, still corked—and presented it at a federal courthouse in Tampa as evidence of the find.

Initial reports indicated that the first coins recovered included gold double eagles and eagles and silver half dollars and quarters, with nearly all being dated between the 1840s and 1865. Reportedly, the coins represented a number of different dates and mints, unlike those recovered from the *SS Central America* and the *SS Brother Jonathan*, for example, which were limited to a small number of dates and largely from the San Francisco Mint. Insiders suggested that based on the quality of the first coins recovered, professionally conserved by Numismatic Conservation Services (NCS), and graded and encapsulated by the Numismatic Guaranty Corporation of America (NGC), the *Republic* treasure may include a number of the finest-known examples from the mid-19th century. Random samples of the gold coins show that most range between AU-50 and MS-65, with some even higher.

As the salvage work began, Dr. Donald H. Kagin, one of the coin experts advising Odyssey, said the cargo could be worth as much as $120 million to $180 million, or an average of between $6,000 and $9,000 per coin. "That value," he said, "would depend on the ultimate quality of the specimens, but if their condition proves to be comparable to other shipwreck coins from the period, it would make this the most valuable documented cargo ever recovered from a shipwreck."

Another coin expert, David W. Akers, noted an important difference between the wreck of the Republic and that of the *SS Central America*. "The coins on board the *Central America* were lying in 8,000 feet of cold water," Akers said. "There's almost no marine life down there, and that environment preserved them for all these years. The *Republic* is in 1,700 feet of water, so who knows what the coins will look like."

Nevertheless, he said, "it's an exciting discovery. Any time there's a news story this big about old coins, it translates into more enthusiasm for coin collecting. And I don't think anything excites collectors more than buried or sunken treasure."

One-Minute Treasure Tip:

John Albanese, founder of NGC and numismatic adviser to Odyssey, anticipates broad marketing of the coins from the *Republic*, through many channels, and wide acceptance. The size of the hoard will facilitate a friendly marketplace where nobody is—or, as a practical matter, *can be*—excluded, Albanese says. In other words, the mistakes made in marketing the *Central America* coins will not be repeated. The sheer magnitude of the treasure will require a massive marketing effort, and that is likely to push up the prices of these and similar coins over the short term through broadening of the collector base. In the long run, natural market equilibrium will govern prices after the coins are fully dispersed.

HMS SUSSEX

HMS Sussex was a 157-foot, 80-gun English warship built during the reign of William and Mary at the close of the 17th century. Its normal mission was combat, not convoy, but it's thought to have been carrying tons of treasure at the time it met its doom in a storm near the Strait of Gibraltar in 1694.

Research has revealed that the *Sussex* was escorting a large merchant fleet to the Mediterranean when she sank. Her admiral had orders to pay a large sum of money to the Duke of Savoy in Spain to finance his involvement in a war then being waged between England and France. Evidence suggests that the payment most likely consisted of more than 2.5 billion pounds sterling in British gold sovereigns, which presumably sank to the bottom with the *Sussex*.

The mission was shrouded in secrecy; the existence of the treasure didn't come to public light, in fact, for more than three centuries. In 1995, a researcher studying dusty archives turned up a diplomatic letter written after *HMS Sussex* sank, in which it was revealed that the ship had been carrying a small fortune. The British government subsequently launched an investigation into the events surrounding the final mission of the *Sussex* and undertook efforts to locate the wreckage of the ship.

Word of the potential windfall also reached Odyssey Marine Exploration Inc. of Tampa, Fla., a private marine salvage company, which spent more than six years and $3 million looking for the wreck. The ship was finally located at a depth of 2,400 feet, although its exact location has not been disclosed. In 2001, Odyssey divers retrieved several artifacts that were used to identify the wreck as the long-forgotten British ship of the line.

In an effort to protect its interest in the treasure and avoid long and costly legal complications, the British government entered into discussions with Odyssey to proceed as partners with the salvage. Under a proposed agreement, Odyssey would be granted exclusive rights to explore, catalog, salvage, and market artifacts from the wreck. It would recognize the United Kingdom as owner of the *HMS Sussex*, but would be entitled to share in the proceeds from the artifacts sold from the salvage operation—from 40 percent to 60 percent, depending on the value.

As of early 2004, the agreement had not yet been finalized, and the government faced some resistance from the British press and public. A spokesman for Odyssey said the contract would mark the first time in history that any government has allowed a private company to explore and excavate a sovereign warship.

The exact nature of the treasure is uncertain, but estimates suggest it could be worth as much as $4 billion in present-day money.

One-Minute Treasure Tip:

Like the Spanish colonial coins of the *Atocha*, the British gold sovereigns from the *Sussex* have limited marketability as collectibles. At this preliminary stage, it appears that their value will be based heavily on their bullion content—much more so than that of the treasure coins from the U.S. shipwrecks. Exercise caution in deciding whether to purchase such coins for significant premiums; the resale market may not justify such an outlay.

SHIPWRECK COINS AND THE LAW

The search for long-lost shipwrecks can be time-consuming and difficult. At times, though, the quest can seem simple, compared with the legal complications that inevitably entangle treasure hunters who find what they are looking for. And the process of gaining free-and-clear title to the treasure retrieved from those wrecks can be every bit as murky as the watery tombs that made them hard to find for so many years.

There have been laws governing shipwrecks for centuries, but such laws have become increasingly important in recent years as advances in technology have led to the discovery of more and more wrecks and sometimes to the recovery of vast riches. With each new discovery and recovery, another court fight ensues over who really owns the newfound treasure. And increasingly, judges have been called upon to apply the laws—and interpret them—in cases that would tax the wisdom of Solomon. Their verdicts show an inconsistent pattern, making each new legal battle a voyage in rough legal seas for the finders.

When shipwrecks are found, recovery of their cargos can be governed by either of two basic precepts of maritime law—the international law of salvage or the law of finds. The difference was explained by a federal judge in Virginia, J. Calvitt Clarke Jr., during a 1998 case involving salvage claims against two 18th-century Spanish naval vessels. "Under salvage law," Judge Clarke said, "the original owners still retain their ownership interests in such property." The law of finds, by contrast, "expresses the ancient and honorable principle of finders, keepers."

The distinction is clear, but it's far less obvious which law should be applied in each specific case. Since many of the shipwrecks date back hundreds of years, the "original owners" are often long since dead if they were individuals, probably long since defunct if they were companies and sometimes much different in structure if they were governments. In the United States, judges must consider claims that may have been paid by underwriters at the time a ship was lost, international treaties that existed at the time and were negotiated in the interim, and federal and state laws regarding offshore wrecks and recent actions by Congress that may have bearing.

David L. Ganz, a prominent New York City lawyer with special expertise on coin-related matters, offered this insight:

> When sunken ships or their cargos are rescued from the bottom of the ocean by anyone other than the owners, courts generally favor applying the law of salvage over the law of finds. Finds law is generally applied, however, where the previous owners were found to have abandoned their property. Abandonment must be proved to the court's satisfaction by clear and convincing evidence, typically by an owner's express declaration abandoning title. It can be proved indirectly through actions, too.

On a number of occasions, District Court judges have decided in favor of the finders, only to be overruled by Circuit Courts, which concluded that the law of salvage should be applied. But as of this writing, in February 2004, there has been no ultimate ruling, since the U.S. Supreme Court has not yet weighed in. In order for a case to reach the highest court, four Supreme Court justices must agree to hear an appeal, and so far that hasn't happened in any of these disputes.

In several high-profile cases, the finders and other claimants have reached out-of-court settlements under which the finders have agreed to give the other parties a portion of the treasure recovered from valuable wrecks. This happened, for example, in the case of the *SS Central America*, a ship laden with gold coins and ingots from Gold Rush California. In order to avert further litigation and hasten the marketing of the treasure, the finder, the Columbus America Discov-

ery Group, agreed to give a portion of the recovered riches to insurance underwriters who had laid claim to the treasure.

Ganz offered this additional observation:

> In the final analysis, treasure-trove seekers will have to look far more
> carefully at the prior status of the ships, ascertain whether or not there is
> an insurable interest—or a national interest—involved, and perhaps
> take on partners before undertaking salvage operations. Negative court
> decisions are not the death knell of treasure hunting, though they do sig-
> nal that the process of bringing sunken treasure to the marketplace will
> be time-consuming and expensive.

> But all concur the result is worth the wait.

EPILOGUE

Rare coins provide rare opportunities. Although they are only pocket-size, they possess enormous attractions: historical significance . . . beautiful art . . . high value . . . great collector appeal . . . and, in some instances, investment potential.

One-Minute Coin Expert has given you all the knowledge you need to harness these assets and make them work for you.

I've shown you how to find a fortune in your pocket change—how to sift through the ordinary coins in your pocket and purse and discover the extraordinary coins that lie hidden there, totally overlooked by most people.

I've shown you what to look for in that long-forgotten cigar box in your attic, or that cookie jar filled with coins on a kitchen shelf—how to identify coins that are worth a small fortune among these seemingly humble family hoards.

Venturing into the far-flung coin marketplace, where rare coins are bought and sold by thousands of entrepreneurs, I've given you vital insights into how to measure the market's current mood—how to size up its psychology—and how to make this knowledge work to your advantage. I've stressed the importance of not simply following the crowd. Remember this advice: When everyone seems to be buying, you should be selling, and when everyone seems to be selling, you should be buying.

I've told you how coins are graded, and how a coin's grade directly affects its market value. I've demonstrated why an improperly graded coin could be just as devastating to you financially as one that is overpriced.

I've shown you how coins can be traded very much like stocks—coins that have been independently certified by grading services such as the Professional Coin Grading Service, the Numismatic Guaranty Corporation, ANACS, and the Independent Coin Grading Company.

I've told you how you can make big profits from small coins and shown you how to cash in those profits. I've even supplied a secret list of twelve "sleeper" coins—coins with high potential to increase in value dramatically.

I've explained how rare coins are related to precious metals, and discussed both the similarities and the differences between rare coins and "bullion" coins. And I've shown how even drug dealers find rare coins and bullion highly appealing.

Back in the 1970s, many investors didn't know how to deal with rampant inflation. The strategies they employed were unsophisticated and smacked of excessive trial and error. Today, the investment market is more mature—and rare coins have assumed an increasingly important role in many investors' plans and portfolios.

Some economic forecasters are predicting that inflation will return in coming years with a vengeance. If inflation does come raging back, rare coins would surely soar in value.

This time people would know how to protect themselves against the ravages of inflation, and that protection would certainly include massive purchases of gold and silver bullion as well as heavy emphasis on rare coins as time-proven hedges.

But many coins have excellent potential for appreciation in value—irrespective of inflation or any other economic variable.

Follow the blueprint in *One-Minute Coin Expert* and you'll be prepared for any marketplace. You'll be ready and able to protect both yourself and your coins.

Reread the book, and enjoy it. Then use it like the expert you've become!

INVITATION FOR CORRESPONDENCE

The author welcomes reports of your pocket-change finds and your questions about coin investing at: Scott Travers Rare Coin Galleries, LLC, P.O. Box 1711, F.D.R. Station, New York, NY 10150. Telephone: 212-535-9135. E-mail: travers@pocketchangelottery.com

INDEX

Scott A. Travers ranks as one of the most influential coin dealers in the world. His name is familiar to readers everywhere as the author of six bestselling books on coins: *How to Make Money in Coins Right Now*, *The Coin Collector's Survival Manual*, *Travers' Rare Coin Investment Strategy*, *Scott Travers' Top 88 Coins Over $100*, *The Insider's Guide to U.S. Coin Values*, and *The Investor's Guide to Coin Trading*. All of them have won awards from the prestigious Numismatic Literary Guild (NLG). In 2002, NLG awarded him its highest bestowable honor, the lifetime achievement Clemy. He was elected vice-president (1997-1999) of the American Numismatic Association, a congressionally chartered, nonprofit educational organization. He is contributing editor to *COINage* magazine and a regular contributor to other numismatic periodicals, and has served as a coin valuation consultant to the Federal Trade Commission. His opinions as an expert are often sought by publications such as *Barron's*, *Business Week*, and The *Wall Street Journal*. A frequent guest on radio and television programs, Scott Travers has won awards and gained an impressive reputation not only as a coin expert but also as a forceful consumer advocate for the coin-buying public. He serves as numismatic advisor to a number of major investment funds and has coordinated the liquidation of numerous important coin collections. He is president and member of Scott Travers Rare Coin Galleries, LLC, in New York City.

AMERICAN
NUMISMATIC
ASSOCIATION

ANA Membership
IT MAKES CENTS AND SAVES YOU DOLLARS.

Members receive:
- The ANA's award-winning monthly magazine, *Numismatist*
- Access to 50,000 titles in the ANA's Dwight N. Manley Numismatic Library
- Discounts on books and supplies
- Low-cost collection insurance
- Plus dozens of other exclusive member benefits

JOIN NOW and SAVE $6! (We'll waive the $6 application fee.)
Photocopy this page and mail to the ANA, or **join online** at www.money.org.

☐ Enclosed is **$33** for first-year membership.

☐ Enclosed is **$29** for first-year senior membership (65 or over).

☐ **Mr.** ☐ **Mrs.** ☐ **Ms.** _____

Street _____

City _____ **State** _____ **Zip** _____

Signature _____ **Birthdate** _____
Required for senior discount.

I herewith make application for membership in the American Numismatic Association, subject to the bylaws of the Association. I also agree to abide by the Code of Ethics adopted by the Association.

Make check payable to the ANA and return application to:
ANA, 818 North Cascade Avenue, Colorado Springs, CO 80903-3279.

Charge my credit card in the amount of . . . . $ _____

☐ Visa   ☐ AmEx   **Card No.** _____ **Exp. Date** _____
☐ MasterCard ☐ Discover **Signature** _____

☐ Periodically, the ANA's mailing list is sold or provided to third parties. If you do not want your information provided to such parties for non-ANA related mailings, please check here. (Previous requests not to provide your information will continue to be honored.)

For more information or to join by phone, call 800-367-9723.   S1